Transparency in Business

Utpal Dholakia

Transparency in Business

An Integrative View

Utpal Dholakia
Jones Graduate School of Business
Rice University
Houston, TX, USA

ISBN 978-3-031-12144-9   ISBN 978-3-031-12145-6 (eBook)
https://doi.org/10.1007/978-3-031-12145-6

© The Author(s), under exclusive license to Springer Nature Switzerland AG 2023

This work is subject to copyright. All rights are solely and exclusively licensed by the Publisher, whether the whole or part of the material is concerned, specifically the rights of translation, reprinting, reuse of illustrations, recitation, broadcasting, reproduction on microfilms or in any other physical way, and transmission or information storage and retrieval, electronic adaptation, computer software, or by similar or dissimilar methodology now known or hereafter developed.

The use of general descriptive names, registered names, trademarks, service marks, etc. in this publication does not imply, even in the absence of a specific statement, that such names are exempt from the relevant protective laws and regulations and therefore free for general use.

The publisher, the authors, and the editors are safe to assume that the advice and information in this book are believed to be true and accurate at the date of publication. Neither the publisher nor the authors or the editors give a warranty, expressed or implied, with respect to the material contained herein or for any errors or omissions that may have been made. The publisher remains neutral with regard to jurisdictional claims in published maps and institutional affiliations.

Cover illustration: © Melisa Hasan

This Palgrave Macmillan imprint is published by the registered company Springer Nature Switzerland AG
The registered company address is: Gewerbestrasse 11, 6330 Cham, Switzerland

Seldom, very seldom, does complete truth belong to any human disclosure; seldom can it happen that something is not a little disguised, or a little mistaken.

—Jane Austen

Preface

According to a widely circulated 2021 New York Times story, if you had gotten a colonoscopy at the University of Mississippi Medical Center that August, the price you'd have paid would have depended on your health insurance provider. If you had health insurance from Cigna, you'd have paid $1,463, whereas with Aetna, your price tag would've been approximately 50% more, or $2,144. However, if you had no health insurance or decided to pay out of your pocket, your colonoscopy price would have been about half the Cigna price and one-third the Aetna price, or $782. What's more, no matter how hard you tried, you would not have discovered the price you'd pay until after you had undergone the procedure and been discharged from the hospital.

Since January 2021, all American hospitals have been mandated by the federal government to post the prices of their services online so that anyone can easily access them. Yet, as of the summer of 2022, only about 14% of hospitals had complied; the other 86% simply flouted the rule without any explanation. Even today, most hospital patients pay widely different prices and don't know what they are until they are handed the bill at the end of their treatment. In any other industry, this would be called extortion or a rip-off, but for hospitals, this was and still is, business as usual. US hospital pricing is about as nontransparent as it gets in business.

Contrast the University of Mississippi Medical Center with the fashion label Everlane and the coffee roaster and retailer Pachamama Coffee. Both brands fall squarely on the other end of the price transparency spectrum. Everlane's motto is to make a difference through "Radical Transparency." It implements this brand promise by providing detailed information about every input cost for each garment it sells so that a curious customer can easily work out its gross profit. Pachamama Coffee not only reveals where its coffee is sourced (Peru, Nicaragua, Guatemala, Mexico, and Ethiopia) and how much coffee farmers are paid (an average of $3.47 per pound in 2020), but also openly shares its financial performance such as revenue earned per pound of roasted coffee ($15.34), net profit ($1.11), and net profit margin (9%). Most businesses would consider costs to be proprietary, but Everlane's and Pachamama Coffee's customers and competitors can easily find this information on their websites.

The transparency of these pricing strategies and the logic behind them couldn't be more different. Yet, the lawless opacity of American hospitals and the idealistic openness of brands like Everlane and Pachamama Coffee both support sustainable business models. On the list of the world's best hospitals, the top three and five of the top ten hospitals are American at the moment. These hospitals treat tens of millions of patients successfully every year, providing excellent care, just like Everlane and Pachamama Coffee sell apparel and coffee and build satisfied, loyal customer bases. Workers find meaningful careers, and investors earn a return on their investments in both settings even though they are so far apart in their price transparency.

In my research and writing on pricing strategy, this paradox fascinated me and first got me interested in the concept of transparency. What exactly is transparency, and how transparent should a business be? Is transparency good or bad? What do we know about business transparency, and what important questions remain unanswered? I wanted to find out the answers to these and many other questions about transparency and learn what scholars in different business disciplines were seeking and had found. That is why I wrote this book.

Houston, USA   Utpal Dholakia

Contents

1 **The Many Faces of Business Transparency** 1
   Dual Perspectives on Business Transparency 2
   The Positive Side of Business Transparency 3
   The Negative Side of Business Transparency 4
   The Purpose of this Book 6
   Selected Business Transparency Definitions 8
   Why Business Transparency is Important 14
   The Book's Roadmap 16
   References 19

2 **Business Operations Transparency** 23
   Supply Chain Transparency 25
      The Value of Supply Chain Transparency 26
      The Drawbacks of Supply Chain Transparency 27
      Core Definitions of Supply Chain Transparency Concepts 29
      Supply Chain Visibility 31
   Operational Transparency 38
      Process Transparency and Customer Transparency 38
      Research Findings Regarding Operational Transparency 39
   References 44

3 Price Transparency — 49

- Conceptual Formulations of Price Transparency — 51
- The Pricing Process, the Buying Journey, and Price Transparency — 53
  - Price Transparency During Price Setting — 54
  - Price Transparency During Communication or Negotiation — 55
  - Price Transparency During Price Realization — 57
- A Typology of Price Transparency — 59
  - Disclosure-Based Price Transparency — 62
  - Accessibility-Based Price Transparency — 63
    - Price Availability — 63
    - Price Offer Complexity — 65
    - Price Change Frequency — 66
    - Perceived Price Negotiability — 68
  - Disclosure-Based Price Transparency — 70
    - Definitions of Disclosure-Based Price Transparency — 71
    - Disclosure of Labor Costs to Pay Fair Wages — 73
    - Disclosure of Purchase Costs for Supplier Welfare — 74
    - Disclosure of Costs and Markups for Brand Differentiation — 75
- References — 76

4 Organizational Transparency — 83

- The Origins of Transparency in Organizational Research — 86
- Definition of Organizational Transparency — 88
  - The Deliberate Orchestration of Information Flows — 89
  - The Quality of Shared Information — 90
- The Building Blocks for Cultivating a Transparent Organizational Culture — 91
  - Setting Clear Expectations of Transparent Conduct — 93
  - Behaving Consistently with Professed Values and Expectations — 94
  - Providing a Work Environment Supporting Transparent Practices — 95
  - Making Employees' Transparent Conduct Observable — 95
  - Encouraging Intra-Organizational Debate and Dissent — 96
  - Sanctioning Non-Transparent Behavior Unequivocally — 97
- Pay Transparency and the Gender Wage Gap — 98
  - The Gender Wage Gap — 99
  - Pay Transparency — 101

	The Disparity of Pay Transparency Regulations	102
	Effects of Pay Transparency on the Gender Wage Gap	102
	The Downsides of Pay Transparency	104
	References	106
5	**Transparent Business Leadership**	**111**
	The Present Significance of Authentic Leadership	113
	What Is Authentic Leadership?	114
	Authentic Leadership in Practice	115
	Relational Transparency	118
	Self-Awareness	120
	Truthful Communication Practices	122
	Humility	123
	Critiques of Authentic Leadership and Relational Transparency	125
	References	130
6	**Algorithmic Transparency and Consumer Disclosure**	**135**
	The Algorithmic Transparency Challenge	137
	Defining Algorithmic Transparency	138
	Transparency in ADM Systems	139
	Warm Human and Institutional Factors	140
	Event Versus Process Algorithmic Transparency	141
	The Algorithmic Transparency Continuum	142
	Enhancing Algorithmic Transparency	145
	The Right to an Explanation	146
	Comprehensibility, Understandability, and Explainability	147
	Customer Transparency	149
	Racial Discrimination on Two-Sided Platforms	152
	The Benefits of Shared Medical Appointments	153
	Effects of Customer Transparency on Crowdfunding and Peer-to-Peer Lending	154
	References	156
7	**An Integrative Perspective on Business Transparency**	**161**
	An Integrative Conceptual Framework of Business Transparency	163
	The Six Forms of Business Transparency	164
	Explanation-Based Transparency	165
	Tactical Transparency	166

    Access-Based Transparency   168
    Process-Based Transparency   170
    Personal Value-Based Transparency   171
    Organizational Value-Based Transparency   173
    The Characteristics of Disclosed Information   174
        Clarity   175
        Precision   176
        Completeness   176
        Interpretation and Contextualization   177
    An Expanded Definition of Business Transparency   179
        Deliberately Designed Disclosure   179
        Negotiated Disclosure   180
        Mutually Beneficial Understanding   180
    References   180

References   185

Index   211

LIST OF FIGURES

Fig. 3.1	Different aspects of price transparency during the pricing process and the customer journey	53
Fig. 3.2	The four components of accessibility-based price transparency	63
Fig. 4.1	Six significant contributors to a transparent organizational culture	92
Fig. 7.1	An integrative framework of business transparency	164

LIST OF TABLES

Table 1.1   Selected definitions of transparency from the business literature   9
Table 3.1   Selected definitions of price transparency from the academic literature   60

CHAPTER 1

The Many Faces of Business Transparency

Abstract This chapter introduces the business transparency concept, exploring the range of its conceptual domain, providing a preliminary omnibus definition, and highlighting the significant scope of its positive and negative effects on business practice. It explores a range of definitions, finding transparency research to be siloed, overly focused on the disclosure of information, and often endorsing a "more-is-better" perspective, referred to here as the *transparency principle*. The chapter concludes by providing a roadmap for the book.

Keywords Transparency · Disclosure · Privacy · Knowledge · Decision Making · Candor

> Publicity is justly commended as a remedy for social and industrial diseases.—Louis Brandeis.

No concept is quite so widely invoked as transparency or has so many different meanings and utilities across so many business contexts. Transparency finds its way into the heart of important questions in virtually every business discipline, from organizational studies, information technology, information systems management, leadership, and corporate governance, to strategy, operations, marketing, human resource management, consumer behavior, business leadership, finance, and accounting.

© The Author(s), under exclusive license to Springer Nature
Switzerland AG 2023
U. Dholakia, *Transparency in Business*,
https://doi.org/10.1007/978-3-031-12145-6_1

We all intuitively understand transparency, and most of us deem it to be a force for good most of the time.

Transparent leaders are regarded as saviors of corporations and the economy and the bastions of present-day virtue. Transparent brands are celebrated as potent, authentic platforms to build engaged and profitable customer bases. Transparent supply chains are designated as crucial for improving efficiency, reducing waste, promoting environmentally and socially sustainable practices, and fostering a safe work culture. Transparent prices are regarded as a way to hold businesses accountable and increase customer welfare. Transparent algorithms are deemed to be fair and inclusive. Transparent organizational cultures are viewed as desirable workplaces for employees and engines of ethical and profitable business models. Transparency implies a managerial mindset that "we have nothing to hide because it's all good."

Dual Perspectives on Business Transparency

Transparency is just as relevant to a company's CEO as it is to its frontline service employees and everyone in between, not to mention its significance to entrepreneurs, consumers, investors, regulators, environmental activists, and others who deal with businesses or are affected by them. As we will see throughout this book, each of the many manifestations of transparency in business is unique; in some respects, transparency is a catchall phrase that can be used to describe various phenomena, intentions, proclivities, orientations, and behaviors. But in others, as the title of this chapter highlights, transparency has many shades of unique meaning in different business contexts.

Business transparency can variously refer to openness, honesty, forthrightness, self-awareness, lucidity, the capacity or need or extent of disclosure, the nature of the underlying motivation for disclosure, an impulse to eschew secrecy, simplicity, comprehensibility, simulability, understandability, legal compliance, accessibility, individual control, interpretability, accuracy, freedom of information, the timely release of all relevant information, authenticity as defined by the concordance between beliefs, values, and actions, and the path to the absolute truth. Its specific meaning depends on which business scholar is writing about transparency, the focus of their investigation, their epistemological stance, their explicitly stated or implied understanding of the concept, and their scientific and political biases (Albu & Flyverbom, 2019; Bernstein, 2017; Heald, 2006;

Larsson, 1998). Indeed, it is virtually impossible to find another concept that is so widely used in so many business disciplines by academics and practitioners—executives, managers, and consultants alike, and with such large established bodies of scholarly literature, that lacks a clear center or consensus in meaning.

The Positive Side of Business Transparency

Transparency has long been viewed as a fundamental building block of modern civil society, deemed to be as essential for the functioning of democracies and market economies as it is for business organizations seeking to build sustainable stakeholder relationships, executive teams wanting to establish effective governance mechanisms, and managers aspiring to become effective leaders. Political scientists and organizational researchers have contended that a critical function of transparency is to stifle the natural, evolutionary impulse that resides in individuals and organizations to exploit and abuse power and take advantage of asymmetries without restraint. They posit that the processes and constraints introduced by the need to be transparent also lead to restraint, necessitating the use of power in measured and constructive ways.

At the societal level, transparency legitimizes government, generates trust in citizens, and allows businesses to establish sustainable practices and employ effective business models. We might even say that a certain minimum amount of transparency is necessary for civil society to function on a day-to-day basis. At the organizational level, transparency allows managers to formulate and execute effective strategies, cultivate and maintain mutually beneficial stakeholder relations, and build trust in dyadic relationships. For individual managers, transparency involves understanding and presenting one's authentic self to colleagues and subordinates, openly sharing information, and behaving in concordance with one's core beliefs and values. By contrast, the lack of transparency at any of these levels produces an environment where corruption, inequity, inefficiency, and exploitation can flourish. It is not a stretch to say that transparency, in its many forms, is the foundation and operating principle of ethical and sustainable business practice.

The transparency principle. Underlying the positive perspectives of business transparency is the fundamental premise, broadly applied whether the subject is an individual, an organization as a whole or certain functions within it, or a particular business initiative, program, or practice, that openness, disclosure, and candor are virtuous principles in and of themselves, and when they are applied to business, they lead to positive outcomes for the practitioners and proponents of transparency through various means. Extended further, such a perspective holds that more transparency is better and that greater degrees of disclosure will shine more light and make businesses more accountable, efficient, and fair. Throughout this book, we will call the idea that more business transparency is better as *the transparency principle*.

The Negative Side of Business Transparency

Yet the reality about business transparency is far more nuanced and decidedly gloomier, with its ramifications dictated by the business context and the issue at hand. Transparency can inhibit, homogenize, and suppress innovation and business success, sanction lengthy debates and undermine executive authority, stifle original and dissenting voices, lead to systematic exploitation and discrimination, and one-sided transparency in a dyadic relation can confer significant benefits to one party at the expense of the other, whether the relationship is between a brand and its customers, a company and its suppliers, or between a manager and their subordinates. Business secrecy, the inverse of transparency, whether it refers to a particular formulation, business process, pricing strategy, intellectual property, or algorithm, can confer long-lasting benefits (Dufresne & Offstein, 2008) and bolster the influence of actors with relatively little power (Toegel et al., 2022). Maintaining secrecy often provides businesses with an insurmountable advantage over the competition.

Transparency strips away privacy and many of its protections for the discloser, shifting power away from them. When customers reveal personal information, they open the door to be exploited and discriminated against by marketers, other customers, and third parties that gain access to the customer's information (Hansen & Weiskopf, 2021; Solove & Citron, 2017). When workers are monitored by digital technology, they suffer physically and psychologically and push back (Bernstein, 2017; Kellogg et al., 2020). Restrained disclosure can be used as a strategic tool in pricing strategy to influence buyers' decision making, distort their valuations, and stimulate impulsive buying (Dholakia, 2019). In two-sided platforms, disclosure can lead to racial and other forms of discrimination (Fisman & Luca, 2016). Injudicious disclosure of wages can result in unfavorable social comparisons, lower job satisfaction, and employee demotivation (Cullen & Perez-Truglia, 2018). In business leadership, injudicious candor by a manager can lead to a loss of credibility and trust among subordinates (Ibarra, 2015). And the list goes on.

The adverse effects of business transparency occur for at least three reasons. First, in business settings, the disclosure and its results, especially when the disclosure is involuntary, derive meaning from and hinge on power disparities between the discloser and the receiver. The receiver routinely benefits more from the disclosure than the discloser and may even increase their power in the dyadic relationship. On the other hand, a powerful discloser can use disclosure strategically to distort the receiver's perceptions, burnish their own reputation, and gain the upper hand. Simply put, in an exchange transaction, divulging information can easily turn into a zero-sum game. Who is transparent to whom, in what sense, and for what purpose reflects the extant power relation and modulates the resultant shift in power. As Pasquale (2015) puts it, "to scrutinize others while avoiding scrutiny oneself is one of the most important forms of power" (p. 3).

Second, claims of transparency can generate an unwarranted and misleading aura of *beneficent openness* for the claimant but have little actual value if they are not backed up by the quality, completeness, and interpretability of the disclosed information and the motivation and ability of receivers to understand and contextualize the information and use it meaningfully. In other words, the *illusion of transparency* is as common, and perhaps more effective in business, than transparency itself, and "real disclosure" (Brandeis, 1913) that provides understanding is elusive and illusory. As developed throughout this book, even with good intentions, meaningful transparency is very difficult, if not impossible, to achieve in many business contexts, and greater transparency simply means the availability of a greater volume of impenetrable information and more confusion. Accordingly, understanding the nature and boundaries of transparency is essential for every affected manager, worker, policymaker, and academic rather than simply embracing the transparency principle.

The third reason is that transparency can backfire in unexpected and significant ways, producing perverse outcomes for the discloser or receiver, and sometimes for both, along with the organization and its constituents. For example, when the outcomes of cardiac surgery and percutaneous coronary intervention started being publicly reported in New York state, instead of motivating surgeons to perform better, it motivated them to avoid the sickest patients (Rosenbaum, 2015), and when pay transparency allows workers to learn how much their coworkers are being paid, they offer less help to those who are being paid more than them (Bamberger & Belogolovsky, 2017). For academic investigations, such unexpected effects are particularly noteworthy because they overturn trite generalizations, deepen understanding, and help to establish boundaries.

The Purpose of this Book

There are dozens of books and review articles, not to mention research papers by the hundreds, covering every conceivable form of transparency in business, many of which are cited throughout this book. Even though they share some commonalities, especially at an abstract level, not surprisingly, the literatures in the different business areas have developed virtually independently from each other, without cognizance of overlapping ideas and concepts. For instance, researchers studying how operational transparency affects service employees have paid little heed to the relevant findings about how employees are affected by transparency initiatives in the organizational transparency literature and vice versa. Similarly, the question of how to make an algorithm explainable has insights to offer on making pricing structures more understandable for customers and pay information more comprehensible to employees, but these researchers rarely talk to each other. Even worse, they hardly ever listen to one another.

Given its importance and the amount of scholarly attention devoted to issues of business transparency, an integrative perspective that examines its different forms and draws connections between them is bound to be valuable. My main goal in writing this book was to provide this integration in a preliminary way by exploring many of the significant ideas, applications, and research findings about transparency that reside in various business areas and trying to understand their common and unique aspects. I have sought to go beyond simplistic, one-dimensional, and mostly positive perspectives of transparency and tried to explore and make sense of some of the knottier, more nuanced investigations wherever they are available.

The primary thesis that emerges from adopting this integrative mindset is twofold. First, business transparency, in its many forms and applications throughout the different business disciplines, is a *double-edged sword* that managers should wield carefully and with due understanding. Managers, the media, and even some researchers routinely take a "more is better" stance when discussing transparency but this *transparency principle* is rarely accurate or applicable. Instead, in most cases, the essence of effective, and we might even say, moral business strategy lies in achieving a reasonable balance between disclosure and concealment, observation and privacy, revealing and hiding, clarity and obfuscation, and transparency and opacity. Transparency can be a boon to the extent that there is correspondence in the power and motivations of the observer and the observed entity, and the disclosure and the observation process benefit both exchange partners. However, such cases are rare. More often, there is a power asymmetry and opposing motivations; in such cases, if transparency is used as a cloak to surveil employees or pit them against one another, exploit suppliers and their workers, hoodwink customers or activists, or signal virtue without actually practicing it, transparency can turn into something that diminishes, and ultimately causes financial harm to its practitioners and the business as a whole. In most business settings, the challenge lies in finding the balance between disclosure and concealment, not maximizing transparency.

The second core insight that emerges is that many scholarly considerations of transparency are framed too narrowly, focusing on concepts such as openness, access, and availability of information. However, openness, access, and availability only take us part of the way toward achieving meaningful transparency. No matter how readily it is available, information can only be of value when its access is accompanied by its comprehension. This can only happen when the receiver can sufficiently interpret, analyze, contextualize, and assess—in other words, they can make sense of the information. Meaningful transparency cannot be achieved, nor can its hoped-for benefits be fully realized unless the disclosure is deliberately made useful.

Thus, understanding the motivations, opportunity, and, most of all, the receiver's ability to make sense of the disclosure are important considerations, as are the good-faith efforts of the discloser in supporting the receiver's sense-making. Even though they are essential to transparency, both these issues, the receiver's receptivity and the discloser's active cooperation, have often been ignored or downplayed in the business transparency literature, being treated as outside the scope of the study. These ideas, and many others, will be developed in greater detail throughout this book. We have a lot of ground, conceptual, empirical, and integrative, to cover. Let's start by first considering a set of transparency definitions from different business disciplines to acknowledge and measure out the vast terrain of our domain of interest.

Selected Business Transparency Definitions

Virtually every business discipline, from accounting, operations, and organizational management to branding, business leadership, and pricing, has significant literatures on transparency; furthermore, each area has dozens of definitions that are not always congruent to one another. As a starting point, Table 1.1 provides a small, curated assortment of transparency definitions taken from reviews and well-cited articles across these business disciplines. Note that I have paraphrased or edited (as lightly as possible) some of the definitions when transparency was not precisely defined in the source. The table's main purpose is to give the reader a sense of the diversity and potential overlap in conceptions of transparency in the vast conceptual domain of business.

Despite the significant range of the conceptual domain covered in these definitions, several common themes emerge from the list. The first row in Table 1.1 provides a preliminary omnibus definition that I constructed with the common aspects of transparency in the other definitions as, "*Business transparency is the degree to which valuable information is deliberately disclosed or made available through an uncovering process to the relevant receiver to achieve a specific purpose.*" Note that this definition will be revised and expanded in Chapter 7.

The definition expresses several useful insights about business transparency. First, the deliberate disclosure of previously unavailable valuable information lies at the core of business transparency (Albu & Flyverbom, 2019). The information itself can be anything—the mechanics of an algorithm and details of the data on which it is implemented for a significant business application, the price or price inputs such as costs of a particular offering, the pay of individual employees or certain groups within an organization, the labor practices or the provenance of ingredients used by a supplier, and so on. The nature of the information, the sources of value embedded with it, the validity, accuracy, and coverage of the disclosed information, and the intentionality or the "why" behind the disclosure are all key defining features of business transparency.

Table 1.1 Selected definitions of transparency from the business literature

Citation	Definition	Discipline
This book—Preliminary definition	Business transparency is the degree to which valuable information is deliberately disclosed or made available through an uncovering process to the relevant receiver to achieve a specific purpose	General Business
Bateman and Bonanni (2019)	Supply chain transparency requires companies to know what is happening upstream in the supply chain and to communicate this knowledge both internally and externally	Operations
Brown et al. (2022)	Pay information disclosure (PID) is defined as the communication of relevant pay information between and among actors	Organizational Culture
Buell (2019)	Operational transparency is the deliberate design of windows into and out of the organization's operations to help customers and employees alike understand and appreciate the value being created	Operations
Colella et al. (2007)	Pay secrecy is a restriction of the amount of information employees are provided about what others are paid	Organizational Culture
Diakopoulos and Koliska (2017)	Algorithmic transparency is defined as the disclosure of information about algorithms to enable monitoring, checking, criticism, or intervention by interested parties	Algorithms
Flyverbom (2016)	The purposeful and strategic production of insight and openness in attempts to position organizations as attractive and willing to engage with their employees and stakeholders	Organizational Culture
Gardner et al. (2005)	Transparent leadership involves both owning one's personal experiences (values, thoughts, emotions, and beliefs) and acting in accordance with one's true self (expressing what you really think and believe and behaving accordingly)	Leadership

(continued)

Table 1.1 (continued)

Citation	Definition	Discipline
Hanna et al. (2019)	The extent to which information about prices is available to buyers that organizes, explains, clarifies, or projects the contextual direction and/or rationale for the seller's pricing	Pricing
Jiang et al. (2021)	The estimates and breakdowns of costs provided by the firm or published by third-party infomediaries	Pricing
Jönsson (1988)	The obligation of firms or agents to disclose their financial circumstances for the benefit of creditors or principals	Accounting
Kaptein (2008)	Ensuring visibility within the organization to allow employees to properly modify or correct behaviors	Organizational Culture
Madhavan et al. (2005)	Market transparency refers to the ability of participants to observe information about the trading process	Finance
Meijer (2014)	Transparency is the availability of information about an actor allowing other actors to monitor the workings or performance of this actor	General Business
Merriam-Webster Dictionary (2022)	An object, issue, or idea characterized by visibility or accessibility of information especially concerning business practices	General Business
Osorio-Vega (2019)	The entrepreneur's idiosyncratic imperatives and associated ethical groundings that translate into stories of deep knowledge and experience adding legitimacy to the entrepreneurial adventure	Entrepreneurship
Rego and Giustiniano (2021)	Relational transparency is defined as showing one's true self to others, expressing true thoughts and emotions, and openly sharing information	Leadership
Schnackenberg and Tomlinson (2016)	Transparency is the perceived quality of intentionally shared information from a sender	Organizational Culture
Sinha (2000)	The ability of buyers to see through seller's costs and determine whether they are in line with the prices being charged	Pricing

Citation	Definition	Discipline
Sodhi and Tang (2019)	A company disclosing information to the public, including consumers and investors, about upstream operations and about the products it sells to consumers	Operations
Walumbwa et al. (2008)	Authentic leadership is a pattern of leader behavior that draws upon and promotes both positive psychological capacities and a positive ethical climate, to foster greater self-awareness, an internalized moral perspective, balanced processing of information, and relational transparency on the part of leaders working with followers, fostering positive self-development	Leadership
Walumbwa et al. (2008)	Relational transparency is presenting one's authentic self (instead of a curated self) to others through judicious disclosures that involve openly sharing personal information and expressing one's true thoughts and feelings while at the same time minimizing displays of inappropriate emotions	Leadership

Second, the directionality of disclosure matters in the sense that the discloser, the receiver, and the nature of their relationship before the disclosure should be clearly defined. In some cases, the receiver may mandate disclosure, such as when managers monitor the activities of workers on an assembly line (Bernstein, 2012). In others, the disclosure may stem from the organization's culture or a particular manager's motivation, such as when a senior business executive makes a candid admission to subordinates about their vulnerability (Ibarra, 2015). Heald (2006) calls these two forms of disclosures "transparency upwards" and "transparency downwards," respectively, persuasively arguing that the key tasks and challenges associated with maintaining transparency, its boundaries, and its upshots are different in the two cases.

Third, the decision making process behind the decision to disclose is a significant aspect of transparency. Consider the case of price transparency, covered at length in Chapter 3. The pricing manager may decide on the degree of availability of their organization's prices after careful consideration of business strategy, follow industry conventions, or decide reactively or in an ad hoc manner. When the decision is deliberate, multiple aspects must be considered: what prices to disclose, when to disclose them, who to disclose them to, and the conditions surrounding the disclosure. More often than not, the disclosure is a multi-factor decision with multiple antecedent considerations, often involving trade-offs.

Fourth, the boundaries or parameters of the disclosure need to be defined. The disclosure may be guided by a set of rules established by laws, codes, or policies adopted widely by a profession (e.g., self-regulation by journalists, physicians, or marketing researchers), industry norms (e.g., best practices or benchmarking), or even as a form of competitive differentiation (e.g., using transparency as a core brand value). In accounting, for instance, transparency can be framed as the degree of adherence to a set of bookkeeping rules, some regulated and others considered to be best practice.

In many settings, the boundaries of the disclosure are naturally established by its feasibility, making it important to distinguish between the organization's intent to be transparent and its ability to do so. A company, or even an entire industry, may be willing to disclose information but may lack the requisite information and the processes to find or gather it. For instance, in an influential study of the traceability of conflict minerals from the Democratic Republic of Congo, Kim and Davis (2016) found that despite being given three years to ascertain and disclose whether their products contained these conflict minerals, nearly 80% of 1,300 corporations, including many of the largest multinational corporations in the world, were not able to determine the country of origin of materials and confidently certify their offerings as "conflict-free." The authors concluded that supply chain complexity, as measured by the size and concentration of the supplier base, was a key hurdle to accomplishing the intended transparency.

Fifth, the actual mechanics of the disclosure, that is, the actions performed by the discloser and the receiver to consummate the disclosure, are material considerations. For example, a public company must publish its financial statements online in the investor section of its website every quarter, and the information is available to anyone who chooses to visit the website. In contrast, an oilfield services company that rents drilling rigs may require potential customers to undergo a vetting process before they supply prices. Other companies may conduct the disclosure using a persuasive mode, such as advertisements or press releases, and accompanied by other components like a sales pitch or a price promotion (Buell & Kalkanci, 2021). For instance, an apparel brand might run an ad that says, "We are the only fashion brand that pays its workers a fair wage in the Dominican Republic, that's why you should buy our garments." This common form of disclosure results in the possibility that the informational aspects of the disclosure are conflated with its persuasive or behavior-inducing components. As these examples illustrate, the processes involved in making the disclosure are as important, if not more so, than the disclosure itself in understanding the ramifications of business transparency.

Finally, a common thread that runs through the definitions in Table 1.1 is an implicit acceptance of the following idealized chain of logic: *The greater the amount of information that is revealed and the more widely it is made available, the closer the users of the information (and the disclosers) are to arriving at the truth.* Under this perspective, transparency is the conduit to idealized outcomes such as accountability, parity, equity, ethicality, and fairness. It is a means of leveling the playing field and shrinking exploitative and ultimately poisonous asymmetries between exchange partners in a business relationship. To be transparent about something is a means of arriving at mutually beneficial decisions involving that thing, whether the decisions are by customers choosing which offer to purchase, managers about where to invest resources or which suppliers to use, employees about which job to accept, or companies about which algorithms to use and how to use them in automating business processes.

Why Business Transparency is Important

At this stage, the divergent manners in which transparency, and its sibling, accountability, are treated in two business disciplines is illustrative in exploring the core question of the significance of business transparency. In business law, some experts view accountability to be a contested concept by defining it as holding a particular entity—individual or organization to account by having to justify their actions, answer questions raised by interested others, and face commensurate consequences (e.g., Edwards & Veale, 2017). Transparency is seen as the starting point of the process for achieving accountability, and in this sense, it is seen as an instrument to strive toward accountability. In contrast, transparency has an entirely different meaning in the pricing discipline, having to do with the disclosure and availability of prices and the provision of information to help contextualize prices for consumers. Price availability is often insufficient because the past three decades of psychological pricing research have shown that shrewd managers can make prices readily available but still make it difficult for customers to process or understand them using methods such as partitioned pricing and drip pricing (Dholakia, 2019).

Other aspects, such as how frequently prices change and the range within which they vary, and whether they are fixed or negotiable, are all significant facets of price transparency; accountability is not a consideration because once prices are disclosed, it is entirely the customer's responsibility to make sense of them and use them effectively. Yet another conceptualization of price transparency sees it as a value proposition that blossoms into an attractive brand promise that engenders emotional responses from customers. To summarize, the business law version of transparency is idealized and aspirational, whereas the pricing transparency version is pragmatic, self-serving, and limited. Although they influence practitioners' day-to-day decisions, these divergent perspectives remain "stranded" and self-referent within business academia, with no bridges spanning the disciplines.

Furthermore, in addition to its ubiquity and the aforementioned coverage of the broad conceptual domain, there are at least four key aspects of business transparency that make it an essential business topic for researchers. First, transparency is part and parcel of numerous critically important unanswered questions in every business discipline. In big data and information systems management, defining and increasing algorithmic transparency is a key challenge with the power to mainstream or scuttle numerous technological advances such as facial and voice recognition, personalized marketing programs (known as customerization), and new financial services. In pricing strategy, transparency is reflected in four distinct aspects, including price availability, pricing offer complexity, the frequency of price changes, and the perceived negotiability of prices, which can make or break pricing success and, consequently, the business's long-term viability. For instance, controlling the ready availability of prices is a key managerial decision that dictates consequential outcomes, whether it is generating an advantage in negotiations, an aura of exclusivity and status, or the profit margin.

In operations management, supply chain transparency is a conduit to quick and decisive, yet fraught, managerial actions in safety–critical industries like food, drugs, and airlines, a way to improve efficiency and productivity in production, and a means of generating customer trust and brand strength. In business leadership, transparency in relations with others is seen by many researchers to be a foundational attribute of career success (Gardner et al., 2005; Walumbwa et al., 2008), although others question the simplicity of this perspective, arguing that it offers a static, decontextualized, and biased picture (Alvesson & Einola, 2019) and fails to demarcate the distinction between intentions to be authentic versus others' attributions of authenticity (Iszatt-White & Kempster, 2019).

Second, the contextual aspects of business transparency, its antecedents, and its consequences make it far more difficult to establish general theories, conceptualizations, or empirical generalizations relative to narrow and well-defined concepts. The phenomenon of transparency in one setting, say, the ready availability of prices in a B2B industry, is structured very differently from another setting, such as establishing the accountability of algorithms in AI and its implications for user trust. Academically, it is far easier to point out the differences in the meaning of transparency in these two settings (and in others) than it is to form a unifying framework. Indeed, many studies of transparency focus on the particular. In analyzing algorithmic transparency (and opacity), for instance, Burrell (2016) points out that "The algorithms in question are studied for the way they are situated within a corporation, under the pressure of profit and shareholder value, and as they are applied to particular real-world user populations (and the data these populations produce)... Such analyses are often particular to an implementation (such as Google's search engine) with its specific user base and uniquely accumulated history of problems and failures with resulting parameter settings and manual tweaking by programmers. Such an approach may not surface important broader patterns or risks to be found in particular classes of algorithms." (pp. 2–3). Remaining optimistic, we may conclude that even though the challenge of developing an integrative framework taken up in this book is formidable, the potential payoffs of doing so are high, with the possibility of contributing to multiple business literatures. This issue forms the focus of Chapter 7.

Third, although the aforementioned transparency ideal is one of uncovering knowledge to get to the truth (Ananny & Crawford, 2018), the reality is that business transparency is essentially *a matter of perception*, not only in the eyes of those affected by the degree of transparency (or lack thereof) but also for those who manage and administer the processes that generate and modulate the transparency, and even lookers-on. Specifically, when we are talking about making something transparent, more often than not, we are really talking about how to manage perceptions of how transparent that something is, whether it is the company's prices, the use of an algorithm, or its CEO's leadership style. In the study of business transparency, the analysis of transparency perceptions is almost as important as the analysis of transparency itself.

Fourth, across disciplines and settings, business transparency is *inherently asymmetric* mainly because the counter-parties—the discloser and the receiver, in most business settings, have different amounts of power and recourse. For example, companies know a lot more about the attitudes, motivations, preferences, and behaviors of their customers than customers know these things about the companies. The antitheses of transparency are secrecy and privacy, and unlike the idealistic principle of "perfect transparency is perfect truth," in most business settings, a balance between transparency, on the one hand, and secrecy and privacy, on the other, is the most desirable condition, with maximal aligned benefits.

The Book's Roadmap

Many concepts studied by business scholars tend to be difficult to pin down, but transparency is notoriously slippery and evanescent even by these standards. As Hood (2006, p. 3) observes, "Like many other notions of a quasi-religious nature, transparency is more often preached than practiced, more often invoked than defined, and indeed might ironically be said to be mystic in essence, at least to some extent." Simply put, there is a great deal of confusion and idealization in the domain of transparency. The fact that our understanding of business transparency is murky is a special irony. Providing some clarity is this book's primary objective and its main intended contribution. To do so, the business transparency literature is first organized and explored by disciplinary area before an integrative summary is provided in the last chapter.

Chapter 2 reviews the extensive research on transparency in business operations. The idea of two-sided operational openness permeates this research, with transparency initiatives directed toward upstream partners such as suppliers and downstream entities such as customers, investors, and activists, but the two sides have been considered in separate siloes, with issues about product-centric transparency covered under *supply chain transparency* and service-centric transparency covered under *operational transparency*. These initiatives are grounded in a number of pragmatic objectives, such as improving efficiency, reducing costs and waste, establishing a culture of safety, and building a strong brand, but for many companies, they are as much about improving performance as they are about managing the perceptions of a particular target group such as regulators or customers. Compared with other areas of business transparency, this literature is rife with inconsistent nomenclature and tenuous nomological linkages. Chapter 2 tries to clarify core concepts of business operations transparency and their relations to each other and identifies significant research findings and implications.

Chapter 3 considers the research on *price transparency*, a form of tactical transparency that companies use to devise complex and effective pricing structures and to build brands with transparency as a core value proposition. Different aspects of price transparency become salient to the company and its customers during each stage of the pricing process and the buying journey, respectively; an original framework is presented in the chapter to consider these meanings and their implications. The chapter also explores the distinction between *accessibility-based price transparency*, which comprises four components—availability, offer complexity, change frequency, and perceived price negotiability, and *disclosure-based price transparency*, concerned with the disclosure of pricing inputs and performance variables. The extensive research and nuances of these concepts are considered in Chapter 3.

Chapter 4 discusses the research on *organizational transparency*, concerned primarily with the open sharing of relevant information within and across functional and hierarchical organizational delineations and its implications. This is a rich literature spanning several decades, much of which has viewed cultivated transparency to be the backbone and governing principle of an organization's corporate culture, guiding the decisions and actions of its executives, contributing to employee productivity and engagement, and leading to positive downstream outcomes. However, an interesting contrarian view considers organizational transparency to justify adopting intrusive monitoring mechanisms to surveil employees and customers under the guise of fostering openness and wellbeing, which is also explored in this chapter. Finally, the research on one particular form of organizational transparency, *pay transparency*, and its relation to the gender wage gap is considered in Chapter 4 to understand better how cultural transparency shapes individual and collective employee outcomes within the organization.

Chapter 5 reviews *authentic leadership*, considered by some as "the gold standard for leadership" (Ibarra, 2015). The authentic business leader is attuned to transparency both for themselves and their organization; the extensive theorizing in this domain posits that the core of this construct comprises transparency-related aspects, including a penetrating self-awareness of one's values, motivations, and attributes, the consistent practice of value and attitude-congruent behaviors, a commitment to truthful practices, the practice of humility, and honesty and openness in one's relationships (called *relational transparency*). As mentioned earlier, vociferous critiques of these ideas are also considered in the chapter. They argue that the authentic leadership paradigm is scaffolded by concepts and assertions that are overly simplistic, one-dimensional, static, decontextualized, anecdotal, and distorted by a positive bias and have yet to be sufficiently tested through rigorous academic scholarship. The criticisms further warn that the advice derived from authentic leadership research for practitioners may mislead and trivialize difficult work.

Chapter 6 covers research on the transparency of algorithms and consumer disclosure. As the cost of gathering, storing, and analyzing data has come down, and companies have embraced data-driven decision making and hyper-personalized offerings for their customers, the use of algorithms has been adopted in numerous business applications. While they seem objective and methodical, algorithm use has the potential to harm users and those affected by their decisions unintentionally. This chapter considers the research on the challenges behind making algorithms and their outputs transparent that hinge on facilitating understanding. As seen from the discloser's side of the information exchange, some of the issues involving consumer disclosure and their nuanced outcomes are also examined in this chapter. The upshot is that disclosure has obvious benefits, leading to more customer-oriented marketing programs, yet it invariably opens the door to discrimination and exploitation of consumers, which is then very hard to close.

Chapter 7, the final chapter, identifies a pervasive tension that dominates transparency research in the business disciplines between the unalloyed positive narratives that emphasize its role in making business more accountable, efficient, and equitable and its dark side that highlights the strategic use of disclosure to gain the upper hand, persuade, mislead, or exploit by either the discloser or the receiver. To reconcile this fundamental inconsistency, a detailed consideration of how the disclosed information is used, by whom, and its interaction with the relevant contextual factors is needed. An original integrative conceptual framework of business transparency is presented in Chapter 7 that identifies the distinct roles of the discloser and the receiver, distinguishes between six forms of transparency, each having certain configurations and structural features that generalize across disciplines and settings, elaborates on five properties that define the role of disclosure as information, and establishes the primary role of business transparency as a mutual striving toward generating meaning from the disclosure. The chapter, and this book, concludes with a reconceptualized definition of business transparency for the reader's consideration that seeks to be balanced, interdisciplinary, versatile, and integrative.

References

Albu, O. B., & Flyverbom, M. (2019). Organizational transparency: Conceptualizations, conditions, and consequences. *Business & Society, 58*(2), 268–297.

Alvesson, M., & Einola, K. (2019). Warning for excessive positivity: Authentic leadership and other traps in leadership studies. *Leadership Quarterly, 30*(4), 383–395.

Ananny, M., & Crawford, K. (2018). Seeing without knowing: Limitations of the transparency ideal and its application to algorithmic accountability. *New Media & Society, 20*(3), 973–989.

Bamberger, P., & Belogolovsky, E. (2017). The dark side of transparency: How and when pay administration practices affect employee helping. *Journal of Applied Psychology, 102*(4), 658–671.

Bateman, A., & Bonanni, L. (2019, August 20). *What supply chain transparency really means*. Harvard Business Review. https://hbr.org/2019/08/what-supply-chain-transparency-really-means

Bernstein, E. S. (2012). The transparency paradox: A role for privacy in organizational learning and operational control. *Administrative Science Quarterly, 57*(2), 181–216.
Bernstein, E. S. (2017). Making transparency transparent: The evolution of observation in management theory. *Academy of Management Annals, 11*(1), 217–266.
Brandeis, L. D. (1913, December 20). What publicity can do. *Harper's Weekly* (pp. 10–13).
Brown, M., Nyberg, A. J., Weller, I., & Strizver, S. D. (2022). Pay information disclosure: Review and recommendations for research spanning the pay secrecy–pay transparency continuum. *Journal of Management, 48*(6), 1661–1694.
Buell, R. W. (2019). Operational transparency. *Harvard Business Review, 97*(2), 102–113.
Buell, R. W., & Kalkanci, B. (2021). How transparency into internal and external responsibility initiatives influences consumer choice. *Management Science, 67*(2), 932–950.
Burrell, J. (2016). How the machine 'thinks': Understanding opacity in machine learning algorithms. *Big Data and Society, 3*(1), 1–16.
Colella, A., Paetzold, R. L., Zardkoohi, A., & Wesson, M. J. (2007). Exposing pay secrecy. *Academy of Management Review, 32*(1), 55–71.
Cullen, Z. B., & Perez-Truglia, R. (2018). *The salary taboo: Privacy norms and the diffusion of information* (Working paper 25145). National Bureau of Economic Research.
Dholakia, U. M. (2019). *Priced to influence, sell & satisfy: Lessons from behavioral economics for pricing success*. Kindle Publishing Group.
Diakopoulos, N., & Koliska, M. (2017). Algorithmic transparency in the news media. *Digital Journalism, 5*(7), 809–828.
Dufresne, R. L., & Offstein, E. H. (2008). On the virtues of secrecy in organizations. *Journal of Management Inquiry, 17*(2), 102–106.
Edwards, L., & Veale, M. (2017). Slave to the algorithm: Why a right to an explanation is probably not the remedy you are looking for. *Duke Law and Technology Review, 16*, 18–84.
Fisman, R., & Luca, M. (2016). Fixing discrimination in online marketplaces. *Harvard Business Review, 94*(12), 88–95.
Flyverbom, M. (2016). Transparency: Mediation and the management of visibilities. *International Journal of Communication, 10*, 110–122.
Gardner, W. L., Avolio, B. J., Luthans, F., May, D. R., & Walumbwa, F. (2005). "Can you see the real me?" A self-based model of authentic leader and follower development. *Leadership Quarterly, 16*(3), 343–372.

Hanna, R. C., Lemon, K. N., & Smith, G. E. (2019). Is transparency a good thing? How online price transparency and variability can benefit firms and influence consumer decision making. *Business Horizons, 62*(2), 227–236.

Hansen, H. K., & Weiskopf, R. (2021). From universalizing transparency to the interplay of transparency matrices: Critical insights from the emerging social credit system in China. *Organization Studies, 42*(1), 109–128.

Heald, D. (2006). Varieties of transparency. *Proceedings of the British Academy, 135*, 25–43.

Hood, C. (2006). Transparency in historical perspective. *Proceedings of the British Academy, 135*, 3–23.

Ibarra, H. (2015). The authenticity paradox. *Harvard Business Review, 93*(1/2), 53–59.

Iszatt-White, M., & Kempster, S. (2019). Authentic leadership: Getting back to the roots of the 'root construct'? *International Journal of Management Reviews, 21*(3), 356–369.

Jiang, B., Sudhir, K., & Zou, T. (2021). Effects of cost-information transparency on intertemporal price discrimination. *Production and Operations Management, 30*(2), 390–401.

Jönsson, S. (1988). *Accounting regulation and elite structures*. Wiley.

Kaptein, M. (2008). Developing and testing a measure for the ethical culture of organizations: The corporate ethical virtues model. *Journal of Organizational Behavior, 29*(7), 923–947.

Kellogg, K. C., Valentine, M. A., & Christin, A. (2020). Algorithms at work: The new contested terrain of control. *Academy of Management Annals, 14*(1), 366–410.

Kim, Y. H., & Davis, G. F. (2016). Challenges for global supply chain sustainability: Evidence from conflict minerals reports. *Academy of Management Journal, 59*(6), 1896–1916.

Larsson, T. (1998). How open can a government be? The Swedish experience. In V. Deckmyn & I. Thompson (Eds.), *Openness and transparency in the European Union* (pp. 39–52). European Institute of Public Administration.

Madhavan, A., Porter, D., & Weaver, D. (2005). Should securities markets be transparent? *Journal of Financial Markets, 8*(3), 265–287.

Merriam-Webster. (2022). *The Merriam-Webster dictionary* (New edition).

Meijer, A. (2014). Transparency. *The Oxford handbook of public accountability* (pp. 507–524). Oxford University Press

Osorio-Vega, P. (2019). The ethics of entrepreneurial shared value. *Journal of Business Ethics, 157*(4), 981–995.

Pasquale, F. (2015). *The black box society: The secret algorithms that control money and information*. Harvard University Press.

Rego, A., & Giustiniano, L. (2021). Are relationally transparent leaders more receptive to the relational transparency of others? An authentic dialog perspective. *Journal of Business Ethics.* https://doi.org/10.1007/s10551-021-047 92-6.

Rosenbaum, L. (2015). Scoring no goal—Further adventures in transparency. *New England Journal of Medicine, 373*(15), 1385–1388.

Schnackenberg, A. K., & Tomlinson, E. C. (2016). Organizational transparency: A new perspective on managing trust in organization-stakeholder relationships. *Journal of Management, 42*(7), 1784–1810.

Sinha, I. (2000). Cost transparency: The net's real threat to prices and brands. *Harvard Business Review, 78*(2), Reprint R00210.

Sodhi, M. S., & Tang, C. S. (2019). Research opportunities in supply chain transparency. *Production and Operations Management, 28*(12), 2946–2959.

Solove, D. J., & Citron, D. K. (2017). Risk and anxiety: A theory of data-breach harms. *Texas Law Review, 96,* 737–786.

Toegel, I., Levy, O., & Jonsen, K. (2022). Secrecy in practice: How middle managers promote strategic initiatives behind the scenes. *Organization Studies, 43*(6), 885–906.

Walumbwa, F. O., Avolio, B. J., Gardner, W. L., Wernsing, T. S., & Peterson, S. J. (2008). Authentic leadership: Development and validation of a theory-based measure. *Journal of Management, 34*(1), 89–126.

CHAPTER 2

Business Operations Transparency

Abstract This chapter examines the research on transparency in business operations, distinguishing between the literature on supply chain transparency, focused on product-centric organizations, and operational transparency, concerned with service-centered organizations. The complex and inconsistent nomenclature and nomological linkages in this literature are clarified as is the growing research emphasis on downstream issues. One significant conclusion reached is that business operations transparency is often as much about managing perceptions of a particular target audience as it is about improving actual performance.

Keywords Transparency · Supply chains · Business operations · Customers · Service operations

> Transparency is not the same as looking straight through a building: it's not just a physical idea, it's also an intellectual one.—Helmut Jahn.

As business strives to be a force for good, transparency is an inherently appealing concept. Within many organizations today, there is a powerful self-evident impulse to *practice two-sided openness* when conducting business operations. One side refers to transparent practices involving suppliers, channel partners, and even employees that provide the raw materials, ingredients, components, and labor used in making the company's products and services. The other side refers to transparency practices directed mainly toward customers, but that may also include other downstream entities such as investors, activists, and after-sales services partners. In the academic business literature, there has been a lot of theoretical and pragmatic interest in studying both these sides of openness in business operations for a number of decades.

Furthermore, there are significant differences in issues and findings related to operational openness (or contrarily, opacity) depending on whether the organization's predominant offering is tangible and product-heavy or intangible and services-centered. For product-centric offerings, the main concerns involve understanding, measuring, and managing suppliers for specific purposes. For service-centric offerings, in contrast, the key decision is about how high to raise the curtain to shed light on previously hidden "backstage" service processes and, contrarily, how visible to make customer reactions to frontline service employees. Extensive but largely siloed literatures have sprung up to examine these two aspects of business transparency, referred to as *supply chain transparency* and *operational transparency*, respectively, in this chapter.

Two core insights are offered in this chapter. The first one is that business operations transparency is often as much about improving performance as it is about managing the perceptions of a particular target audience such as customers or regulators. For example, learning about the manufacturing processes, ingredient sources, and suppliers' labor practices may provide ideas about how to increase manufacturing efficiency or react when an adverse event occurs. Still, it may also provide fodder to signal virtue or to establish a conscientious or eco-friendly brand association directed toward consumers. Managers need to be clear about why they are adopting transparent operations practices for their organization to derive the maximum value from their efforts.

Second, the literature covered here is rife with complex and even inconsistent nomenclature and nomological linkages employed to parse the different forms of operational transparency. For instance, some authors see traceability as one form of visibility, whereas others treat the two concepts as synonymous. Additionally, there are industry-specific conventions that further muddy the waters. The upshot is that it is difficult to form a coherent or comprehensive theoretical understanding of operational transparency given the current state of the literature. Finally, the research on operational transparency in services has evolved virtually independently of the older and larger literature on supply chain transparency. All of this is to say that while I have tried hard to establish clarity around how the concepts are defined and linked here, a more comprehensive effort to unify these literatures into a conceptual whole is needed. The next section considers the research on supply chain transparency, and this discussion is followed by one examining operational transparency research.

Supply Chain Transparency

Supply chain transparency, broadly characterized as finding out and then deliberately disclosing information about various aspects of the functioning of the organization's supply chain, has moved to the forefront of managerial decision making over the past fifteen years or so (Bateman & Bonanni, 2019; New, 2010). Depending on the primary target and the underlying purpose of the disclosure, researchers demarcate supply chain transparency initiatives into two broad categories. *Internal transparency initiatives* focus on gathering and disseminating proprietary information about suppliers and the company's operations and service delivery processes to employees. The emphasis is on gathering hitherto ignored or unavailable data and performance measures to understand and manage the social and environmental impacts of the company's operations. *External transparency initiatives*, in contrast, are mainly concerned with the disclosure of proprietary information about the supply chain and the processes behind it to specific external constituents such as customers, regulators, activists, investors, or others (Buell & Kalkanci, 2021; Parmigiani et al., 2011). The information to be disclosed externally may already be available within the organization, or in some cases, the disclosure may involve gathering new information.

Supply chain transparency initiatives serve a variety of strategic and tactical organizational goals, including improving efficiency through various means, reducing costs and waste, maintaining and encouraging a culture of safety within the organization as well as for its suppliers, speeding up reactions to adverse events to minimize their ramifications, validating the company's standing as a responsible and law-abiding entity to regulators, industry groups, investors, etc., building the company's brand by making "a virtue of provenance" (New, 2010), preparing for or meeting the requirements of Environmental, Social, and Governance (ESG) reporting, attracting high-quality conscientious employees, proactively managing the organization's reputation, and strengthening customer engagement and relationships (Bateman & Bonanni, 2019; Parmigiani et al., 2011; Sodhi & Tang, 2019). Note that this is still a partial list; as political tastes, corporate cultural norms, and other environmental factors evolve, and movements for issues such as social justice, wage inequality, and conscious capitalism grow, the nature of disclosures and the types of supply-chain-related information that warrant disclosing will also continue to evolve.

The Value of Supply Chain Transparency

Broadly speaking, the lengthy list can be distilled into three significant reasons that account for the heightened significance of supply chain transparency, all of which support greater levels of transparency as defined by the breadth of criteria and the depth of disclosed information: (1) the need to react quickly and decisively in safety-critical settings to minimize the financial costs and sometimes even loss of lives when an adverse event occurs such as incidents of foodborne illness, food or drug contamination, failure of an aerospace part in service, or a manufacturing accident, and the ability to apportion liability afterward, (2) to improve the efficiency of the company's supply chain by being able to analyze, monitor, and track supplier inputs and performance precisely to make business decisions, and (3) to alleviate consumers' distrust and strengthen consumer-brand relationships through judicious and meaningful disclosures about operations, especially when such revelations are extraordinary and offer a competitive advantage, or when they are about issues that target customers are really concerned about such as conflict minerals or greenhouse emissions (Aung & Chang, 2014; Kim & Davis, 2016; New & Brown, 2011; Sodhi & Tang, 2019; Symonds, 2007).

Studies show that companies that exhibit greater supply chain transparency achieve greater profitability, realize improved sales performance, and have higher stock market valuations than comparable firms with lower levels of transparency (Swift et al., 2019). Furthermore, telling customers about its supply chain sustainability efforts, such as paying a living wage to workers, is at least as persuasive as advertisements about the organization's corporate social responsibility and cause marketing efforts measured by customer purchases (Buell & Kalkanci, 2021). Recently, this positive logic behind supply chain transparency has been extended to attempts to measure and report the financial value of the impacts and dependencies of business operations on natural resources. This so-called forward-looking *natural capital accounting* aims to take a longer-term perspective on sustainability and provide more realistic, future-oriented valuations to investors and other stakeholders (Mohr & Thissen, 2022).

The Drawbacks of Supply Chain Transparency

On the other hand, some scholars have argued that supply chain transparency can negatively affect the company. Some of these arguments are grounded in the logic that internal information about demand, capacity utilization, manufacturing processes, supplier capabilities, orders, prices, costs, and margins at different points in the supply chain constitutes valuable proprietary information, and revealing this in an uncontrolled way (such as making it available on a website) cedes competitive advantage (e.g., Bateman & Bonanni, 2019; Marshall et al., 2016). Furthermore, providing this information without sufficient context can lead to misinterpretation, resulting in a negative assessment and even backlash from consumers, activists, and other stakeholders. As Bateman and Bonanni (2019) succinctly put it, "supply chains were not designed to be transparent." More practically, increasing supply chain transparency can be costly without yielding an adequate return on the money spent.

Another reason for caution is that the widespread adoption of RFID, the Internet of Things (IoT), and blockchain technologies to track materials through the supply chain has gained enthusiasm in many companies in recent years (Astill et al., 2019; Hastig & Sodhi, 2020; New, 2010). Yet, these technologies and tracking methods come with significant challenges that include an inordinate increase in costs and labor resources, the lack of coordination, the lack of standards, the unavailability of information in the appropriate form and in a timely fashion, and bureaucratic, political and executive resistance, all of which dampen the movement toward greater supply chain transparency (Bosona & Gebresenbet, 2013). Simply put, adopting unproven, buggy, and constantly innovating technologies without a corresponding infrastructure and organizational culture to support this innovation orientation and manage the risks stemming from it may produce more harm than good in many organizations.

Given this mixed outlook, as noted earlier, a considerable amount of the managerial interest in supply chain transparency is driven by consumers. In particular, because of a lack of trust in brands and businesses and a rising interest in social and political issues, more consumers today want to know where the products they consume come from, how they are made, who makes them, and the sources of their ingredients (Amed et al., 2019; Markenson & Orgel, 2022). In analyzing the fashion industry, for instance, Amed and colleagues (2019) lay out the challenge in this way: "Fashion companies must come to terms with the fact that a more distrusting consumer expects full transparency across the value chain" (p. 60).

What's more, compounding the difficulty, many consumers in categories such as apparel and food have a poor or inaccurate understanding of core issues such as the science behind the food grown with genetically modified organisms or the economics of fast fashion, that is often gleaned from non-expert and biased sources like social media influencers. The fault outlook expands the transparency challenge from just publishing factual information to providing the information and then persuading customers that it is valid (e.g., Kale, 2021; Wunderlich & Gatto, 2015).

The core challenge of supply chain transparency. In the research literature on supply chain transparency, however, the focus is squarely on the organization's gathering information and increasing its accessibility. When seen from the consumer's perspective, supply chain transparency can mean the availability of information about many things, from proof of ownership of the intellectual property utilized and embedded in the brand's offerings, to the employment of fair labor practices, including such things as fair wages and diversity and inclusion initiatives, to the use of ethical and sustainable sourcing practices, and proactive environmental conservation activities (Campbell & Winterich, 2018; Mohan et al., 2018; Thompson, 2021). To deliver these expectations to consumers and other stakeholders, New and Brown (2011) frame the core imperative for managers regarding supply chain transparency broadly but meaningfully as: "*How much should organizations know about their extended supply base, and what should they do with this information?*" They further elaborate on this question by describing a four-pronged set of challenges for managerial decision making about supply chain transparency: (1) Does the company have supply chain visibility; (2) how much supply chain visibility does the company share; (3) how does the company face risk when they find it in their supply chain; and (4) what does the company need to organize to provide supply chain visibility?

Core Definitions of Supply Chain Transparency Concepts

To parse the New and Brown (2011) set of challenges clearly, operations management researchers commonly distinguish between the concepts of *visibility*, *disclosure* (also referred to as *transparency* by some researchers), and *traceability* (also called *provenance*) in supply chains (Kraft et al., 2018; New, 2010; Sodhi & Tang, 2019), that mirrors the way in which disclosure and availability of information are conceptualized in other business areas such as pricing and organizational culture covered in this book. However, there is one additional wrinkle.

Unlike prices or organizational reporting structures, the information about supply chains resides entirely outside the organization; the managerial challenge of finding out the requisite information from partners can be significant and costly, involving the core choices of *who* and *what*, and these questions repeat for the subsequent decisions regarding the targets of the disclosure. Although the organization's culture may significantly affect fact-finding decisions and processes, the literature on organizational cultural transparency, covered in Chapter 4, has evolved in parallel with very few bridges spanning them. Examining some of the definitions offered by researchers for the core concepts provides a useful starting point to dig deeper into supply chain transparency.

Starting with *supply chain visibility*, Sodhi and Tang (2019) define it as "managers' efforts to gather information about operations upstream and downstream in their supply chains," and they define *supply chain transparency* as "a company disclosing information to the public, including consumers and investors, about upstream operations and about the products it sells to consumers" while Bateman and Bonanni (2019) define it in somewhat broader terms by noting that "Supply chain transparency requires companies to know what is happening upstream in the supply chain and to communicate this knowledge both internally and externally," where the relevant audience may not only be customers but also be governments, NGOs, investors, and others. In the domain of food production, Astill and colleagues (2019) define supply chain transparency somewhat ambiguously as involving "access to non-distorted, factual, relevant, and timely information about supply chain products" where the subject and object are both unclear.

Sodhi and Tang (2019) define *supply chain traceability* as one facet of visibility, as "the capability of a company for ascertaining provenance" (p. 2946), while Astill and colleagues (2019) define traceability as "the ability to track the history, location, and function of an entity." In the domain of food management, Bosona and Gebresenbet (2013) define food traceability as "a part of logistics management that capture, store, and transmit adequate information about a food, feed, food-producing animal or substance at all stages in the food supply chain so that the product can be checked for safety and quality control, traced upward, and tracked downward at any time." As these definitions suggest, the larger the organization, the more complex the products it sells, and the larger its product portfolio, the more difficult and costly the process of traceability will be. Significantly, traceability is dynamic and continuous, much like other significant business variables such as customer satisfaction or employee engagement.

Understanding the distinctions between these transparency-related concepts is crucial. Sodhi and Tang (2019) distinguish between *visibility* and *transparency* in this way: "Visibility initiatives aim at stakeholders internal to the company and its immediate supply chain partners. By contrast, transparency efforts target external stakeholders by way of consumers, investors, and regulators, among others" (p. 2948). While this distinction is clear-cut and useful, it is not universally used in this literature; in fact, it is common for the word *transparency* to be used to define supply chain initiatives that Sodhi and Tang (2019) refer to as *visibility*.

Upstream and downstream transparency. This literature also distinguishes between *upstream* and *downstream* supply chain transparency, with downstream transparency gaining importance in recent years. Upstream transparency refers to the extent of disclosure by the company about its upstream operations and supply chain and is covered by the set of definitions provided above. These disclosures can pertain to a variety of factors such as the names, locations, and business practices of the company's main suppliers (also known as tier-1 suppliers; see, e.g., fashion brand Patagonia's "Footprint Chronicles"), the provenance or source of its raw materials, ingredients, or parts, the degree of compliance of its suppliers to environmental regulations as well as well-accepted norms about resource use, information about various costs such as expenses for materials, labor, transportation, and taxes (also covered in Chapter 3 under price transparency), the degree of supplier compliance to Environment, Health, and Safety (EHS) standards, and information in all these categories about the supply chains of the core suppliers (i.e., the extent to which the suppliers can track and gather information about *their* suppliers).

In contrast, *downstream transparency* refers to relevant disclosures about post-purchase issues that involve the company's extended services and supply chains, such as how the company and its partners make delivery and packaging decisions to minimize waste and post-purchase customer inconvenience, the access to repair and refurbishment services, and how the company will handle information regarding the used, failed, or expired product at the end of its life, such as through recycling, disassembly, destruction after it has been consumed (e.g., Butler, 2022; Jovane et al., 1993; Sodhi & Tang, 2019). Downstream transparency is explored in greater detail later in this chapter.

Supply Chain Visibility

The concept of supply chain visibility is nuanced and conceived of in a number of different ways, with some degree of overlap between the different treatments. Some researchers consider visibility simply as the current state of managerial knowledge about an organization's supply chain. For instance, Kraft et al. (2018) define visibility as "the extent to which a company [i.e., its managers and employees] has information about the social responsibility practices in the supply chain." In contrast, as described earlier, others like Sodhi and Tang (2019) consider visibility to be a matter of managerial effort (that has already been expended plus future behavioral intentions) in gathering information such that greater visibility corresponds to greater effort. In this definition, perceptions of effort by relevant stakeholders are as often the focus of attention as actual effort (e.g., Kraft et al., 2018). Still others view visibility as a matter of managerial judgment and decision making about which informational elements of the supply chain to track and report and putting in place the processes to implement these strategic choices (New & Brown, 2011).

The primary reason for an organization's supply chain to be traceable in many industries is pragmatic. One vital consideration is to maintain high levels of safety. Consequently, in industries such as aerospace, pharmaceuticals, specialty chemicals, and medical equipment, regulations, and complex legacy processes instituted at the industry level ensure that materials and components are rigidly and minutely tracked through the supply chain, irrespective of the prohibitive cost of doing so (New, 2010). In the food industry, for example, traceability is seen both as a tool for implementing food safety actions such as executing a recall of a particular food item and also as a way to establish proof of authenticity of food, to use as a marketing message (Hastig & Sodhi, 2020). Despite the potential benefits and the significant resources devoted to it, traceability is still a challenge in this industry because of the fragmented nature of the industry, the complex, multi-sourced, and multi-staged processing, the lack of comprehensive regulations and enforcement, and the opportunities for subverting traceability processes (Astil et al., 2019; Aung & Chang, 2014). For example, counterfeiters can relabel fake products to inject them into legitimate business channels, and tracking packages is easier than tracking their actual contents, leaving them vulnerable to misidentification or appropriation (Hastig & Sodhi, 2019).

Visibility is a meaningful organization-specific strategic variable in that the organization's leaders must deliberately decide how to pursue and implement visibility initiatives involving their supply chain. However, as New and Brown (2011) point out, the context matters; much of the disparity in visibility initiatives across organizations can be attributed to structural features of the business and supply chains, such as the complexity of the company's offerings, the nature of the technology used for tracking and reporting and the rate of technological change, the complexity and fluidity of the specific organization's supplier network, and the degree of commoditization at each point in the supply network. Considering these different elements, the manager must make common decisions about what data to collect from the supply chain and how to do so, how to verify the data, i.e., what standards of evidence to use, and how to store and handle the proprietary data.

Visibility and supplier risks. Furthermore, exchange relationships between companies and their suppliers are often marked by conflicting motives and power dynamics resembling the relationships between companies and their customers. As one example, in the pursuit of the highest profit, or even because of sustained pressure from the organization itself to cut costs, raise quality, and speed up delivery, suppliers may engage in risky behaviors that, in the long run, may produce adverse downstream consequences for the organization.

In particular, Sodhi and Tang (2019) identified six types of supplier risks that require the organization to attend to visibility diligently and consider it in a nuanced way instead of using a simplistic "more is better" approach: (1) *materials risks*, which involves suppliers using unsafe or illegal materials or ingredients such as lead or phthalates in toys that are prohibited in the markets where the final products will be sold, or which are known to cause harm to consumers, (2) *product risks*, which involves unsafe design or shoddy manufacturing practices that make products such as strollers hazardous to users (e.g., Fowler, et al., 2016), (3) *reputation risk*, whereby the endorsement of unethical or illegal activities such as using child labor by suppliers affect the company's brand reputation, (4) *environmental risks*, whereby suppliers violate environmental regulations in their own countries or in countries where the products will be sold, (5) *product development risks*, whereby suppliers promise the logistics and manufacturing capabilities to deliver the product but are either unable or unwilling to do so, and (6) *time risk*, which involves failure on the suppliers' part to deliver the product on time. To this list, we can add (7) financial risk, whereby a supplier's illegal, unsafe, and self-serving behaviors result in adverse financial consequences for the company, from diminished goodwill and lost sales to outraged customers and fines by regulators.

Consistent with the list, many managers view supply chain visibility as a structured approach to mitigate supplier risks using a range of industry-specific auditing, inspection, and monitoring mechanisms that are either entirely managed by the company or implemented as part of an industry consortium or private–public engagement. As one example of the latter, after a building collapse killed 1,134 garment workers in Bangladesh, over 220 global apparel and retailer brands coordinated with worker unions to develop and enforce a set of regulations called the Accord on Fire and Building Safety in Bangladesh that mandate periodic safety inspections, safety training programs for all workers, and detailed reporting of these inspections (Ashwin et al., 2020).

Visibility and actionable insights. Another benefit of supply chain visibility, much like the adoption of price input disclosures covered in Chapter 3, is that it provides actionable insights to managers for operational improvement (e.g., they could sever ties with underperforming or law-flouting suppliers) or strategic decision making (e.g., bring a particular capability like logistics services or the production of a particularly significant component in-house). For instance, armed with an understanding of its extant supply chain's potential weaknesses and future prospects, Apple has worked systematically for over a decade to design and manufacture many components of the semiconductors it uses in its products, replacing suppliers like Broadcom and Skyworks (Gartenberg, 2021). This issue has become even more significant in the aftermath of the supply chain disruptions caused by the COVID-19 pandemic, as organizations shift from emphasizing cost and operating efficiency to placing greater weight on resilience and redundancy in their supply chains (Wellener et al., 2022).

For suppliers, the effects of transparency are a mixed bag. On the one hand, when reputable brands practice supply chain transparency, say by publishing a list of their suppliers or reporting specific aspects of their performance such as (lack of) accidents, this can provide direct benefits to the supplier by publicizing its strengths, and generating instant credibility in a manner similar to validation from a credible third party; this, in turn, burnishes the supplier's brand image, making it easier to acquire other customers, reduce NGO scrutiny, and so on. On the flip side, when such disclosures shed light on the supplier's shortcomings, such as relatively low wages being paid to employees or past environmental violations, it can produce significant and even irreversible reputational harm (Kalkanci & Plambeck, 2020). Not surprisingly, then, the net impact of disclosure depends on the supplier's track record and customer orientation, along with structural industry characteristics.

Supply chain transparency as a consumer trust-building strategy. In an overall business environment that is marked by "a rising trust deficit" (Amed et al., 2019) and suspicion about the motives of professional managers, supply chain transparency practiced voluntarily using judicious disclosure offers a powerful way for an organization to signal its good intentions and to show that it is "walking the walk." Many customers today are more interested in learning the source and authenticity of their purchases, choosing to support brands that have shown themselves to be socially responsible (New, 2010). As Sodhi and Tang (2019) put it, supply chain transparency "helps [the organization] gain consumer trust, create consumer awareness, solicit feedback from consumers, and communicate their efforts for environmental and social sustainability" (p. 2951). At the least, even in low-involvement contexts, they will use such disclosures as a signal of competence and authenticity. In other words, consumers' psychological responses stimulated by disclosure yield significant changes in their buying behavior.

Supporting this idea, in impressive field experiments, Buell and Kalkanci (2021) found that telling customers about the company's supply chain initiatives, such as the fact that an apparel company pays living wages to its employees in the Dominican Republican, and this has been verified by Worker Rights Commission, an independent organization that monitors labor rights, or that a coffee roasting company values environmental sustainability and composts the chaff from its roasting process, converting it into organic compost, not only increased customers' willingness to purchase the disclosing company's products, but also resulted in tangible increases in buying behavior as evidenced by the market share, quantity purchased, the average price paid, and the total spend for the brand.

Consumers also derive practical benefits from an organization's supply chain transparency. In food production, precisely knowing the source of a particular item and being able to track it through the supply chain from "farm to fork" can quell outbreaks of foodborne illness and food adulteration incidents, allow brands and regulators to orchestrate well-defined and quick recalls that minimize wastage, and provide consumers with the requisite information in a timely fashion to make smarter and personally relevant buying decisions (Astill et al., 2019).

While this research provides a solid understanding of the efforts of companies to provide information to customers about the supply chain, except for the aforementioned studies, it is mostly silent on how customers make sense of this information and integrate it into their buying decisions. In particular, there are some concerns about customers' motivation and willingness, not to mention their ability to make sense of company-generated disclosures. As one example of this issue, New (2010) points out that providing customers with online verification codes generated by third parties that can be used to learn in-depth information about the regions, companies, and factories and trace the route from raw materials to finished products has become popular among retailers like Asda and Tesco. However, as evident in other business settings throughout this book, it is not clear that the customers to which this disclosure is targeted can make sense of these codes or that they use them in any meaningful way in their buying decisions.

To the extent that this information affects buying decisions (itself an open question), two distinct possibilities arise based on high versus low motivation and ability to make sense of the disclosed information (Petty & Cacioppo, 1984). Is it, as seems more likely, that simply the presence of a verification code, or more generally, knowledge of the fact that the brand has taken the trouble to disclose information about its supply chain, serve as a positive heuristic conveying reputation? If this is the case, the company's efforts and money expended on supply chain transparency initiatives may serve as useful virtue signals but nothing more. Or is it that customers take the trouble to learn what the information provided in the disclosure means and use more complex decision rules to incorporate this information with their other quality- and price-based buying criteria? Without richer and definitive answers to these questions, a key component of the value and functioning of supply chain transparency and its impact on the organization's financial performance will remain unclear.

Downstream supply chain transparency. Downstream transparency is concerned with how the organization manages its offering in the customer's post-purchase journey (Dholakia, 2022) and includes a variety of issues such as the use and disposal of packaging in an environmentally and customer-friendly manner, offering customers or other entities the capability and the resources to repair the product (vs. discard it), extend the product's life as much as possible, and dispose of it at the end of its life responsibly and safely.

Relative to the research on upstream transparency covered earlier, the academic thinking on downstream transparency disclosures and their consequences is much less organized or elaborate. In practice, such disclosures are often non-strategic and ad hoc, executed reactively to manage potential reputational harm. As one example, a number of fashion and retailer brands such as Burberry, Louis Vuitton, Nike, and H&M have admitted to destroying or intentionally damaging products such as perfume, bags, shoes, and clothes worth tens of millions of dollars to protect their brand cachet and prevent old inventory from cannibalizing new sales (Cernansky, 2021). They make such disclosures reactively when a viral video showing slashed shoes or burnt clothes emerges on social media and causes outrage among environmental activists and even their loyal customers. Investors or reporters demand that they respond (Dalton, 2018; Napier & Sanguineti, 2018). Furthermore, in response to the blowback from such disclosures, these same brands promise to stop such practices or adopt alternative business models taking visible stances with varying degrees of follow-through (Butler, 2022; Paton, 2018).

Anecdotal evidence suggests that the impulse for downstream transparency within an organization arises from the values and championship of its leaders, usually the founders or owners of the business, which then leads to multi-pronged and innovative approaches to delivering these disclosures. Accordingly, an organization that emphasizes downstream transparency is fashion brand Patagonia, through innovative programs like *Worn Wear*, aimed at moving away from throwaway culture and planned obsolescence by making well-built, durable products with long lives and deliberately extending the lives of the products they sell. The program encourages customers to repair their Patagonia apparel by providing access to detailed guides to teach DIY customers to do repair work themselves and a well-staffed repair center run by company employees (Shankar & Canniford, 2016). The company has also adopted several other unique business practices, such as 100% renewable energy throughout its operations (except manufacturing), using substantial recycled and organic materials in its products, active participation in industry coalitions to champion its values such as the Fair Labor Association and the Sustainable Apparel Coalition.

Relevant to us, the company actively communicates these activities through detailed disclosures to its customers, lays out its goals for the future publicly (e.g., to use 100% reusable, home compostable, renewable, or easily recyclable packaging by 2025), and invites their customers and other stakeholders to hold them accountable (Patagonia, 2022). In many respects, Patagonia sets the current standard for the state-of-the-art best practice of downstream transparency. As the business environment evolves and the challenges of dealing with climate change, changing consumer expectations and social norms, and competitor initiatives, among others grow stiffer, downstream transparency practices and the standards for assessing them are bound to evolve.

Rigorous research on the consequences of transparency initiatives such as those adopted by Patagonia, the challenges of inadvertent transparency faced by brands such as Burberry and Nike, and other downstream transparency issues such as designing and making durable products, adopting sustainable and minimalist packaging approaches, building and supporting a repair ecosystem, engaging with right to repair movements, practicing responsible recycling and circular economy business models, changing customers' replacement mindset, and so on, is scarce at the moment, but is likely to be extremely useful and impactful in the future (e.g., Godfrey et al., 2022).

OPERATIONAL TRANSPARENCY

Thus far, much of the discussion in this chapter has focused on manufacturing industries and supply chain transparency for offerings comprised primarily of tangible products. Buell and colleagues (Buell, 2019; Buell & Norton, 2011; Buell et al., 2017, 2021) expanded the scope of business operations transparency by considering its use by managers and its implications for customers in predominantly service settings where customer value is created through coproduction of mostly intangible benefits. In service settings, the demarcation between actions performed in the view of customers by *onstage*, visible employees or technology interface activities and actions that are hidden from customers and conducted by *backstage*, invisible employees and the support infrastructure comprised of mechanical and digital technologies to create and deliver the service is significant (Bitner et al., 2008). This visible-invisible demarcation affects service design processes, the infrastructure, costs, and resources involved, and ultimately the nature of customer experience. Importantly, the demarcation, and therefore the degree of transparency in services, is a design choice and deliberately determined by managers.

Is it useful (and profitable) to reveal some or all of the activity and effort behind the scenes into creating the service, or is it a case of too much information and is counterproductive? Buell (2019) calls the issue of making visible the effort expended by typically backstage activities as *operational transparency*, defining it as "the deliberate design of windows into and out of the organization's operations to help customers and employees understand and appreciate the value being created." Where supply chain transparency applies to backstage disclosure for tangible products, operational transparency applies to backstage disclosure about intangible services.

Process Transparency and Customer Transparency

Buell further distinguishes between *process transparency* and *customer transparency* as two distinct and complementary aspects of operational transparency. *Process transparency* involves making the actions of backstage employees, and the support and operations processes more salient and visible to customers. For example, some online travel agents like Kayak display a list of the airline sites that are being included and searched and details of the fares that are being found in real-time after the customer has requested a search for a particular travel plan (Buell & Norton, 2011) while some restaurants use an open kitchen concept whereby patrons can see their meal being prepared by line cooks and chefs (Buell et al., 2017). The typical barrier that hides the backstage processes from customers is broken down, leading to more challenging operational processes and a qualitatively different customer experience deemed to be more authentic. As the owner of a restaurant with an open kitchen concept put it, "If you walked by right now through the courtyard [next to the restaurant], you're going to see us breaking down a whole fish. You're going to see us breaking down or putting away all the fresh vegetables. Being exposed on the front and back side has been a huge plus to us" (O'Brien, 2021).

Customer transparency is the inverse of process transparency and often goes hand in hand with it. In this case, the service organization deliberately makes its customers' engagement, participation, and reactions visible or salient to service employees as they go about their jobs of producing or cocreating the service; this, in turn, affects employee behaviors and performance outcomes. Customer transparency can occur in service organizations either naturally because the customer actively participates in service creation or it can be deliberately orchestrated through service design steps to make the process transparent. As an example of the former, the waitstaff in any full-service restaurant will see their customers' reactions as they order, share, and consume their meal, responding to the unfolding experience. As an instance of deliberate service design, the same open restaurant kitchen concept that allows customers to see kitchen staff also allows the staff to see customers' eating the food they have prepared. For kitchen staff, the scrutiny heightens the saliency of expectations of skill and cleanliness that customers have of them and affects their performance (O'Brien, 2021). As a general rule, the more actively the customer participates in cocreating the service, the more opportunities there will be to orchestrate customer transparency.

Research Findings Regarding Operational Transparency

Academic research on operational transparency is relatively new and growing quickly. As its popularity has increased, so has its practical value, as digitalization leads organizations to incorporate intangible service components into more and more hitherto tangible products (Dholakia, 2022). This research has found a number of findings that deepen our understanding of how consumers perceive and make sense of transparency in service encounters. On the whole, they show that operational transparency benefits consumers' perceptions of value and their relational orientation, whereas customer transparency contributes to the output quality and efficiency of service workers. Furthermore, these effects can be economically meaningful.

The positive effects of operational transparency. In Buell et al. (2017) main study conducted in a university dining hall, adding customer and process transparency by allowing diners and chefs to see each other on strategically located iPads resulted in an increase of 22.2% in customer perceptions of quality and reduced throughput times by 19.2%. The authors explained their findings this way: "Customers who observed process transparency perceived greater employee effort and thus were more appreciative of the employees and valued the service more. Employees who observed customer transparency felt that their work was more appreciated and more impactful and thus was more satisfied with their work and more willing to exert effort. By visually revealing operating processes to consumers and beneficiaries to producers, we find that transparency generates a positive feedback loop through which value is created for both parties" (p. 1673). Consistently, restaurant consultant O'Brien (2021) put it like this: "Despite the difficulties that a visible kitchen can sometimes present, it can heighten the drama of the dining experience, reinforce a restaurant's concept or emphasize its food safety procedures."

Mejia et al. (2019) found similar effects on crowdfunding platforms for charitable projects where operational transparency, as measured by the provision of updates by the project's organizer, was associated with more donations. Buell et al. (2021) extended these findings to services provided by the government, finding that when the government employed greater operational transparency, it not only engendered trust in citizens but also encouraged them to perform more work themselves in reciprocation. The study's context was a mobile app provided by Boston's city government to citizens to submit service requests such as fixing potholes, cleaning graffiti, and so on. Using two years of data from this app, the authors found that when the government showed the images of the work done in response to the citizen's request, citizens used the app more for thirteen months afterward, submitting 60% more requests in 38% more categories of issues. This allowed the Boston city government to provide service more efficiently, focusing more on solving problems than identifying them. The persistence of citizen engagement is particularly noteworthy;

the seemingly minor and inexpensive act of enhancing operational transparency by the local government simply by following through led to sustained citizen engagement. This echoes the advice given to marketing researchers to close the loop after a customer survey and explain how their responses were used by the organization (Dholakia & Morwitz, 2002). In this case, giving customers a window into the organization's response also enhances the relational engagement of customers.

The labor illusion effect. Furthermore, Buell and Norton (2011) also found evidence of a "labor illusion" effect whereby introducing a form of explanatory "this is why it is taking so long" transparency to technological service interfaces such as websites and apps while customers are waiting has beneficial effects on their perceptions of value. In the authors' words, "although an automated solution may objectively deliver faster performance, we suggest that customers may perceive that service as less valuable because of the absence of labor. Adding that labor back in via operational transparency, therefore, has the potential to increase perceptions of value" (p. 1564).

As one example of the labor illusion effect, displaying which sites are being accessed during a search while the consumer is waiting for results increases preference relative to a comparable website that produces instantaneous results. Counterintuitively, making the customer wait and displaying hitherto black-box service processes that signify effort is better than providing quick service. Importantly, the authors distinguished between *labor illusion*, defining it as customers' perceptions of the effort exerted by the service provider, and *operational transparency*, which they defined as the revelation of the actual operations that underlie a service process, and suggested that operational transparency has to be orchestrated, explained, or contextualized by the service provider for the beneficial consumer effects of labor illusion to occur. The "illusion" aspect of transparency is telling here: It's not real disclosure. It is a fake, carefully engineered disclosure designed explicitly to persuade and impress customers.

Dirty work. These findings also raise the interesting questions of whether and to what degree these positive findings about operational transparency may transfer to service occupations involving "dirty work," defined as tasks involving the taint of a physical, moral, or social nature leading workers and consumers to try and psychologically distance themselves from them (Ashforth et al., 2007). Examples of dirty work services include debt collection, lab animal research, sex work, and policing (Simpson & Simpson, 2018). Relevant to the current discussion, Ashforth and colleagues (2007) found that some managers in professions involving substantial dirty work confront public perceptions of taint by explaining the value derived from the work, challenging specific public misconceptions, and sometimes using humor.

While these strategies may implicitly contain some elements of disclosure, the question of whether raising the curtain and shining the light on certain "dirty" aspects of the job and linking them directly to beneficial buyer outcomes is effective warrants investigation. Indeed, there is some evidence that this is the case. One study examining perceptions of lab animal researchers found that when their employer increased transparency by allowing access to the public through open houses, tours, and school visits, providing access to experimental animals and research protocols, and allowing staff to answer questions, public perceptions of these workers and their work became more positive (Mills et al., 2018). Understanding how operational transparency can be used to mitigate the negative effects of dirty work on workers and bystanders is a consequential and high-potential research issue.

In a rare study that considered different forms of business transparency concurrently, Mohan et al. (2020) compared cost transparency with price and operational transparency. The authors argued that cost and operational transparency work on customers differently. Specifically, compared to operational processes in service settings, costs are more sensitive, proprietary, and closely guarded, and disclosing them holds the potential for backlash, supplier reaction, and competitive disadvantage (see Chapter 3 for details about cost and price transparency). Because it makes the disclosing firm more vulnerable, customers deem cost transparency to be a stronger form of business transparency. Unlike operational transparency, which increases relational customer behaviors by engendering reciprocity because of heightened perceptions of effort by the firm, the authors argued that cost transparency enhances consumer trust in the company.

The dark side of operational transparency. While the corpus of findings paints a mostly rosy picture of operational transparency functioning as a positive feedback loop through which value is created for the organization and its customers, there is also a relatively unexplored dark side to delivering operational transparency (e.g., Guda et al., 2021).

For service employees, once the novelty of seeing and being seen by customers wears off, the frequent social interactions and the resultant emotional labor from constantly being "on stage" could not only be fraught with stress, dissonance, and self-alienation, but it may also result in a degradation of efficiency and the potential to make mistakes because of distraction (Ashforth & Humphrey, 1993; Hochschild, 1983). Atypical customer behavior during service coproduction, in particular, dysfunctional behavior that has continued to be common in many service settings, may further accentuate the potential negative effects on frontline workers from being exposed to abusive language, threats, physical violence, and so on (e.g., Dholakia, 2022; Gong et al., 2014; Khazan, 2022).

For customers, too, peeking behind the scenes or being made aware of the effort the service provider is undertaking for them may not necessarily resonate. For instance, research conducted in the context of targeted online advertisements has found that when the marketers' deliberately exposed practices violate *norms of practice*, defined as how customers think marketers *should* behave (e.g., not using consumers' personal information collected from an external source but instead only using personal data that consumers have given them), transparency can backfire, particularly for companies and brands that are not well-trusted by customers, to begin with (Kim et al., 2019). Along similar lines, if the exercise of operational transparency exposes flaws, weaknesses, or even just unpleasant aspects of the service creation process from ingredients or equipment used or from the actions of service employees, it may turn customers away instead of triggering their appreciation.

As Bruni (2005) observes, "In many New York restaurants, the wall between dining room and kitchen has tumbled to the point where the kitchen is not merely open to your view... The kitchen demands your attention, bears down on you, wrests the focus of an evening from the beets before you to the beads of perspiration on a not-so-distant line cook's brow." Do patrons out for a fine dining experience appreciate seeing sweaty cooks in an open kitchen preparing their meal, and does this really contribute positively to their service experience? Or does it just arouse disgust?

Summary It can be argued that the operational transparency findings, in particular, the labor illusion effect, have encouraged, or at the least supported, the widespread adoption of so-called *dark patterns* by many online businesses such as e-tailers, gaming sites, and stock trading apps

(Schüll, 2012; Wursthorn & Choi, 2020). Dark patterns are defined as "interface design choices that benefit an online service by coercing, steering, or deceiving users into making unintended and potentially harmful decisions" (Mathur et al., 2019), and many of them involve creating the illusion of process or customer transparency such as when shoppers are informed about the (artificially inflated) simultaneous buying and browsing activities of other shoppers on the site or provided with seemingly real-time inventory levels of merchandise indicating artificially low levels, or messages indicating that a particular product is in high demand and will sell out soon. These are just some findings from a scarce handful of studies; more research on the downsides of operational transparency is sorely needed.

References

Amed, I., Balchandani, A., Beltrami, M., Berg, A., Hedrich, S., & Rölkens, F. (2019). What radical transparency could mean for the fashion industry. *McKinsey Insights*. https://www.mckinsey.com/industries/retail/our-insights/what-radical-transparency-could-mean-for-the-fashion-industry

Ashforth, B. E., & Humphrey, R. H. (1993). Emotional labor in service roles: The influence of identity. *Academy of Management Review*, 18(1), 88–115.

Ashforth, B., Kreiner, G., Clark, M., & Fugate, M. (2007). Normalizing dirty work: Managerial tactics for countering occupational taint. *Academy of Management Journal*, 50(1), 149–174.

Ashwin, S., Kabeer, N., & Schüßler, E. (2020). Contested understandings in the global garment industry after Rana Plaza. *Development and Change*, 51(5), 1296–1305.

Astill, J., Dara, R. A., Campbell, M., Farber, J. M., Fraser, E. D., Sharif, S., & Yada, R. Y. (2019). Transparency in food supply chains: A review of enabling technology solutions. *Trends in Food Science & Technology*, 91, 240–247.

Aung, M. M., & Chang, Y. S. (2014). Traceability in a food supply chain: Safety and quality perspectives. *Food Control*, 39, 172–184.

Bateman, A., & Bonanni, L. (2019, August 20). What supply chain transparency really means. Harvard Business Review. https://hbr.org/2019/08/what-supply-chain-transparency-really-means

Bitner, M. J., Ostrom, A. L., & Morgan, F. N. (2008). Service blueprinting: A practical technique for service innovation. *California Management Review*, 50(3), 66–94.

Bosona, T., & Gebresenbet, G. (2013). Food traceability as an integral part of logistics management in food and agricultural supply chain. *Food Control, 33*(1), 32–48.

Bruni, F. (2005, July 27). Yes, the kitchen's open. Too open. *New York Times.* https://www.nytimes.com/2005/07/27/dining/yes-the-kitchens-open-too-open.html

Buell, R. W. (2019). Operational transparency. *Harvard Business Review, 97*(2), 102–113.

Buell, R. W., & Kalkanci, B. (2021). How transparency into internal and external responsibility initiatives influences consumer choice. *Management Science, 67*(2), 932–950.

Buell, R. W., & Norton, M. I. (2011). The labor illusion: How operational transparency increases perceived value. *Management Science, 57*(9), 1564–1579.

Buell, R. W., Kim, T., & Tsay, C. J. (2017). Creating reciprocal value through operational transparency. *Management Science, 63*(6), 1673–1695.

Buell, R. W., Porter, E., & Norton, M. I. (2021). Surfacing the submerged state: Operational transparency increases trust in and engagement with government. *Manufacturing and Service Operations Management, 23*(4), 781–802.

Butler, S. (2022, October 21). Zara enters resale market with pre-owned service. *The Guardian.* https://www.theguardian.com/business/2022/oct/21/zara-enters-resale-market-pre-owned-service.

Campbell, M. C., & Winterich, K. P. (2018). A framework for the consumer psychology of morality in the marketplace. *Journal of Consumer Psychology, 28*(2), 167–179.

Cernansky, R. (2021, October 18). *Why destroying products is still an "Everest of a problem" for fashion.* Vogue Business.

Dalton, M. (2018, September 6). Why luxury brands burn their own goods. *Wall Street Journal.* https://www.wsj.com/articles/burning-luxury-goods-goes-out-of-style-at-burberry-1536238351

Dholakia, U. M. (2022). *Advanced introduction to digital marketing.* Edward Elgar.

Dholakia, U. M., & Morwitz, V. G. (2002). The scope and persistence of mere-measurement effects: Evidence from a field study of customer satisfaction measurement. *Journal of Consumer Research, 29*(2), 159–167.

Fowler, E., Kobe, C., Roberts, K. J., Collins, C. L., & McKenzie, L. B. (2016). Injuries associated with strollers and carriers among children in the United States, 1990 to 2010. *Academic Pediatrics, 16*(8), 726–733.

Gartenberg, C. (2021, December 16). *Apple is reportedly going to make more of its chips.* The Verge. https://www.theverge.com/2021/12/16/22839850/apple-office-develop-chips-in-house-broadcom-skyworks

Godfrey, D. M., Price, L. L., & Lusch, R. F. (2022). Repair, consumption, and sustainability: Fixing fragile objects and maintaining consumer practices. *Journal of Consumer Research, 49*(2), 229–251.

Gong, T., Yi, Y., & Choi, J. N. (2014). Helping employees deal with dysfunctional customers: The underlying employee perceived justice mechanism. *Journal of Service Research, 17*(1), 102–116.

Guda, H., Dawande, M., & Janakiraman, G. (2021). *The economics of process transparency*. Available at SSRN. https://doi.org/10.2139/ssrn.3715037

Hastig, G. M., & Sodhi, M. S. (2020). Blockchain for supply chain traceability: Business requirements and critical success factors. *Production and Operations Management, 29*(4), 935–954.

Hochschild, A. R. (1983). *The managed heart: Commercialization of human feeling*. University of California Press.

Jovane, F., Alting, L., Armillotta, A., Eversheim, W., Feldmann, K., Seliger, G., & Roth, N. (1993). A key issue in product life cycle: Disassembly. *CIRP Annals, 42*(2), 651–658.

Kale, S. (2021, , October 6). Out of style: Will Gen Z ever give up its dangerous love of fast fashion? *The Guardian*. https://www.theguardian.com/fashion/2021/oct/06/out-of-style-will-gen-z-ever-give-up-its-dangerous-love-of-fast-fashion

Kalkanci, B., & Plambeck, E. L. (2020). Reveal the supplier list? A trade-off in capacity vs. responsibility. *Manufacturing & Service Operations Management, 22*(6), 1251–1267.

Khazan, O. (2022, March 30). Why people are acting so weird. *The Atlantic*. https://www.theatlantic.com/politics/archive/2022/03/antisocial-behavior-crime-violence-increase-pandemic/627076/

Kim, T., Barasz, K., & John, L. K. (2019). Why am I seeing this ad? The effect of ad transparency on ad effectiveness. *Journal of Consumer Research, 45*(5), 906–932.

Kim, Y. H., & Davis, G. F. (2016). Challenges for global supply chain sustainability: Evidence from conflict minerals reports. *Academy of Management Journal, 59*(6), 1896–1916.

Kraft, T., Valdés, L., & Zheng, Y. (2018). Supply chain visibility and social responsibility: Investigating consumers' behaviors and motives. *Manufacturing and Service Operations Management, 20*(4), 617–636.

Markenson, S., & Orgel, D. (2022). *Transparency in an evolving omnichannel world*. NielsenIQ—FMI Report.

Marshall, D., McCarthy, L., McGrath, P., & Harrigan, F. (2016). What's your strategy for supply chain disclosure? *Sloan Management Review, 57*(2), 37–45.

Mathur, A., Acar, G., Friedman, M. J., Lucherini, E., Mayer, J., Chetty, M., & Narayanan, A. (2019). Dark patterns at scale: Findings from a crawl of 11K shopping websites. *Proceedings of the ACM on Human-Computer Interaction, 3*, 1–32.

Mejia, J., Urrea, G., & Pedraza-Martinez, A. J. (2019). Operational transparency on crowdfunding platforms: Effect on donations for emergency response. *Production and Operations Management, 28*(7), 1773–1791.

Mills, K. E., Han, Z., Robbins, J., & Weary, D. M. (2018). Institutional transparency improves public perception of lab animal technicians and support for animal research. *PloS One, 13*(2), e0193262.

Mohan, B., Buell, R. W., & John, L. K. (2020). Lifting the veil: The benefits of cost transparency. *Marketing Science, 39*(6), 1105–1121.

Mohr, J., & Thissen, C. (2022). Measuring and disclosing corporate valuations of impacts and dependencies on nature. *California Management Review, 65*(1), 91–118.

Napier, E., & Sanguineti, F. (2018). Fashion merchandisers' slash and burn dilemma: A consequence of over production and excessive waste? *Rutgers Business Review, 3*(2), 159–174.

New, S. (2010, October). The transparent supply chain. *Harvard Business Review*. https://hbr.org/2010/10/the-transparent-supply-chain

New, S., & Brown, D. (2011). The four challenges of supply chain transparency. *European Business Review*, 4–6. https://www.europeanbusinessreview.com/challenges-supply-chain-transparency/

O'Brien, T. (2021, February). *The move to kitchen transparency*. Foodservice Equipment and Supplies. https://fesmag.com/topics/trends/18984-the-move-to-kitchen-transparency

Parmigiani, A., Klassen, R. D., & Russo, M. V. (2011). Efficiency meets accountability: Performance implications of supply chain configuration, control, and capabilities. *Journal of Operations Management, 29*(3), 212–223.

Patagonia (2022). Our environmental responsibility programs. https://www.patagonia.com/our-responsibility-programs.html. Accessed on 25 November 2022.

Paton, E. (2018, September 6). Burberry to stop burning clothing and other goods it can't sell. *New York Times*. https://www.nytimes.com/2018/09/06/business/burberry-burning-unsold-stock.html

Petty, R. E., & Cacioppo, J. T. (1984). The effects of involvement on responses to argument quantity and quality: Central and peripheral routes to persuasion. *Journal of Personality and Social Psychology, 46*(1), 69–81.

Schüll, N. D. (2012). *Addition by design: Machine Gambling in Las Vegas*. Princeton University Press.

Shankar, A., & Canniford, R. (2016, September 29). *If Patagonia's business model is a paragon of virtue, should more companies follow suit?* The Conversation. https://theconversation.com/if-patagonias-business-model-is-a-paragon-of-virtue-should-more-companies-follow-suit-66188

Simpson, R., & Simpson, A. (2018). "Embodying" dirty work: A review of the literature. *Sociology Compass, 12*(6), e12581.

Sodhi, M. S., & Tang, C. S. (2019). Research opportunities in supply chain transparency. *Production and Operations Management, 28*(12), 2946–2959.

Swift, C., Guide, V. D. R., Jr., & Muthulingam, S. (2019). Does supply chain visibility affect operating performance? Evidence from conflict minerals disclosures. *Journal of Operations Management, 65*(5), 406–429.

Symonds, M. (2007). The traceability advantage. *Quality, 46*(10), 36–41.

Thompson, S. (2021, May 30). *Your customers want to know the progress you've made in diversity, inclusion and belonging*. Forbes, CMO Network. https://www.forbes.com/sites/soniathompson/2021/05/30/your-customers-want-to-know-the-progress-youve-made-in-diversity-inclusion-and-belonging/?sh=7db84c113abc

Wellener, P., Hardin, K., Gold, S., Leaper, S., & Parrott, A. (2022, September). *Meeting the challenge of supply chain disruption*. Deloitte Insights.

Wunderlich, S., & Gatto, K. A. (2015). Consumer perception of genetically modified organisms and sources of information. *Advances in Nutrition, 6*(6), 842–851.

Wursthorn, M., & Choi, E. (2020, August 20). Does Robinhood make it too easy to trade? From free stocks to confetti. *Wall Street Journal*. https://www.wsj.com/articles/confetti-free-stocks-does-robinhoods-design-make-trading-too-easy-11597915801

CHAPTER 3

Price Transparency

Abstract This chapter reviews the literature on price transparency to gain a better understanding of its significance. The multiple, context-dependent meanings of price transparency are identified and explored, an original framework capturing the different elements of price transparency from the organization's and customer's points of view throughout the pricing process is presented, and the distinction between accessibility-based and disclosure-based price transparency is investigated. Whereas the former emphasizes the ready accessibility of prices, the latter has to do with availability of pricing inputs and price performance variables to external constituents.

Keywords Transparency · Pricing Strategy · Buying Journey · Price Availability · Price Knowledge

> More than half could not correctly name the price of the item just placed in the shopping cart and more than half of the shoppers who purchased an item that was on special were unaware that the price was reduced—Peter Dickson and Alan Sawyer

Effective pricing strategy provides the scaffolding to execute a successful marketing strategy and lies at the heart of every organization's long-term financial success. Determining the prices of the products and services to be sold by the organization and establishing nuanced and customer-focused pricing structures that detail the overall assortment of prices, price-benefit combinations, price variations, and price offers provided to customers are the core functions of pricing strategy (Dholakia, 2017). Transparency plays a significant role in developing successful pricing structures not only in the simple sense that modulating price availability has a significant impact on customer behaviors but in the more nuanced sense that price structures can be assembled, communicated, and contextualized to carefully calibrate how easy or difficult customers find it to comprehend and utilize price information in their buying decisions.

Simply put, the most significant and widely used form of tactical business transparency lies in the provision and contextualization of price information by organizations to their customers. Price transparency has received extensive scholarly exploration for several decades in economics as well as in consumer psychology, not to mention from practitioners and consultants; accordingly, exploring this research for a better understanding of the meaning and significance of price transparency will be the focus of this chapter.

Three principal insights are advanced here. First, price transparency is a concept with multiple meanings that are heavily context-dependent and reliant on elaboration; the particular connotation is not only based on the user's perspective (e.g., their role as a manager, customer, industry analyst, and so on), but it also depends on the industry setting and the specific underlying purpose for which price transparency is invoked.

Second, the concept of price transparency must go beyond commonly held views of availability and disclosure (although these are important) to include considerations of interpretation and understanding by the recipient. Simply put, the seller can make prices readily available or disclose them in itemized detail, yet they may remain impenetrable and, therefore, unserviceable if they are not properly explained and contextualized for users. Savvy sellers can create an illusion of price transparency yet reduce the accessibility of prices for consumer decision making (White, 2020). Third, the relation between price transparency and the welfare of consumers (and other stakeholders) is complex and non-monotonic. Whichever particular way price transparency is defined, it is almost never the case that "more is better" for stakeholder well-being. "How" the price is made transparent often matters just as much if much more than "how much" it is so for customers, investors, employees, and others.

Conceptual Formulations of Price Transparency

Price transparency is a concept with significant practical value to managers, consumers, and policymakers because of its informational, diagnostic, communicational, and regulatory significance. At first glance, the meaning of price transparency, like other domains of business transparency covered in this book, seems unambiguous, more or less in line with the core dictionary definition of transparency as *an object, issue, or idea characterized by visibility or accessibility of information especially concerning business practices*.[1] Using this definition, transparent prices are prices that are widely visible or accessible. However, when we dig deeper into the literature and consider its applications in practice, price transparency is a rather knotty and unwieldy pricing idea for at least two reasons.

First, transparency can mean a number of different things in pricing strategy, depending not only on whether we take the seller's or the buyer's perspective but also based on the stage of the pricing process. Furthermore, depending upon the context, non-transparent pricing can either imply the unavailability of prices or a lack of knowledge on the customer's part to make sense of available prices at key stages in their buying journey, each taking different forms and having multiple antecedents. The prices may be hidden from access and require customer effort or a qualification process to find; or prices may be presented in a complex manner that makes it difficult for the customer to process and understand; or the seller may change prices far too frequently (e.g., several times a day) using automated algorithm-based methods, and use a wide price range complicating the buyer's purchase decision; or there may be tacit opportunities for customers to negotiate seemingly fixed prices, or even to decide the price unilaterally when the seller offers a participative method like Pay What You Want pricing; or the seller may not be able to obtain the necessary

---

[1] This is the Merriam-Webster definition of transparency that seems most relevant to the pricing context. Transparency also has other meanings such as "having the property of transmitting light without appreciable scattering so that bodies lying beyond are seen clearly," "fine or sheer enough to be seen through," "free from pretense or deceit," "easily detected or seen through," and "readily understood." For pricing, these meanings coalesce to produce a positive aura around the concept of transparent pricing. In marketing, transparent pricing is perceived as customer-focused and authentic, and therefore an effective business strategy.

inputs such as accurate measures of costs or customers' economic valuations to be able to set a reasonable and sustainable price; or the rationale for prices or price changes may not be provided to customers or frontline employees, leaving them confused. Clarity, or the lack thereof, is relevant in different forms throughout the pricing process and affects both process and outcomes of pricing activities.

Furthermore, a completely different but well-accepted use of the term "price transparency" in marketing is to denote a brand promise or a core value of a business within the larger conceptual framework of *radical transparency* (Turco, 2016). At its heart, radical transparency involves laying open the most significant inner workings of the business, from details about its supply chains and environmental impacts to interactions between employees and every component of its cost structure and labor practices to outside scrutiny.

For instance, the US-based fashion label Everlane has adopted *radical transparency* as a value proposition, making cost and price transparency the fundamental pillars of its promise to stakeholders. In this sense, price transparency may refer to the fact that a company deliberately chooses to disclose some or all of its costs or other pricing inputs, or it may mean that the company is candid about the unit economics of its business model, including costs, markup factors, margins, unit sales, and revenues to all or selected constituents for reasons of establishing a differentiated brand that is attractive to its targeted customers, or that it chooses to disclose some of its most meaningful costs such as the prices it pays certain suppliers or the minimum or average wages it pays its employees to establish its ESG credentials. Where price transparency is concerned, meanings abound.

The second reason for the potential confusion about price transparency follows from the first. The different aforementioned meanings often remain obscured or unexplained. Without a proper explanation of the context or purpose, it is impossible to decode the precise meaning of price transparency, its antecedents, or its upshots. Compounding the problem, managers, consultants, and customers, not to mention academic researchers, use price transparency or terms related to it, such as cost transparency, interchangeably across different contexts and areas without defining what they mean. For managers, in particular, this routine lack of clarity can make it difficult to understand what works and what doesn't work and to choose an effective price transparency strategy for their brand or organization.

Next, the different specific meanings of price transparency for the business and its customers at each stage of the pricing process and the customer journey are considered in detail. Figure 3.1 shows the graphic depiction of an original framework providing a deeper understanding not only of the consequences of the accessibility and disclosure of prices to buyers and sellers but also of their interpretability and contextualization throughout the pricing process from the organization's perspective and the buying journey from the customer's perspective.

THE PRICING PROCESS, THE BUYING JOURNEY, AND PRICE TRANSPARENCY

Within every business, an essential task is to establish, communicate, negotiate, and realize prices. In pricing strategy, we can make the broad distinction between price setting, price communication and negotiation, and price realization as the three core stages of the pricing process. Transparency plays a significant role in each stage, with different meanings and nuances. A good starting point for our investigation is to understand the three stages and the relevant forms of price transparency in each stage.

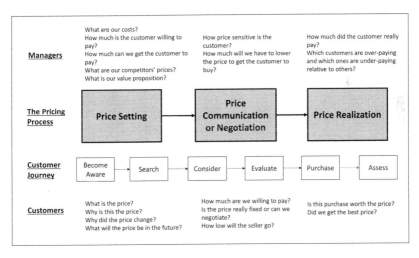

Fig. 3.1 Different aspects of price transparency during the pricing process and the customer journey

Price Transparency During Price Setting

The pricing process begins with *price setting*, defined as establishing prices for a new offering or changing existing prices. It involves considering the decision inputs of *costs* (e.g., which costs are incurred, which ones are fixed and variable, and how costs change as a function of the price), *customer valuation* (e.g., the economic value assigned by the customer to the offering's benefits), and *reference prices* (e.g., competitors' prices for similar offerings and the company's own previous prices) and weighting these three inputs based on the *brand's value proposition* deliberately chosen by the firm (Dholakia, 2017).

Availability. During this process, the availability of relevant information is critical for managers and customers. For managers tasked with setting prices, the significant challenge is to compile and integrate information about each decision input. The main cost inputs are typically the easiest to obtain, as are the company's historical prices because they are usually available in the company's accounting systems. Information about the other two inputs, customer valuation, and competitors' prices, may be more difficult to find. In many B2B industries, for example, prices tend to be viewed as proprietary knowledge and are therefore hidden from easy access. Prices are only provided to potential customers after a screening process or to current customers as part of account management activities by sales staff. Similarly, the economic valuation of customers is private information, and the manager may have to conduct research to learn customers' willingness to pay (Schmidt & Bijmolt, 2020).

The rationale for the price. During price setting, customers are in the awareness and search stages of their buying journeys (see Fig. 3.1) and will be concerned with access to prices and the company's rationale for them. Perhaps the most ubiquitous transparency-related questions that arise for customers at this point are "What is the price?" and "Why is this the price?" which they must answer satisfactorily to progress in their decision making (Vanhuele & Drèze, 2002). The "Why" question's importance, in particular, increases with the consequentiality of the customer's buying decision. Relatedly, customers' knowledge and expectations about future prices are also important, particularly in turbulent environments. In an inflationary environment, for example, consumers tend to become more inclined to purchase durable products such as furniture and electronic items hastily, even at inflated prices, concerned that prices will go up even further (D'Acunto et al., 2022).

A different version of transparency is relevant to customers making cheaper, frequent purchases. In such instances, because of relatively poor price knowledge (Vanhuele & Drèze, 2002), many customers need help answering the question, "Is this a good price?" For example, it may not be clear to grocery shoppers whether $7 is a reasonable price for a 10 oz bottle of tomato ketchup at the point of purchase. Despite the clearly displayed price tag, the price may be opaque with respect to its meaning and evaluation. In such cases, providing customers with context for the price (e.g., regular price = 10, sale price = $7, or tomato ketchup of this quality usually costs $1.50 per ounce) is tantamount to making the price more transparent to customers. For both consequential and everyday products, while making prices available, many companies fail to provide sufficient context for the price or explain the rationale behind price changes, leaving customers to draw their own inferences (Dholakia, 2019). In such cases, prices may be readily available to consumers, but they remain impenetrable as inputs into consumer decision making.

Price Transparency During Communication or Negotiation

During the "consider" and "evaluate" stages of the customer's decision making process, the seller must communicate the established price to the customer. In many B2B settings and for consumer durables, both parties may engage in an elaborate negotiation process to finalize the price and other terms of the purchase transaction. At this stage, the managerial concern about price transparency centers around understanding the customer's situational mindset, particularly their price sensitivity and price tolerance (Mazumdar et al., 2005). Specific insights into how much the customer is willing and able to pay *for that transaction* are helpful, which in turn is dictated by how much they want the offering and their reference prices, as is their skill and experience with conducting negotiations and even their emotional mindset (Bazerman et al., 2000). For the manager involved at this stage, perfect transparency would mean discovering the maximum amount the customer is willing to pay in that context.

Discovering value and price. One price mechanism that permits this level of transparency for high-demand products and services is an English or second-price auction (Cox, 2008). For unique items like a highly valued artwork or a rare antique car, as well as in larger markets with strong demand and weak supply, such as the US housing market in early 2022, auctions make the buyer's willingness to pay transparent to the seller through bidding (e.g., Ashenfelter & Graddy, 2003; Friedman, 2021). When using auctions is not possible, another strategy to discover the buyer's genuine willingness to pay is to start with a very high price and gradually lower prices until the buyer accepts the offer, a pricing method called *price skimming* in the marketing literature (Besanko & Winston, 1990) by which buyers expose their economic valuation through their purchase timing. As these cases show, specific pricing methods can and do moderate the level of transparency of the customer's price sensitivity to the seller.

Price comprehensibility. For buyers, the transparency challenge is different at this stage. In many situations, they may still have difficulty answering fairly basic questions such as "What is the price?", "Is this a good price?", and "Is the quoted price fixed or is it negotiable?" especially if they have bypassed the awareness and search stages and are close to the point of purchase (Ahearne et al., 2022). Understanding and processing the total price may become demanding because the seller can structure the same price differently, making it easy or challenging to comprehend and use in decision making.

For instance, one alternative available to sellers is to either rely on a relatively simple aggregate or "all-inclusive" price (e.g., buy a pair of shoes from our site for $100, including shipping and returns) or to use a more complicated pricing structure with methods such as *partitioned pricing* or *drip pricing* where the quoted price is readily available but comprises of a base price and several mandatory or optional surcharges (e.g., shoes = $75, shipping = $15, handling = $10, returns will cost extra depending on when and why the product is returned), that make it very difficult for customers to calculate exactly how much they are paying for their purchase (Greenleaf et al., 2016; Santana et al., 2020; Seim et al., 2017; White, 2020). In essence, the seller calibrates the usefulness and interpretability of price information while holding price availability constant.

Furthermore, the issue of whether it is possible to negotiate prices arises because, in more and more settings, including those where prices used to be fixed, such as supermarkets or home improvement stores, they are now often negotiable (Ahearne et al., 2022; Dholakia, 2021). The possibility of negotiable prices reduces price transparency for buyers. The extant research and research opportunities on both issues, the complexity of the price offer, and the perceived negotiability of prices will be considered in more detail later in this chapter.

Price Transparency During Price Realization

Interestingly, the challenges with price transparency continue for buyers and sellers even during and after purchase. It is especially significant for contracts, service agreements, condition-based subscriptions, and other complex pricing structures. For sellers, the issue of *price execution* comes to the forefront at this stage, reflecting the fact that regardless of industry, the prices posted on websites or catalogs or quoted to customers differ significantly from the prices actually paid by customers (Dholakia, 2017) which are called *realized prices* or *pocket prices* (Baker et al., 2010).

Consider the case of Airbus and Boeing. When the major airlines purchase airplanes from these major airplane manufacturers, the prices they actually pay are far lower than the prices quoted by these companies by as much as 40–50% (Michaels, 2012). Furthermore, these realized prices are entirely hidden. In the words of Michaels (2012), "The aviation industry's code of silence on pricing is notable in this era of information overload. Thousands of people worldwide are involved in airplane purchases, yet few numbers spill out. That yields much mystery and speculation." Note that price opacity here is not a matter of availability; list prices for new airplanes are readily available and commonly reported in the media (e.g., Saigol & Root, 2022); it is the prices realized by airplane manufacturers that are virtually impossible to learn; they are shrouded in secrecy, often behind iron-clad non-disclosure agreements.

The price realization gap. In many industries, particularly in B2B sectors, even managers in charge of pricing may not know the price that each customer pays once all the different incentives, allowances, contract-specific terms, and cost-to-serve differences are fully taken into account (Baker, et al., 2010; Dholakia, 2017). This results in a "price execution gap" or a "price realization gap," which reduces the effectiveness of the company's pricing strategy and lowers price transparency. Dholakia (2017) points out that the main reason for the price realization gap is that many B2B customers are offered multiple incentives to close the deal, often by salespeople not under the direct purview of pricing managers (Keiser, 1988). Depending on the industry, the number and size of these incentives can be significant. As an example, Baker, Marn, and Zawada (2010) document the case of a furniture manufacturer that gave numerous incentives to customers, including a discount for paying in cash, a co-op advertising allowance, an annual volume rebate, free freight, special competitive deals, dealer discounts, order size discounts, and customer pickup allowances. Together, these incentives led to customers paying 47% less than the listed prices.

The price realization gap also occurs in consumer markets, when retailers may offer "buy one get one" deals, run flash sales, give free or subsidized shipping, and so on, which bring down the actual price paid by customers. Even in higher education, there is a significant gap between listed tuition prices and what students pay after accounting for scholarships and financial aid (Lieber, 2022); in 2020, for instance, undergraduates received an average discount of 48.1% off the listed prices, with significant variability in prices paid (NACUBO, 2021). Much like passengers in an airplane, two students sitting side by side in a class may be paying dramatically different prices to attend a university. In all these cases, the publicized prices, such as the list or catalog prices, are transparent but inaccurate and misleading, hiding significant customer differences. The relevant degree of price transparency has to do with the fact that the actual prices paid by buyers are hidden or unknown, even to sellers themselves.

Dholakia (2017) suggests that the price realization gap and the accompanying opacity of realized prices occur for at least three reasons. First, in many organizations, there is a lack of communication and coordination stemming from the fact that pricing decisions are made centrally, whereas price realization occurs peripherally at the organization's frontlines by order takers, salespeople, store managers, and others who work directly with customers (e.g., Keiser, 1988; Lal, 1986; Schaerer et al., 2020). Often these frontline employees have considerable discretion in offering incentives but are not given sufficient guidelines or instructions about how to offer incentives or provided with an understanding of the company's pricing philosophy (assuming the company has one), leaving them to make decisions about incentives idiosyncratically (Gijsbrechts, 1993).

Second, significant organizational challenges are associated with measuring, recording, and tracking incentives given at the customer level. This is because many costs are difficult to track and allocate precisely to individual customers. Compounding this challenge, different functional departments may use different labels or funding sources for incentives. Furthermore, customer incentivization methods such as loyalty programs that bring realized prices down may be challenging to track, making information about realized prices unavailable within the organization.

The third reason stems from problems with customer pushback during price negotiations and after price increases and the resultant enforcement and compliance of concessions (or lack thereof). For instance, many customers continue to receive incentives even when they don't qualify or meet the conditions to do so. Many opportunistic customers continue availing expired or non-applicable incentives by threatening to sever ties. Savvy customers find creative ways to lower the amount paid, contributing to a price realization gap.

Post-purchase price evaluation. For buyers, the relevance of price transparency during and after the purchase has to do as much with assessing the total price they paid and whether they received good value as it has to do with the ready availability of prices during the decision making process. During the post-purchase phase, customers engage in numerous behaviors such as reviewing, complaining, referring, and returning in customer journey models (Dholakia, 2022). Complex price offers, frequently changing prices, a lengthy and contentious negotiation process, and even knowing about lower prices received by other customers can affect price transparency perceptions negatively, in turn affecting the customer's satisfaction with the price offer and the purchase process adversely.

In consumer settings, these assessments are often subjective and imbued with belief-based cognitive content and emotional reactions. In contrast, in B2B settings, especially where sellers use value-based pricing methods in setting prices, the post-purchase evaluation may have to do with a post hoc assessment of the purchase's economic value, including the validation of claims made by the seller during the sales process. In both settings, post hoc judgments of the seller's price transparency feed into the customer's repurchase decisions and loyalty and advocacy intentions.

A Typology of Price Transparency

The academic literature that explicitly studies price transparency, either as a central concept or as an explanatory concept to explore other issues, is not quite as nuanced as the framework developed in the previous section. Nevertheless, there are at least two distinct ways in which researchers and pricing experts have conceived price transparency. To unpack the differences, let's examine a set of selected definitions from the academic literature, shown in Table 3.1. Note that this is by no means a comprehensive listing; there are literally dozens of studies on price transparency, cost transparency, and other less-clearly specified forms of price-related transparency in the marketing literature alone, not to mention the vast economics, operations management, and other literatures. My goal here is to simply illustrate the different ways in which different pricing scholars conceive of price transparency.

In Table 3.1, when providing the definition, I used the authors' exact words when the definition was given. When not available, I have edited

Table 3.1 Selected definitions of price transparency from the academic literature

The degree to which market participants know the prevailing prices and characteristics or attributes of goods and services on offer (Soh, Markus, & Goh, 2006). (1)
The degree to which pricing information is sufficient and valid. Giving lots of options with prices attached increases sufficiency by allowing customers to form an understanding of available prices, making it easy to compare prices increases diagnosticity by supporting the customer's decision making process. (Miao & Matilla, 2007). (1)
The extent to which firms provide price information that allows consumers to readily understand what they are purchasing from the firm and how that compares to competitors' offerings (Seim et al., 2017). (1)
The extent to which information about prices is available to buyers that organizes, explains, clarifies, or projects the contextual direction and/or rationale for the seller's pricing. (Hanna et al., 2019). (1)
The ability of buyers to see through seller's costs and determine whether they are in line with the prices being charged. (Sinha, 2000). (2)
The one-way sharing of cost information from a firm to its customers. It refers to the disclosure of the variable costs associated with a product's production purchase to customers. In its strong form, the company divulges the variable costs associated with each component of producing a good. In a weaker form, the total variable costs to produce the good is disclosed. (Mohan et al., 2020). (2)
The practice of revealing the unit costs of production to consumers. (Truong & Masopust, 2021). (2)
The voluntary disclosure of cost information up front by the salesperson at the front end of a negotiation. (Atefi, et al., 2020). (2)
The estimates and breakdowns of costs provided by the firm or published by third-party infomediaries. (Jiang et al., 2021). (2)
An infographic highlighting the costs and processes involved in manufacturing various products. Revealing costs allows the company to showcase the otherwise hidden work that goes into making the product to customers. Customers are shown the markup charged by the company and compared favorably to the markup charged by competitors. (Buell, 2019). (2)

the original words from the source text as lightly as possible to stay close to the authors' meaning. There is also a number 1 or 2 next to each definition to indicate whether the definition has to do with accessibility or disclosure.

Based on these definitions, we can distinguish between two types of price transparency in the academic literature: price transparency that has to do with the accessibility of prices (i.e., how much) and price transparency that concerns the disclosure of costs or pricing performance variables such as sales, margins, etc. (i.e., what). In both cases, price transparency is a matter of degree rather than a binary indicator. Finally, it is worth noting that this form of two-dimensional conceptualization of transparency can also be found in other literatures. In work on transparency in decision modeling of medical decisions, for example, Sampson and colleagues (2019) propose that completeness of information and accessibility of information are two distinct forms of transparency and argue that there may be an inherent tradeoff between the two "because ensuring the clarity and accessibility of information may become more challenging as the amount of information shared is increased" (p. 1356).

Accessibility-based price transparency. Soh, Markus, and Goh (2006) define price transparency as "the degree to which market participants know the prevailing prices and characteristics or attributes of goods or services on offer" (p. 706). Similarly, Hanna et al. (2019) define it as "the extent to which information about prices is available to buyers that organizes, explains, clarifies, or projects the contextual direction and/or rationale for the seller's pricing" (p. 228). Both these definitions exemplify what I call *accessibility-based price transparency*, defined as *the degree to which prices are readily accessible to current and potential customers and others such as suppliers, investors, channel partners, and competitors.* In addition to price availability, there are three significant aspects of accessibility-based price transparency that are orthogonal to price availability, *price offer complexity* dictating how easy the price is for the customer to process and interpret, the *price change frequency* reflecting how quickly prices change, and these changes are transmitted and publicized by the seller, and perceived price negotiability, which concerns the extent to which prices are negotiable and the modes by which negotiation occurs (see Fig. 3.2).

Even when prices are readily provided, sellers can make the price offer complex by breaking it up into different components, presenting only one part of the price first and then introducing other components. Likewise, in many industries or for particular brands, prices change rapidly, often daily or even hourly. In contrast, in others, typically B2B industries, dollar stores, etc., prices may change less often on a monthly, quarterly, or annual basis. Furthermore, digital technologies and changing norms have made prices fluid and negotiable in more settings than ever before. The four measures of accessibility-based price transparency together provide a richer understanding of price transparency from the customer's point of view.

Disclosure-Based Price Transparency

In contrast to accessibility-based price transparency, Atefi and colleagues (2020) conceive of price transparency as the voluntary disclosure of *costs* by the salesperson at the front end of a negotiation, and Buell (2019) sees it as giving customers a "behind-the-curtains" perspective through information about costs, markups, and the processes involved in producing a product or service. These conceptualizations are exemplars of what I call *disclosure-based price transparency*, defined here as *the degree to which some or all costs, other pricing inputs, and price performance variables (e.g., markup factors, margins, unit sales, and revenue) are actively disclosed by the seller to current and potential customers and others such as suppliers, investors, channel partners, and competitors.*

The critical distinctions between accessibility- and disclosure-based forms of price transparency lie in the nature of the information provided by the seller and their motivations for doing so. Over the past three decades, several trends, such as the widespread adoption of digital technology, the empowerment of customers, and the changing cultural and political norms, have increased both forms of price transparency. Yet, these same factors have allowed managers to make prices more complex, change them more frequently, and manage the mode and interpretation of price-related disclosures. They can determine not only how easy or challenging to make it for customers to find prices or learn about the seller's costs, markups, and so on but also to learn and comprehend current prices, compare prices in different channels, evaluate the total price, contextualize the price to make sense of it, and so on. While seeming to increase accessibility and disclosure of prices, managers still retain considerable discretion in how usable and meaningful this information is. There are significant nuanced differences between accessibility- and disclosure-based price transparency that are explored next.

ACCESSIBILITY-BASED PRICE TRANSPARENCY

As developed in the previous section, there are four distinct components of accessibility-based price transparency that affect how readily customers can access and use current prices in their buying journeys: (1) price availability, (2) price offer complexity, (3) price change frequency, and (4) perceived price negotiability (see Fig. 3.2). Each factor is considered separately.

Price Availability

In many settings, how readily available to make prices to customers is a strategic managerial decision driven by the nature of the customer relationship and the stage of their buying journey. For example, the ready availability of prices is a cornerstone of the business strategy of many retailers and online travel agencies (OTAs). These sellers display prices front and center in their stores, websites, and apps. This is because

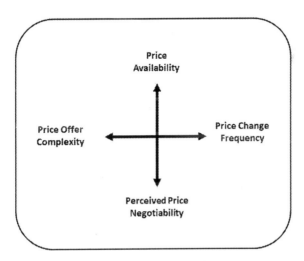

Fig. 3.2 The four components of accessibility-based price transparency

they are intermediaries and sell the offerings of competing brands (e.g., different fashion labels or CPG brands for retailers, and different airlines, hotels, and car rental agencies for OTAs) and want their customers to be able to use prices to compare the different available options. Similarly, customers can walk into a supermarket or a fast-food restaurant and find current prices easily. These are examples of high price availability, meaning that prices are readily available to customers throughout their buying journey, regardless of their specific journey state and motivation (Dholakia, 2022).

Furthermore, high price availability is usually not target-specific. When prices are openly available to customers, they are also equally accessible to vendors, investors, regulators, and in particular, competitors. In such settings, the price gains greater weight in the customer's choice process. It tends to be used by customers (and others) in different ways, such as to prescreen alternatives to form a smaller consideration set, to find the cheapest option meeting specific criteria, or to avoid extreme options and settle on a middle one (Dholakia, 2019; Hanna et al., 2019). Competitors can also track and use price information to a greater extent. For instance, it is common for airlines to monitor competitors' prices and react with carefully orchestrated price changes (e.g., Goolsbee & Syverson, 2008).

In many B2B industries, such as oilfield services, specialty chemicals, and certain governmental services, prices are not published, nor can they be found easily (e.g., Maxwell, 2015). The customer must reach out and request the price, signaling a certain seriousness. Industries such as high-end real estate, medical devices, industrial equipment, and many upscale restaurants go one step further in reducing price availability. Prices are only provided after the prospective customer is vetted or screened, typically by providing evidence of their interest and wherewithal. In some industries, like medical devices, customers may even have to sign non-disclosure agreements acknowledging they are prohibited from sharing prices they have learned with others. In all these examples, sellers push the provision of prices further along the customer's buying journey to the evaluate or purchase stage (see Fig. 3.1).

In some extreme cases, usually for nefarious reasons, prices remain entirely hidden, even up to and even after consumption. As an extreme example, many US hospitals (referenced in the preface) do not provide prices to patients until they are handed the final bill with itemized prices after they are discharged (Kliff & Katz, 2021). This sort of price opacity also occurs in many auctions, but the reason is different. Because of their participatory and dynamic nature, establishing the final price coincides with the act of purchase (Cheema et al., 2005). This is also the case for restaurants or software companies that use Pay What You Want pricing, where the discretion of how much to pay is left entirely to customers after they have consumed the offering (Dholakia, 2019). Prices are unavailable because they don't exist; the customer may find it difficult to establish a price even though they are the decision maker.

Price Offer Complexity

Even when prices are readily available, their availability is a *necessary but not sufficient* condition to generate meaningful price transparency for customers. A large body of consumer psychology research has found that the seller can increase the price offer's complexity by using various methods, such as partitioned pricing and drip pricing, while maintaining high price availability. In both methods, prices are broken up into different components (which may include mandatory or optional charges) and presented to customers step-by-step. Compared to a case when a simple all-inclusive price is presented, these more complex price offers typically lead to underestimation by customers because they fail to account for some portion of the disaggregated price.

This creates the *illusion of price transparency* in the sense that although they are available, the way prices are structured, or their mode of presentation makes the price offer too complex to process and use reasonably in customer decision making, ultimately leading to customers being misled and manipulated into making suboptimal purchase decisions. Both methods are discussed in Chapter 7 when considering the different characteristics of disclosed information, such as clarity, interpretability, and completeness, and their effects on the receiver's understanding.

A recent meta-analytic study found that these methods of exploiting customers (which the authors framed as "consumers responding more favorably") are particularly effective in certain settings such as utilitarian products like modes of transportation (e.g., a rental car lease with a fuel surcharge), higher-priced items, when all the sellers in a category or industry use this price communication method (e.g., all resorts in a particular beach community), and when the surcharges (even if they are mandatory) are perceived as offering valuable and substantial benefits (Abraham & Hamilton, 2018). Interestingly, it is still unclear whether sellers benefit from using these pricing methods over the longer term;

however, anecdotal evidence points to the seller's brand and credibility taking a hit when customers realize that they are being exploited by the seller (Consumer McGinnis, 2019; Reports, 2019).

Price Change Frequency

The third dimension of accessibility-based price transparency, orthogonal to price availability, and price offer complexity, is the frequency with which sellers change prices, which in turn affects price stability and downstream consumer outcomes. A significant and growing number of businesses today use algorithm-based pricing methods that link the company's internal costs and production data to data points about customers' preferences, demand, and buying patterns to recommend frequent price changes. Many of these methods go so far as to calculate the best prices to charge in real-time, changing them moment-by-moment based on how much customers are buying, what competitors are charging, and other market variables (Sjolin, 2015). These price changes propagate instantaneously to customer touchpoints such as apps, websites, and electronic shelf price tags (e.g., Garaus et al., 2016). The popularity of price promotions with relatively short lives, such as daily or hourly deals, flash sales, and single-offer marathons, also reduces price stability (Dilmé & Li, 2019; McCoy, 2020). Research has found that frequent price changes lower price transparency and hinder customers' buying decision processes in at least four ways:

Difficulty in accumulating price knowledge and forming a reference price. Consumers' price knowledge is relatively poor in most product categories (Vanhuele & Drèze, 2002). Only when they buy the same item repeatedly, do they acquire some understanding of its acceptable range (Monroe, 1973), and over time, customers form a reference price (Mazumdar et al., 2005). This process is disrupted when a product's price changes frequently and fluctuates over a wide range (e.g., Gatter & Hüttl-Maack, 2020; White, 2020), and many consumers find it hard to form a stable and coherent reference price.

The buying decision becomes more complex. Under normal circumstances, consumers use relatively simple decision heuristics when purchasing everyday items such as groceries. They look at the item's price first, then think of their reference price or the range of acceptable prices to gauge whether it is reasonably priced. They either buy the item or walk away based on this relatively rapid evaluation. When prices change frequently, however, this process becomes much more challenging. The reference price is no longer readily available, and when deciding whether to buy, the person has to search in different channels, remember what they paid last time, check when the price changed and by how much, and so on. A previously habitual, straightforward process taking a few moments transforms into a cognitively taxing, time-consuming activity where the customer is prone to misjudgments and bad decisions.

Consumers extend their decision journey and delay purchase. In a complicated buying situation, consumers question, "Should I buy now, or should I wait longer in case the price goes lower?" They do not know when to pull the trigger. Even when prices have dipped, for instance, they will wait for them to go down even further and may end up missing out on what would have been a great deal (Barber et al., 2009). Consumer psychology research shows that when decisions become complex, many people delay deciding or back out of it altogether (Greenleaf & Lehmann, 1995). When the price of a jacket, handbag, or pair of shoes goes up and down several times a day on an online retailer's site, for instance, the best option for many customers may be to tune out and postpone the purchase (Dholakia, 2015).

Consumers give more weight to prices and less weight to non-price features. Another consequence of constantly changing prices is shifting the consumer's attention away from the product's features to its price (Bertini & Wathieu, 2010). As Rotemberg (2005) points out, "...consumers use nominal price changes as a trigger for reflection about whether producers are fair or not." We are hard-wired to pay attention to stimuli that change and to ignore the stimuli that remain relatively stable. When prices fluctuate constantly, but the product's other features remain unchanged, consumers naturally turn their attention away from the product's functional and experiential aspects and focus on its price, often becoming more price sensitive.

To summarize, the present thrust of academic research suggests that although technological advances permit the execution of frequent price changes, customer reactions to such actions may make rapid fluctuations unproductive at best and perhaps even inflict lasting damage to financial performance at worst. Prices should only be changed as often as the company's tactical objectives and over-arching goals dictate.

Perceived Price Negotiability

In many B2B settings, prices are considered fluid and negotiable. Contracts for purchasing machinery, chemicals, or enterprise software are signed only after lengthy and often intense negotiations (Ahearne et al., 2022). In contrast, for the past century and a half, most everyday consumer goods and services, such as consumer packaged goods, restaurant meals, books, appliances, utilities, or gym memberships, have been sold using posted fixed prices in the United States with no opportunity for haggling. Most consumers today perceive the prices of products and services they buy to be fixed (Poort & Zuiderveen Borgesius, 2021; Zhang et al., 2021).

Using a business history perspective, Norris (1962) found that by 1830, country store proprietors in the United States had begun adopting a fixed price system for staples like flour and sugar. The period between 1860 and 1920 was one of transition from negotiated prices to set prices in many industries. By the early 1900s, posted fixed prices became popular, and US retailers used them widely because of their convenience. Fixed prices sped up the purchase transaction by an order of magnitude or more, increased trust in retailers, and were at least partly responsible for building the most robust retail and CPG brands of the era, marked by standardized products and high-quality service.

After over a century, the tide is turning again. Supported by digital technologies, greater consumer power in dyadic relationships with CPG brands and retailers, changing cultural norms, and the widespread adoption of dynamic pricing (also known as personalized prices; Poort & Zuiderveen Borgesius, 2021), fixed posted prices are becoming increasingly rare to find, only sustained by consumer inertia, reticence, or ignorance. The price of virtually every product, even a bruised banana in a national supermarket chain store, or a double espresso in a coffee shop, is negotiable (e.g., Keefe, 2019). The only hurdle to making seemingly fixed prices negotiable is that, in most cases, the buyer must initiate the negotiation process with the seller by stepping up and asking to pay a lower price than the price quoted on the posted tag (Shelegia & Sherman, 2022). A small minority of consumers is aware that prices are negotiable in many supermarkets, department stores, and coffee shops; even among those who are aware, fewer still are motivated and behaviorally inclined to do so.

Price transparency, characterized by the perceived negotiability of prices and an understanding of the factors that drive the quotation process and the negotiation heuristics employed, has come full circle. The same type of information that sellers and buyers learned about one another through a life-long interpersonal relationship in the 1800s can be acquired at present through the intensive collection of attitudinal and behavioral consumer data by organizations, on the one hand, and through intensive online research by potential customers. Information is abundant, cheap, and exploited in different ways by buyers and sellers to "complexify" (in Gelber's [2005] words) the transaction.

Where transparency is concerned, we are reverting to the "deep knowledge" of the pre-industrial era insofar as understanding the momentary value of the transaction is concerned (e.g., Eggers, 2015). For example, when consumers conduct repeated searches for a particular airfare within a short window, they are likely to encounter increased prices on the sites of online travel agencies, a form of real-time price calibration (Shen, 2017). The seller learns something specific about the potential customer's needs, motivations, and valuation from their observed behavioral pattern and adjusts its price quote instantaneously. In this example, a form of negotiation has occurred even without the knowledge of the affected customer.

Relative to simple, steady prices, a complex and unstable price schedule creates more opportunities and greater openness for both parties involved in the exchange to negotiate prices. For instance, if a particular offering was available at a 20% discount yesterday and today's discount is only 10%, many consumers may believe it is reasonable to ask the frontline retailer employee for yesterday's 20% off the promotional price (e.g., Keiser, 1988; Schaerer et al., 2020). The insertion of online intermediaries in many consumer product categories further encourages customers to negotiate. These entities are less invested in maintaining the manufacturer brand's image and are more open to offering on-the-spot discounts to move inventory or close the sale (Byrne et al., 2022). They don't have the same emotional reluctance to vary prices as the manufacturer-brand owner, who may be more concerned about the potentially harmful effects on their price image.

Separately, spurred on by the Great Recession of 2008–2009, cultural trends encouraging decluttering, frugality, and minimalism became very popular and remained so (Donnelly, et al., 2017; Hampson, et al., 2018; Kondo, 2015). Movements that support frugality, minimalism, and decluttering are based on the principles that consumers should make purchase decisions carefully, buy and consume less, and use every avenue at their disposal to pay the least amount and get the most value for their money when making purchases. Accepting such an *extreme value mindset* means that consumers want to play an active role in establishing prices. More consumers are becoming amenable to bargaining, even in product categories where everyone viewed prices as fixed until recently (Shelegia & Sherman, 2022), spurring the popularity of so-called participative pricing mechanisms (Spann et al., 2018).

For example, a New York Times article recounted the experience and perspective of an upscale department store shopper who was approached by a salesperson, informed that a private sale was underway, and offered a discount on a garment he was inspecting. The article reported that such discount offers became common in the years after the Great Recession. Consumers with higher perceived price negotiability savor the opacity afforded by the seemingly fixed prices and see their willingness to negotiate as a competitive advantage over more reluctant customers and as a way to enjoy a customized discount.

DISCLOSURE-BASED PRICE TRANSPARENCY

As discussed in Chapter 2, the research on operational transparency suggests that targeted, partial disclosure of costs within the company can have significant benefits. As an exemplar, Wilken and colleagues (2010) studied the role of cost disclosure on salespeople's negotiation tactics and outcomes. They found that in many B2B settings, when salespeople with authority to establish the final price in negotiation with customers were explained the full costs of the offerings they were selling, they negotiated more effectively, using higher reference prices and more aggressive bargaining strategies, which resulted in their making lower price concessions and realizing higher prices and profits. However, even in such internal disclosures, too much transparency can backfire in that providing aggregate cost information is more valuable than providing itemized cost information (Plinke, 1985).

Disclosing costs and other pricing variables outside the organization is entirely different. The disclosure of costs, markup factors, and margins by companies is rooted in the philosophy of *radical corporate transparency* that various influential business thinkers have advanced in recent years.

The tenets of radical transparency are still evolving, and the implementation of its principles is often choppy, ad hoc, and incomplete; as such, it can be hard to distinguish companies paying lip service to the idea from those practicing its principles in earnest. Nevertheless, the fundamental principle behind radical transparency is alluring and timely, expressing an honest and complete openness in business operations, both internally with employees and externally with everyone in the wider world (e.g., Blodgett, 2017; Goleman, 2009; Heemsbergen, 2016). Organizational openness manifests in different ways depending on the context as covered throughout this book, but in the pricing context, the openness is about the disclosure of costs and other pricing inputs, along with pricing performance outcomes, that is facilitated by digital technology (Dholakia, 2017).

Relevant to the present discussion, a core idea behind radical transparency is that once market participants, managers, consumers, policymakers, and others, begin to consider the different impacts of products and services beyond immediate consumer responses and seek and share a broader range of data, the consideration of a company's costs is likely to be at the top of the list. Few business variables are as informative as costs in decoding, diagnosing, and conveying business impacts to external observers in and of themselves. For example, knowing the cost of labor incurred in manufacturing a consumer product helps answer whether the workers making the product were paid a fair wage.

Along similar lines, the costs of raw materials shed light on whether the company is compensating its suppliers fairly, a relevant issue in many global supply chains where there is a glaring asymmetry in the power of buyers (multinational corporations) and sellers (impoverished farmers, developing country entrepreneurs, etc.). And then, of course, there are the companies that take this disclosure a step further and make it part of their brand identity, core value proposition, and in some cases, even their raison d'être.

Definitions of Disclosure-Based Price Transparency

When price transparency comes up, many laypeople equate it to cost transparency. On the one hand, divulgences of costs often stem from the self-righteousness of one or a handful of company executives based on their own firmly held principles or views of running their business and are premised on the promise of resultant worker, supplier, and consumer welfare. However, in practice, cost disclosure is an elusive and relatively rare pricing strategy. It raises more questions than it answers, and we might even say that it is not a pricing strategy at all; instead, it is a managerial ideology that has profound consequences on the company's pricing strategy. Considered strictly from a narrow business performance standpoint, there are at least four reasons *for not* disclosing costs or margins.

First, few pieces of proprietary information are as valuable to a business as costs. For most companies, costs are the building blocks of a brand's competitive advantage, and if not, at the least, they are the yardsticks of incremental, day-to-day operating competence. Radical transparency notwithstanding, revealing this valuable proprietary information to potentially adversarial entities like competitors and customers can cause significant harm, diminishing leverage, and competitive advantage. Note that the disclosure of profit margins is a bit trickier; it depends on which margins are being disclosed and for what reason; business-level margins are commonly reported in public domains, while product- or item-level margins are hidden but provide more insight.

Second, revealing costs, even partially, can provide powerful insights into a company's business model, shining light on things such as which features and services it is marking up, which ones it is subsidizing, the sources of its revenue, the logic and calculation behind its pricing structure, and so on. Third, disclosing costs may also increase the company's legal exposure. For instance, when a company's costs are transparent, a smaller customer may claim they are being over-charged compared to a more significant customer, even when the costs to serve them are the same. Fourth, even if its purpose is different and only tangentially related to pricing strategy, cost disclosure inevitably affects the company's pricing strategy, not all of which are welcome or positive. When costs are disclosed, it puts a restraint on price levels that can be charged and the types of price structures that the company can employ. Customers may notice price increases immediately, and raising prices successfully may require considerable effort, including stronger, more ardent justifications. Value-based pricing may become virtually impossible to carry out because this method removes costs from the price-setting calculus. Price promotions may become subject to vetting by customers and other observers looking for evidence of unfairness or exploitative intent. In a nutshell, cost disclosure adds constraints and reduces the pricing strategy's flexibility.

Despite these obvious disadvantages, many organizations have adopted cost and margin disclosure as part of their business operations. While academic research studying disclosure-based price transparency is scarce, three distinct motivations behind disclosing costs and other pricing inputs and performance variables to customers and others can be identified. Each of these motivations is explored using brief case studies next.

Disclosure of Labor Costs to Pay Fair Wages

There are several movements, typically initiated by smaller, niche, socially conscious brands, to increase labor cost transparency that goes into their products and services. Consider the #LowestWageChallenge instituted by Able, a fashion brand that presently makes and sells jewelry and apparel. As indicated by the hashtag, this is a particular form of price-related disclosure in which the seller publishes the lowest wages it pays its workers instead of the average or the median wage. The logic is that the lower bound is more informative to determine whether the company pays a fair wage to its lowest-paid workers. Able developed a reporting system providing the lowest-wage information in a concise format resembling a nutrition facts label.

To explain its motivation, the brand observed, "If we are to move the fashion industry to paying fair wages to its workers, we must first acknowledge where we are, and how far we have to go. In an industry where only 2% of manufacturing labor earns a living wage, and an estimated 75% are women, Able believes that publishing the lowest wages at our manufacturers protects the most vulnerable workers and gives consumers clear data to make an informed choice. If they know what the bottom earns, everyone else from there is protected - not an average wage, or a labor cost per garment, but the lowest wage.... We think customers are ready for brands to be honest about the challenges facing fashion, and deserve to know whether or not the people who made the clothes on our body have been paid enough to meet their basic needs and live a life of dignity." It is noteworthy that like Patagonia in Chapter 2, Able acknowledges that it is far short of its objective of providing a living wage to workers and offers disclosure as a way of holding itself accountable and tracking its progress. The company also audited some of its suppliers, including three in Ethiopia, reporting similar metrics for each.

Interestingly, despite research finding that customers value such initiatives (e.g., Buell & Kalkanci, 2021; Kim et al., 2020), Able does not use the lowest-wage disclosure as part of its pricing strategies or pricing communications. Their promotions are similar to other low-transparency fashion retailers, such as "extra 20% off already reduced items" and "Give $50, Get $50" rewards. It appears that at present, the #LowestWageChallenge is endorsed by the founders and owners of private companies but is divorced from meaningfully impacting customer behavior or even heightening consumer concerns about worker welfare in the apparel industry appreciably.

Disclosure of Purchase Costs for Supplier Welfare

The coffee industry has been concerned with sustainability issues for several decades and has viewed price transparency as a way to achieve sustainability goals (Giovannucci & Ponte, 2005). Some niche, upscale coffee brands have recently formed a collective to measure and report purchase cost transparency on their websites and through social media. As of the summer of 2022, a total of seventy-nine coffee companies have adopted the *Transparency Pledge* (Fråne et al., 2021; Perkins, 2022). Upon signing the pledge, the coffee company commits to generate and publicly share purchasing reports that include all its suppliers, the specific types and volumes of coffee purchased from each one, and the FOB price paid on a per-pound basis. Many signatories provided this information on their websites and in printed catalogs even before signing the pledge.

Much like the brands utilizing disclosure-based price transparency to highlight labor costs and lowest wages paid, businesses providing detailed purchase cost information only appear to have a tangential interest in influencing or even informing their customers about this initiative. Their primary interest lies in reporting the purchase cost information from farmers in places like Ethiopia, Kenya, Peru, Honduras, and Guatemala to hold themselves and their peers accountable. Whether their customers read and process this information and how they react is of secondary concern.

Like the fashion labels that practice labor cost disclosure, the pricing strategies of the coffee companies do not appear to support other forms of transparency covered in this chapter. Specifically, these companies do not utilize methods such as making prices readily available and easy to process and interpret, nor do they substantially consider whether customers are using the supplier cost transparency information in their buying journeys.

Disclosure of Costs and Markups for Brand Differentiation

A third distinct goal of practicing disclosure-based price transparency lies in its utility as a brand differentiation strategy. Consider the case of the upscale fashion brand Everlane to illustrate this role. Everlane is presently a niche, relatively new, upscale apparel brand whose founders and senior executives decided to implement radical transparency as a value proposition and have employed disclosure-based transparency practices to do so (Gerlick, 2019; Richards, 2021). When compared to the fashion and the coffee companies embracing the transparency pledge, Everlane goes further in some respects and not as far in others. Unlike relatively focused concerns about worker welfare or the welfare of low-power suppliers, Everlane is concerned with the welfare of *all* its constituents, including its suppliers, workers, and customers, and uses a variety of practices that include sustainability and welfare concerns. In the pricing domain, the company discloses costs for every item including materials, hardware, labor, duties, and transportation. For many of its core products, the company additionally tallies the total variable costs and reports what its competitors charge for an equivalent item. The idea is to give customers as much information as is reasonable about the company's pricing inputs.

Combined with other core values like making high-quality apparel that will last for years, not using virgin plastics anywhere in its supply chain, and working with factories that pass a compliance audit to evaluate factors like fair wages, reasonable hours, and environmental impact, this radically transparent pricing strategy forms a compelling and comprehensive value proposition that many customers find attractive. Another distinctive aspect is that the radical transparency principle is also used in some of Everlane's price promotions. For example, in its annual "Choose What You Pay" Winter event in late December each year, Everlane sells a considerable proportion of its merchandise using this transparent, customer-empowered promotion. Items are offered for one of three prices that are all lower than the regular price. Each price explains how much of Everlane's costs it covers, giving customers a choice to support Everlane's operations at different levels.

On the flip side, evidence uncovered by investigative reporters showed that Everlane did not deliver fully on its promises of radical transparency. Testa, Friedman, and Paton (2020) reported the mistreatment of employees and unethical behavior by the company's senior executives. Among other things, former employees reported union busting, a culture of favoritism, a lack of consistent policies around promotions, and behaviors such as referring to Black models with inappropriate terms, violating subordinates' personal space, and punishing employees for speaking up (Gold, 2020; Testa et al., 2020).

In contrast to the other two functions of disclosure-based price transparency explored earlier in which adopting businesses were hard-pressed to convert their good intentions into practical customer-directed pricing actions based on transparency, Everlane's promise of radical transparency appears to be entirely customer-focused with little regard for the well-being of its employees. Even with meaningful cost disclosures and clever transparency-driven price promotions, the disclosures fail to translate to authentic transparency (e.g., Gold, 2020).

Summary. In a nutshell, the present state of practice suggests that disclosure-based price transparency is impelled by two distinct and incompatible managerial motivations, one to provide this information openly as an expression of the firm's and its founders' values, and the second to use disclosure-based price transparency as the cornerstone of a company's branding strategy. In all the cases considered here, disclosure-based price transparency is an intriguing idea with the potential to fit, ideologically and economically, into a company's digital marketing activities and synergize with other forms of business transparency.

Above all, perhaps, this form of transparency is inherently appealing to consumers, yet the information it generates is hard to comprehend. Disclosure often requires a detailed explanation to contextualize the information to assess it meaningfully, which is often beyond the scope of branded communications strategies that deliver disclosure-based transparency. As it stands, disclosure-based price transparency seems to be more of a *managerial ideology*, often initiated by company founders enamored with virtue signaling or social activism but often not backed up by considering their customers' reactions to these disclosures. As this discussion should make clear, much remains to be studied and known about disclosure-based price transparency, its promise, and its pitfalls.

References

Abraham, A. T., & Hamilton, R. W. (2018). When does partitioned pricing lead to more favorable consumer preferences? *Meta-Analytic Evidence. Journal of Marketing Research, 55*(5), 686–703.

Ahearne, M., Atefi, Y., Lam, S. K., & Pourmasoudi, M. (2022). The future of buyer–seller interactions: a conceptual framework and research agenda. *Journal of the Academy of Marketing Science, 50*, 22–45.
Ashenfelter, O., & Graddy, K. (2003). Auctions and the price of art. *Journal of Economic Literature, 41*(3), 763–787.
Atefi, Y., Ahearne, M., Hohenberg, S., Hall, Z., & Zettelmeyer, F. (2020). Open negotiation: The back-end benefits of salespeople's transparency in the front end. *Journal of Marketing Research, 57*(6), 1076–1094.
Baker, W. L., Marn, M. V., & Zawada, C. C. (2010). The price advantage (2nd ed.). Wiley.
Barber, B. M., Lee, Y. T., Liu, Y. J., & Odean, T. (2009). Just how much do individual investors lose by trading? *The Review of Financial Studies, 22*(2), 609–632.
Bazerman, M. H., Curhan, J. R., Moore, D. A., & Valley, K. L. (2000). Negotiation. *Annual Review of Psychology, 51*(1), 279–314.
Bertini, M., & Wathieu, L. (2010). How to stop customers from fixating on price. *Harvard Business Review, 88*(5), 84–91.
Besanko, D., & Winston, W. L. (1990). Optimal price skimming by a monopolist facing rational consumers. *Management Science, 36*(5), 555–567.
Blodgett, H. (2017, January 7). Ray Dalio offers a radical solution to the threat of 'fake news' and details life inside Bridgewater, Business Insider. https://www.businessinsider.com/ray-dalio-interview-henry-blodget-1-2017
Buell, R. W. (2019). Operational transparency. *Harvard Business Review, 97*(2), 102–113.
Buell, R. W., & Kalkanci, B. (2021). How transparency into internal and external responsibility initiatives influences consumer choice. *Management Science, 67*(2), 932–950.
Byrne, D. P., Martin, L. A., & Nah, J. S. (2022). Price Discrimination by negotiation: A field experiment in retail electricity. *The Quarterly Journal of Economics, 137*(4), 2499–2537.
Cheema, A., Leszczyc, P. T., Bagchi, R., Bagozzi, R. P., Cox, J. C., Dholakia, U. M., Greenleaf, E. A., Pazgal, A., Rothkopf, M. H., Shen, M., & Sunder, S. (2005). Economics, psychology, and social dynamics of consumer bidding in auctions. *Marketing Letters, 16*(3), 401–413.
Consumer Reports (2019, January 3). WT fee survey research report. https://advocacy.consumerreports.org/wp-content/uploads/2019/09/2018-WTFee-Survey-Report-_-Public-Report-1.pdf
Cox, J. C. (2008). First price independent private values auctions. *Handbook of Experimental Economics Results, 1*(1), 92–98.
D'Acunto, F., Hoang, D., & Weber, M. (2022). Managing households' expectations with unconventional policies. *The Review of Financial Studies, 35*(4), 1597–1642.

Dholakia, U. M. (2022). *Advanced introduction to digital marketing*. Edward Elgar.
Dholakia, U. M. (2021). If you're going to raise prices, tell customers why. Harvard Business Review, June. https://hbr.org/2021/06/if-youre-going-to-raise-prices-tell-customers-why
Dholakia, U. M. (2019). Priced to influence, sell & satisfy: Lessons from behavioral economics for pricing success. Kindle Publishing Group.
Dholakia, U. M. (2017). How to price effectively: A guide for managers and entrepreneurs. Kindle Publishing Group.
Dholakia, U. M. (2015, July 6). The risks of changing your prices too often. Harvard Business Review. https://hbr.org/2015/07/the-risks-of-changing-your-prices-too-often
Dilmé, F., & Li, F. (2019). Revenue management without commitment: Dynamic pricing and periodic flash sales. *The Review of Economic Studies*, 86(5), 1999–2034.
Donnelly, G. E., Lamberton, C., Reczek, R. W., & Norton, M. I. (2017). Social recycling transforms unwanted goods into happiness. *Journal of the Association for Consumer Research*, 2(1), 48–63.
Eggers, J. P. (2015). Focus on the customers you want, not the ones you have. Harvard Business Review, June 15. https://hbr.org/2015/06/focus-on-the-customers-you-want-not-the-ones-you-have
Fråne, A., Dahlbom, M., Sanctuary, M., Malmaeus, M., Fjellander, L., & de Jong, A. (2021). Towards sustainable consumption in the Nordic Region. Nordic Council of Ministers.
Friedman, N. (2021, November 11). Homes now typically sell in a week, forcing buyers to take risks. *Wall Street Journal*. https://www.wsj.com/articles/homes-typically-sell-in-a-week-forcing-buyers-to-take-risks-11636632000
Garaus, M., Wolfsteiner, E., & Wagner, U. (2016). Shoppers' acceptance and perceptions of electronic shelf labels. *Journal of Business Research*, 69(9), 3687–3692.
Gatter, S., & Hüttl-Maack, V. (2020). Any item, only $10! When and why same-price promotions can reduce regret and the pain of paying. *Advances in Consumer Research*, 48, 357–358.
Gelber, S. (2005). Horseless horses: Car dealing and the survival of retail bargaining. In P. N. Stearns (Ed.), American Behavioral History, New York University Press, 118–140.
Gerlick, J. (2019). Transparency in apparel: Everlane as a barometer for global positive impact. *The International Journal of Ethical Leadership*, 6(1), 87–95.
Gijsbrechts, E. (1993). Prices and pricing research in consumer marketing: Some recent developments. *International Journal of Research in Marketing*, 10(2), 115–151.

Giovannucci, D., & Ponte, S. (2005). Standards as a new form of social contract? Sustainability initiatives in the coffee industry. *Food Policy, 30*(3), 284–301.

Gold, H. (2020, March 30). Bernie Sanders calls out Everlane. The Cut. https://www.thecut.com/2020/03/bernie-sanders-calls-out-everlane.html

Goleman, D. (2009). Winning in an age of radical transparency. *Harvard Business Review*. https://hbr.org/2009/05/radical-transparency

Goolsbee, A., & Syverson, C. (2008). How do incumbents respond to the threat of entry? Evidence from the major airlines. *Quarterly Journal of Economics, 123*(4), 1611–1633.

Greenleaf, E. A., & Lehmann, D. R. (1995). Reasons for substantial delay in consumer decision making. *Journal of Consumer Research, 22*(2), 186–199.

Greenleaf, E. A., Johnson, E. J., Morwitz, V. G., & Shalev, E. (2016). The price does not include additional taxes, fees, and surcharges: A review of research on partitioned pricing. *Journal of Consumer Psychology, 26*(1), 105–124.

Hampson, D. P., Grimes, A., Banister, E., & McGoldrick, P. J. (2018). A typology of consumers based on money attitudes after a major recession. *Journal of Business Research, 91*, 159–168.

Hanna, R. C., Lemon, K. N., & Smith, G. E. (2019). Is transparency a good thing? How online price transparency and variability can benefit firms and influence consumer decision making. *Business Horizons, 62*(2), 227–236.

Heemsbergen, L. (2016). From radical transparency to radical disclosure: Reconfiguring (in) voluntary transparency through the management of visibilities. *International Journal of Communication, 10*, 138–151.

Jiang, B., Sudhir, K., & Zou, T. (2021). Effects of cost-information transparency on intertemporal price discrimination. *Production and Operations Management, 30*(2), 390–401.

Keefe, J. (2019, June 18). Haggle on the high street: Tips & tricks for hidden discounts, Money Saving Expert. https://www.moneysavingexpert.com/shopping/how-to-haggle-successfully/

Keiser, T. C. (1988). Negotiating with a customer you can't afford to lose. Harvard Business Review, November. https://hbr.org/1988/11/negotiating-with-a-customer-you-cant-afford-to-lose

Kim, N. L., Kim, G., & Rothenberg, L. (2020). Is honesty the best policy? Examining the role of price and production transparency in fashion marketing. *Sustainability, 12*(17), 6800.

Kliff, S., & Katz, J. (2021, August 22). Hospitals and insurers didn't want you to see these prices. Here's why. *New York Times*. https://www.nytimes.com/interactive/2021/08/22/upshot/hospital-prices.html

Kondo, M. (2015). The life-changing magic of tidying: The Japanese art. Random House.

Lal, R. (1986). Delegating pricing responsibility to the salesforce. *Marketing Science, 5*(2), 159–168.

Lieber, R. (2022). The discount data that some colleges won't publish. New York Times, September 24. https://www.nytimes.com/2022/09/24/your-money/college-common-data-set-merit-aid.html

Maxwell, P. (2015). Transparent and opaque pricing: The interesting case of lithium. *Resources Policy, 45*, 92–97.

Mazumdar, T., Raj, S. P., & Sinha, I. (2005). Reference price research: Review and propositions. *Journal of Marketing, 69*(4), 84–102.

McCoy, E. (2020). Struggling Napa wineries offer deep discounts and virtual tastings, Bloomberg, April 2. https://www.bloomberg.com/news/articles/2020-04-02/struggling-napa-wineries-offer-deep-discounts-and-virtual-tastings?sref=d3S20v77

McGinnis, C. (2019). Hotel resort fees anger readers. SFGate, January 24. https://www.sfgate.com/travel/article/Hotel-resort-fees-anger-readers-13559852.php

Miao, L., & Mattila, A. S. (2007). How and how much to reveal? The effects of price transparency on consumers' price perceptions. *Journal of Hospitality & Tourism Research, 31*(4), 530–545.

Michaels, D. (2012). The secret price of an airliner. Wall Street Journal, July 9. https://www.wsj.com/articles/SB10001424052702303649504577494862829051078

Mohan, B., Buell, R. W., & John, L. K. (2020). Lifting the veil: The benefits of cost transparency. *Marketing Science, 39*(6), 1105–1121.

Monroe, K. B. (1973). Buyers' subjective perceptions of price. *Journal of Marketing Research, 10*(1), 70–80.

NACUBO (2021, November 11). National Association of College and University Business Officers 2021 tuition discounting study. Available online at: https://www.nacubo.org/Research/2021/NACUBO-Tuition-Discounting-Study

Perkins, C. (2022, July 27). Wonder about the impact of your daily cup of coffee on the planet? Here's the bitter truth. TED Ideas. https://ideas.ted.com/truth-about-coffee-impact-on-environment-planet/

Plinke, W. (1985). Cost-based pricing: Behavioral aspects of price decisions for capital goods. *Journal of Business Research, 13*(5), 447–460.

Poort, J., & Zuiderveen Borgesius, F. (2021). *Personalised pricing: The demise of the fixed price? Data-driven personalisation in markets, politics and law* (pp. 174–189). Cambridge University Press.

Richards, H. (2021). Rethinking value: 'Radical transparency' in fashion. *Continuum, 35*(6), 914–929.

Rotemberg, J. J. (2005). Customer anger at price increases, changes in the frequency of price adjustment and monetary policy. *Journal of Monetary Economics, 52*(4), 829–852.

Saigol, L., & Root, A. (2022). Boeing gets good news: It flipped ab Airbus customer. Barron's, May 19. https://www.barrons.com/articles/boeing-737-max-jets-iag-51652951588

Sampson, C. J., Arnold, R., Bryan, S., Clarke, P., Ekins, S., Hatswell, A., Hawkins, N., Langham, S., Marshall, D., Sadatsafavi, M., & Sullivan, W. (2019). Transparency in decision modelling: What, why, who and how? *PharmacoEconomics, 37*(11), 1355–1369.

Santana, S., Dallas, S. K., & Morwitz, V. G. (2020). Consumer reactions to drip pricing. *Marketing Science, 39*(1), 188–210.

Schaerer, M., Schweinsberg, M., Thornley, N., & Swaab, R. I. (2020). Win-win in distributive negotiations: The economic and relational benefits of strategic offer framing. *Journal of Experimental Social Psychology, 87*, 103943.

Schlegelmilch, B. B., & Öberseder, M. (2010). Half a century of marketing ethics: Shifting perspectives and emerging trends. *Journal of Business Ethics, 93*(1), 1–19.

Schmidt, J., & Bijmolt, T. H. (2020). Accurately measuring willingness to pay for consumer goods: A meta-analysis of the hypothetical bias. *Journal of the Academy of Marketing Science, 48*(3), 499–518.

Seim, K., Vitorino, M. A., & Muir, D. M. (2017). Do consumers value price transparency? *Quantitative Marketing and Economics, 15*, 305–339.

Shelegia, S., & Sherman, J. (2022). Bargaining at retail stores: Evidence from Vienna. *Management Science, 68*(1), 27–36.

Shen, L. (2017). The truth about whether airlines jack up prices if you keep searching the same flight. Time, September 18. https://time.com/4899508/flight-search-history-price/

Sinha, I. (2000). Cost transparency: The net's real threat to prices and brands. Harvard Business Review, 78(2), Reprint R00210.

Sjolin, S. (2015). In this London pub, drink prices rise and fall like stocks. MarketWatch, July 26. https://www.marketwatch.com/story/when-this-market-crashes-traders-get-trashed-2015-07-17.

Soh, C., Lynne Markus, M., & Goh, K. H. (2006). Electronic marketplaces and price transparency: Strategy, information technology, and success. *MIS Quarterly, 30*(3), 705–723.

Spann, M., Zeithammer, R., Bertini, M., Haruvy, E., Jap, S. D., Koenigsberg, O., Mak, V., Popkowski Leszczyc, P., Skiera, B., & Thomas, M. (2018). Beyond posted prices: The past, present, and future of participative pricing mechanisms. *Customer Needs and Solutions, 5*(1), 121–136.

Testa, J., Friedman, V., & Paton, E. (2020, July 26). Everlane's promise of 'radical transparency' unravels. New York Times. Available online at: https://www.nytimes.com/2020/07/26/fashion/everlane-employees-ethical-clothing.html

Truong, N. A., & Masopust, G. (2021). Cost transparency: A sales tool or a solid brand component? *Innovative Brand Management II Special Issue*, 39–61.
Turco, C. J. (2016). The conversational firm: Rethinking bureaucracy in the age of social media. Columbia University Press.
Vanhuele, M., & Drèze, X. (2002). Measuring the price knowledge shoppers bring to the store. *Journal of Marketing, 66*(4), 72–85.
White, S. (2020). When shrouded prices signal transparency: Consequences of price disaggregation (Doctoral dissertation). The University of Chicago.
Wilken, R., Cornelißen, M., Backhaus, K., & Schmitz, C. (2010). Steering sales reps through cost information: An investigation into the black box of cognitive references and negotiation behavior. *International Journal of Research in Marketing, 27*(1), 69–82.
Zhang, X., Manchanda, P., & Chu, J. (2021). "Meet me halfway": The costs and benefits of bargaining. *Marketing Science, 40*(6), 1081–1105.

CHAPTER 4

Organizational Transparency

Abstract This chapter examines the research on organizational transparency considering observability, a culture of candor, the so-called conversational firm, and deliberately orchestrated and consensually shared information that is useful, undisguised, and unbiased. Drawing upon a range of scholarly sources, six significant contributors to building a transparent organizational culture are enumerated. The chapter concludes by considering research on pay transparency and its relation to the gender wage gap to explore the nuanced (positive and negative) implications of cultural transparency on the organization as a whole and its members.

Keywords Transparency · Organizational Culture · Employee Engagement · Pay Transparency · Wage Gap

> Every organization needs to be introspective, transparent, and honest with itself. This only works if everyone is unified on the goals and purposes of the organization and there is trust within the team—Colin Powell

Transparency has a significant place in the academic study of organizational culture. It is seen variously by organizational scholars as the backbone and governing principle of an organization's corporate culture guiding managerial decisions and actions, a legitimate means of revising traditional bureaucratic and hierarchical management models, a barometer of the organization's moral character, a template for establishing, updating, and implementing its governing mechanisms, a set of practices contributing to employee productivity and engagement and leading to accountability and trust, a means to break through hurdles like conformity, impression management, and organizational silence, and an idealized value for employees, and particularly for corporate leaders, to strive for. Furthermore, consistent with the transparency principle, observers often view organizations perceived as having a more transparent culture to be more virtuous, moral, and high performing.

In one sense, organizational cultural transparency, defined as *the open sharing of relevant information within and across functional and hierarchical organizational delineations*, is a conduit to the development and fostering of shared understanding and values among its members, ultimately leading to dialogue, camaraderie, cohesion, social identification, and trust, which are all signifiers of a healthy corporate culture. Indeed, consistent with this definition, many business theorists have viewed transparency to be a critical contributor to organizational performance, a core component of organizational culture (e.g., Detert & Burris, 2007; Schnackenberg & Tomlinson, 2016), and the foundation of the so-called conversational firm that utilizes the affordances of digital technology, particularly social media, to revise bureaucratic hierarchies (Turco, 2016). Despite its significance, however, organizational transparency is a slippery concept. Bernstein (2017) points out that organizational transparency is particularly difficult to measure because the conceptual idea of a completely transparent organization is impossible to operationalize, and consequently, any organization's degree of transparency cannot be calibrated, compared, or tracked meaningfully.

While a generally positive view supporting the transparency principle dominates in the organizational studies literature, there also exists a contrarian, somewhat cynical perspective on organizational transparency that sees it as providing the justification for an organization's leaders to adopt intrusive mechanisms and tools to track, monitor, and in many cases even surveil employee and customer actions under the guise of fostering openness and well-being (Albu & Flyverbom, 2019; Bernstein, 2012, 2017; Gilliom & Monahan, 2013; Thiel et al., 2022).

The adopters of this perspective define organizational transparency more narrowly as the "accurate observability of an organization's low-level activities, routines, behaviors, output, and performance" (Bernstein,

2012; p. 181), view "the metaphor of shedding light [as] a gross simplification of the complex labor involved in the manufacture of transparency" (Albu & Flyverbom, 2019, p. 280), and consider measures to increase the transparency of behaviors of employees, suppliers, or customers with caution and skepticism. With this perspective, the manager's desire to observe and the subordinate's desire to maintain privacy are constantly at war with each other, with each party devising more ingenious and technologically-dependent methods to counter the other (Anteby & Chan, 2018).

In reviewing the negative effects, Bernstein (2017) finds that increased organizational transparency leads employees to engage in posturing, pandering, and impression management and inhibits open dialog, all of which potentially negatively affect downstream behaviors and, ultimately, organizational performance. Albu and Flyverbom (2019) point out that transparency can be used to advance particular ideological or political agendas, and in some cases, making information available can undermine trust instead of increasing it if the disclosure violates organizational norms for communicative activities. This skeptical scholarly perspective is particularly informative not only because of the non-intuitive and penetrating insights it often generates beyond trite assertions about the benefits of organizational transparency but also because it opens the door to promising future research opportunities that are especially relevant in today's tough, unforgiving, and rapidly evolving corporate environment (e.g., Albu & Flyverbom, 2019; Anteby & Chan, 2018; Bernstein, 2017; Turco, 2016).

While the bullish perspective on organizational transparency focuses on the psychological and performance rewards derived from it (e.g., Turco, 2016), the bearish perspective highlights the significance of the power disparity that routinely governs the hierarchical work and exchange relationships found in organizations and its potentially detrimental consequences (e.g., Bernstein, 2017; Coser, 1961). While both these perspectives will be touched upon, this chapter focuses on the positive aspects of organizational transparency discovered by extant research; its potentially exploitative power and harmful individual and group-level aspects will be discussed in Chapter 7. The core insight advanced in this chapter is that extant research finds organizational transparency to be a double-edged sword; both the positive-broad and negative-narrow perspectives of its study provide complementary insights into the different ways transparency affects organizational culture and performance.

We will consider core questions about what exactly organizational transparency is, briefly consider its origins, and seek to understand its contributors and consequences. In addition, the research on one significant, well-researched, and currently relevant form of organizational transparency, *transparency about wages*, will be explored in greater detail. Succinctly reviewing and synthesizing the research on pay transparency and understanding its relation to the gender wage gap allows us to consider the nuances behind how one particular form of organizational transparency shapes individual and collective employee outcomes within an organization both positively and negatively.

THE ORIGINS OF TRANSPARENCY IN ORGANIZATIONAL RESEARCH

From the outset, the concept of *observability*, the degree to which a worker's behaviors are visible and what is done with this information, has been central to organizational research. More recently, the impact of observation on those so observed has also generated interest. While Bernstein (2017) provided an elaborate historical timeline of the evolution of observation of human behavior in science, tracing it back to the Greek philosophers, more narrowly, Schnackenberg and Tomlinson (2016) traced the origins of transparency in organizational science to a sociological analysis of observability and its agent-dependent effects based on the individual's status and type of social conformity conducted by Coser (1961). Coser's (1961) position was that the social control facilitated by established and predictable observability procedures contributes to the stability of an organization. Indeed, the bulk of early organizational transparency research viewed transparency as a positive force, and the trajectory established early on with its emphasis on the positive has influenced many researchers to the present day. The following selected examples of scholarly perspectives over the years illustrate this emphasis.

In Denison and Mishra's (1995) grounded theory-based *model of cultural effectiveness*, the organization's members developed a commonly agreed upon and widely shared understanding of collectively significant behaviors, systems, rituals, resources, and unique meanings, all of which led to their so-called normative integration with the organization. The transparency afforded by the widespread availability of mutually developed forms of knowledge within the organization was conceptualized to be a significant organizational cultural trait driving its effectiveness.

In their widely read and cited book on organizational transparency, Bennis et al. (2008) posited that on the grounds of ethicality and pragmatism, embracing transparency provides the organization with the most straightforward path to accomplish its goals. These scholars saw transparency primarily as *consistently practiced candor* by individuals and advocated for building a *culture of candor* within the organization that rewards truth-telling by every employee, even when it runs contrary to their (and the organization's) self-interests and natural inclinations.

More recently, Bernstein (2017) came up with yet another perspective on organizational transparency, consistent with Coser's (1961) original development, viewing transparency through the lens of "practices of observation" and distinguishing between its different forms in the organizational context as monitoring, disclosure, process visibility, and at the extreme end, surveillance. Bernstein (2017) pointed out that in conventional frameworks of organizational transparency, increased transparency is seen as productive to the extent that it supports the generation of comprehensive, accurate information about workers. The fundamental premise of these established paradigms is that greater and more accurate awareness of others, from the observer's vantage point, leads to improvements in learning and control, which in turn improves performance. For example, a plant manager may revise manufacturing processes once they learn points of time-wasting activities by workers on an assembly line to gain efficiency. Finally, for Turco (2016), the open dialog fostered by transparency leads "managers and workers [to] continually confront one another's knowledge, developing a mutual appreciation for each other's wisdom" (p. 171). The result, according to her, is more empathetic executives with an accurate understanding of what they can delegate and what they cannot and more informed and understanding employees.

Yet, transparency in an idealistic, primarily positive, "honesty no matter the consequences" structure that is endorsed in the established literature is hard to find in practice for the simple reason that employees at all hierarchical levels often derive significant personal benefits from withholding information, rationing disclosure, and essentially eschewing transparency. Even in today's environment that normalizes social sharing activities, few employees want to be monitored constantly or report every work-related thought, opinion, and feeling to their supervisors and coworkers. A static, decontextualized, rosy-eyed perspective of organizational transparency lacks face validity (Alvesson & Einola, 2019). Accordingly, far more rank- and-file employees, managers, executives, and organizations pay lip service to transparency and its associated values of openness, access, and candor than practice them, especially in morally ambiguous or personally consequential circumstances where the tenets of transparency matter the most, leading to cynicism and loss of morale among frontline employees, and to the conclusion that organizational transparency in practice is little more than an empty buzz phrase or a vacuous virtue signal.

As a counterpoint to the positive views of organizational transparency, Bernstein (2014) elaborated on the potential downsides of too much transparency on employee performance. He forcefully argued in favor of establishing boundaries so to achieve a middle ground between privacy and openness and for changing the research vantage point from the *observer* to the *observed* so as to obtain a more complete and accurate picture of transparency's effects (Bernstein, 2017), the main point being that certain forms of disclosure in organizational contexts may asymmetrically disenfranchise, subjugate, and harm employees, especially those at the lower ends of the corporate hierarchy, instead of doing good; even for the organization, this may result in degradation of performance.

Definition of Organizational Transparency

As the discussion thus far implies, transparency within an organization essentially has to do with the flows of information within it. Thus, acknowledging the positive slant of extant research and drawing upon extant perspectives, we will adopt the following conceptualization for further consideration: The fundamental meaning of organizational transparency has to do with the *deliberately orchestrated, consensual, individually and collectively beneficial, and unimpeded flow of useful, undisguised, and unbiased information within different parts of the organization*, and in the two-way information flows with other relevant stakeholders and constituents that may include a wide range of entities depending on the organization (Bennis et al., 2008). It is related to available definitions that emphasize *hierarchical observability*, that is, the degree to which employees' conduct and its consequences can be seen by their supervisors or managers (Kaptein, 2008), but goes further in the sense that flows of candid information in the opposite direction, from leaders to followers, are also included.

To be clear, this way of thinking about organizational transparency assigns it a broad and influential role in supporting an organization's effective functioning. It also assigns a wide and disparate range of information types as falling within its aegis. For example, as part of organizational governance mechanisms, a publicly-traded company may be mandated to report certain information to financial market participants regularly, or after elaboration in employment contracts, the activities of workers may be tracked with wearable devices, cameras, and point-of-sale systems (Anteby & Chan, 2018), or on their own initiative, or prodded by regulation, an organization's leaders may adopt pay transparency practices by disclosing average pay (or lowest pay of its workers, see Chapter 3) for different job roles and by gender to its employees. These practices, and many others, and the emergent issues they entail, form the core interest of organizational transparency research. We can further unpack the organizational transparency concept by separately considering its two key components, the deliberate orchestration of information flows and the quality of the shared information within the organization.

The Deliberate Orchestration of Information Flows

Bennis and colleagues (2008) point out that secrecy is a reflexive instinct in many organizations and the default course of action adopted by managers. In other words, withholding information is the status quo. Managers often support this tendency using post hoc rationalization about why limiting access to information is in the organization's (or their department's or group's) best interests. Information is culturally treated as a resource that retains value when hoarded and controlled by those who have it and a way to exert influence over those who do not. Under this prevailing view, the intra-organizational flows of information are dammed up, regulated, and when they do occur, they are unstructured, intermittent, and non-strategic, resulting from idiosyncratic events within or outside the organization or occurring because of a particular manager's whims.

In stark contrast, a transparent organizational culture encourages information sharing between employees and groups, embraces the deliberate orchestration of information flows, and minimizes the creation of obstacles. For information to flow freely, *observation processes*, a set of mechanisms to observe and record data about the opinions and behaviors of employees, and *communication and feedback processes* that allow these data in their raw, or more often, in their processed forms, along with executive assessment and commentary, and tidings about corporate decisions and the rationale behind them to flow throughout the organization, are adopted and implemented with forethought and consideration (Bernstein, 2014; Detert & Burris, 2016).

Finally, where relevant, the cooperation and even active consent of employees whose information is being gathered, processed, and shared is also obtained. Such a practice has clear benefits, and its absence can backfire. In an influential study, Bernstein (2012) introduced the notion of a *transparency paradox*, finding that observing workers' activities continually without their knowledge through various monitoring processes (called "transparency tools") in a Chinese factory reduced their performance by inducing them to conceal their activities; they used codes and other productivity-diminishing techniques to maintain their privacy during their work shift. Bernstein (2012) called this phenomenon the "reverse Hawthorne effect." In a follow-up field study conducted at the same site, creating *zones of privacy* by reducing worker observability with a curtain increased their productivity.

Other research has examined the role of active employee consent to information disclosure. When the productivity metrics of employees were made more transparent by using novel methods such as gamification tools in a field study, the employees who consented to the greater transparency by exercising their agency and agreeing to cooperate actively experienced positive affect; however, affect declined for those who did not consent (Mollick & Rothbard, 2014a, 2014b), presumably affecting employee morale and productivity in turn. In another recent paper, Thiel and colleagues (2022) found that employees monitored at work without consent were more likely to engage in reactive behaviors like disregarding supervisors' instructions, working slowly, and taking unapproved breaks. The authors ascribed these performance-undermining behaviors to a diminished sense of agency, leading to moral disengagement and displacement of responsibility.

The Quality of Shared Information

The operation of observation, communication, and feedback processes is necessary but not sufficient in an organization's path toward performance-enhancing transparency. Several researchers have pointed out that genuine transparency arises when information flows are two-sided, rank-and-file employees have a voice and can communicate frankly with peers and supervisors (Detert & Burris, 2007; Morrison, 2011), such as when they can share ideas for improvement, speak their minds, bring up worrisome signals they may have encountered, voice their concerns, shed light on episodes involving unfairness, inappropriate behaviors or misconduct, criticize decisions made by supervisors and senior executives (by engaging in *principled dissent*) and suggest alternative solutions, and are heeded and rewarded for these activities instead of being punished or ignored entirely (Detert & Burris, 2016). In contrast, *employee silence*, whereby employees withhold information or refrain from calling attention to significant issues, even if it is entirely voluntary, is a form of organizational opacity that can lead to missed or distorted information for decision making, improvement, and innovation (Morrison & Milliken, 2000). With this understanding of what a transparent organizational culture entails and does not entail, the next question is: *how can an organization cultivate a culture of transparency?*

THE BUILDING BLOCKS FOR CULTIVATING A TRANSPARENT ORGANIZATIONAL CULTURE

A number of organizational scholars have proposed conceptualizations of transparency that help to answer the question of how to cultivate a transparent culture and the pitfalls therein. Three insightful perspectives by Schnackenberg and Tomlinson (2016), Bernstein (2017), and Kaptein (2008) are considered here. First, Schnackenberg and Tomlinson (2016) define *organizational transparency* as "the perceived quality of intentionally shared information from a sender" (p. 1788) and propose that it consists of three dimensions: information disclosure, clarity, and accuracy. Second, Bernstein (2017) distinguishes between different forms of transparency related to organizations, such as monitoring, process visibility, surveillance, and disclosure, treating each form as a distinctive construct worthy of a balanced exploration that emphasizes the experience of the observed, that is, the monitored employees.

Third, Kaptein's (2008) *Corporate Ethical Virtues* model focuses on the factors contributing to an organization's virtuousness or the extent to which the organizational culture encourages virtuous employee behavior and penalizes unvirtuous conduct. Although a detailed exposition of what virtue means in this context or its boundaries is beyond the scope of the present discussion, the properties of virtuous organizations laid out by Kaptein (2008) based on extensive qualitative work provide a robust scaffolding to identify the conditions that instill and cultivate transparency in organizations. We will rely on these three scholarly sources and others to enumerate and briefly explore six significant contributors to building a transparent organizational culture. These are graphically shown in Fig. 4.1.

Underlying this discussion are two core ideas. The first one is that transparency generally benefits all employees, contributes to organizational performance, and *can be deliberately cultivated within an organization as a core, persistent value by adopting a set of managerial signals, practices, and mechanisms.* The second one is that to build a transparent culture, actions trump talk. As Beer (2001) points out (quoting executive Vince Forlenza), "Culture gets changed by doing real work in line with the new strategy, a new governance model, business processes, or performance management systems. Not much happens from pure culture conversations because they don't result in a clear idea of what needs to change and how it will be changed to reinforce key strategic priorities."

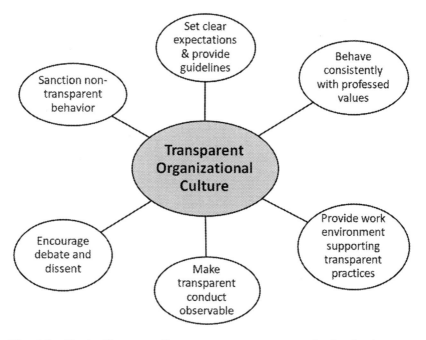

Fig. 4.1 Six significant contributors to a transparent organizational culture

Setting Clear Expectations of Transparent Conduct

Once, we get beyond new employee handbooks describing general behavioral expectations, rules, and policies, which tend to be written for broad applicability (e.g., Flyverbom, 2016; Smith & Harris, 2014), the unwritten norms, expectations, and standards for behaving transparently are hidden from rank-and-file employees in many organizations. This can be due to different reasons, such as the difficulty of precisely describing every form of transparent behavior, the potentially unlimited avenues to be covered where organizational transparency manifests and influences, and the challenge of describing ethical dilemmas and their resolutions. Additionally, as Kaptein (2008) points out, employees may face many challenges unique to their particular work setting for which there is no parallel. As we've seen throughout this book, the context needs attention for transparency to be beneficial.

In these instances, simply letting employees rely on their moral intuitions may not be sufficient to ensure they will behave ethically or transparently to a standard that is deemed acceptable. Furthermore, when norms and expectations are not articulated or understood, many employees may use the lack simply as an excuse or rationalization to behave in unethical or self-serving ways (Bovens, 1998). Starting with a clear explanation of what is and is not considered transparent behavior within the organization and providing employees with concrete, comprehensive, and understandable guidelines about how they *should behave* establishes the boundaries of acceptable behavior (e.g., Flyverbom, 2016). We can think of guidance as *role clarity* in the domain of organizational transparency.

However, like other ethical challenges, acting transparently often involves a constellation of fuzzy, potentially intimidating, and personally challenging activities requiring fortitude, selflessness, and group cohesion. The availability of detailed guidelines, such as a corporate ethics framework (Arkan et al., 2022), documented in operating procedures where suitable, and the occurrence and acknowledgment of visible practices, especially from the organization's leaders, reflecting these guidelines are both important, providing employees with evidence that the organization values authentic information sharing and supports and rewards transparency-enhancing behaviors.

Practically, they encourage employees to engage in normative deliberation, that is, to consider and apply a normative standard based on explicitly considering ethical obligations and stakeholder interests (Arkan et al., 2022). The literature on authentic leadership covered in Chapter 5 also underscores this point. For instance, reinforcing the idea that engaging in dissent and reporting instances of wrongdoing to the appropriate department or supervisor is encouraged, and when it is based on justifiable arguments, will be rewarded through repeated communication and supporting actions will increase the work role clarity of employees (Brown et al., 2014; Landler et al., 2009).

Behaving Consistently with Professed Values and Expectations

Simply stated, a core constituent of transparent organizational culture that an organization's leaders often violate is the principle of "Don't just talk, but *behave* as you expect and want your subordinates to behave." For virtuous behavior, Kaptein (2008) calls this managerial practice "congruency," conceiving of it as visible, sustained, and unalloyed compliance by the organization's leaders with the normative expectations of conduct they have themselves chosen and established. Congruent executive behavior contributes to cultivating a transparent culture because employees look to leaders for cues or explicit direction about what is acceptable behavior in the organization (and what is not) and emulate them (O'Reilly et al., 2021). What's more, such emulation extends to the acceptance of the principles and values conveyed by these norms. In the leadership literature, congruency is considered an essential attribute of authentic leaders.

In theory, congruency appears straightforward. For instance, if a senior executive asserts support for inclusive, merit-based hiring practices, they should hire inclusively and based on merit. In practice, however, congruency with the principles of transparency is often challenging to implement, and there are numerous cases of executives who profess one value but behave contrarily (Van Scotter & Roglio, 2020). For example, the fashion brand Everlane was founded on principles of radical transparency and ethical sourcing, but its culture was rife with favoritism, discriminatory conduct and harassment of employees, and union-busting efforts by its executives (Testa et al., 2020). One consulting study found that 39 percent of CEOs who left their posts in 2018 did so for reasons having to do with unethical conduct rather than unsatisfactory job performance (Karlsson et al., 2019). The idea that business leaders should be consistent in their attitudes, talk, and actions, not only with the organization's transparency guidelines but also with their personal core beliefs and values, is also a core component of relational transparency covered in Chapter 5 (e.g., Gardner et al., 2005).

Providing a Work Environment Supporting Transparent Practices

It is not sufficient to provide clear guidelines about how to act and model expectations through the behaviors of the organization's senior leaders. Rank-and-file employees should be able to adopt and use transparency-enhancing behaviors in the workplace regularly; for this, employees' activities need to be supported by the organization's work environment. Kaptein (2008) calls this organizational characteristic as *feasibility* because it concerns the extent to which the organization generates the working conditions that allow its employees to comply with the deliberately established normative expectations and fulfill their tasks and responsibilities as per expectations.

Providing an environment conducive to organizational transparency involves giving employees adequate resources, time, information, and autonomy, setting reasonable targets for their performance and conduct, and generally creating a climate that gives them confidence in their capability to act in accordance with the organization's corporate ethics framework. In some cases, this may additionally involve establishing feedback processes that reinforce and encourage desired practices, such as sharing authentic information within the organization. Finally, it can also include establishing rituals that emphasize and support transparent work practices and reinforce guidelines provided to employees. In essence, this factor lies at the heart of organizational culture because it concerns the practical design of the work processes and mechanisms that facilitates transparent employee conduct.

Making Employees' Transparent Conduct Observable

Transparent conduct by employees is often not itself transparent in the sense that it may not be visible or publicized within the organization. Even though executives talk up the value of behaving transparently, when employees act transparently, their actions often remain unacknowledged and hidden. Without appreciation or reinforcement, employees will take the guidelines and expectations conveyed to them less seriously over time. They will stop believing that the organization cares about transparency and become unmotivated to pursue transparency-enhancing activities, especially if they are effortful. Over time, they will drift away from transparency-enhancing routines and volitional behaviors. Eventually, the organization's professed culture of transparency will be diluted.

To prevent such a downward spiral, in addition to processes that support transparency, research shows that mechanisms that involve monetary reward, as well as social recognition for transparent employee behaviors, can be effective (e.g., Allen, 2006; Wayne et al., 2002). Kaptein (2008) calls this aspect of support the organization's *visibility*, defining it as the degree to which employee conduct and its effects are observable to those tasked with responding to it in any fashion, whether it is colleagues collaborating on a project, subordinates following directives, or supervisors assessing performance. The timing of visibility efforts also matters; publicizing employee efforts strategically "at advantageous moments or for political purposes" (Flyverbom, 2016, p. 115) is likely to increase their impact.

Kaptein (2008) further makes the useful distinction between *horizontal and vertical visibility*, depending on whether mechanisms that engender visibility of transparent practices by rank-and-file employees are hierarchical, involving supervisors rewarding or punishing subordinates, or lateral, which are mechanisms to facilitate and acknowledge employees observing peers, respectively. Hierarchical and lateral communication and acknowledgment mechanisms are part and parcel of Turco's (2016) *conversational firm* as executives share sensitive information broadly to the organization's employee base, and all employees are encouraged to share their knowledge and opinions in public events that foster firmwide conversation. Not only do such conversational events provide voice to employees, but they solidify hierarchical and lateral mechanisms of visibility in the organization, which through formal and informal means, contribute to fostering an organizational culture of transparency.

Encouraging Intra-Organizational Debate and Dissent

A core requirement of sustainable organizational transparency is that employees at all levels have voice. Voice in this context includes not only having the ability to debate, raise, and discuss potentially controversial topics of import to the organization, or to express critical or skeptical opinions, including about executive discussions or decisions, but also ample opportunities to do so without censure. In this context, employee motivation is to be supported by ability and opportunity. From her ethnographic study, Turco (2016) provides a vivid example of an organizational setting "where employees can step outside the formal chain of command to question their leaders, challenge corporate policies and decisions, and share and discuss their own ideas in a forum visible to the entire organization" (p. 45). Kaptein (2008) refers to this aspect of the organization's culture as *discussability*.

Discussability is particularly significant in today's corporate environment where many employees wish to express their opinions about social and political issues vocally, not only in intra-organizational communication channels but also publicly on social media such as Twitter, and expect their employers to conform to their values, and criticize employer decisions when there is a conflict with a personal value (e.g., Flint, 2021). There are numerous examples of visible and high-profile dissent by employees, from dozens of Netflix employees staging a walkout to protest an offering they perceived to be transphobic to Disney workers walking out to protest their employer's response to state legislation (Koblin & Sperling, 2021; Whelan & Sayre, 2022). Extant research shows that such dissent is often accentuated by employee perceptions of the issue's seriousness, the attribution of personal responsibility for making a difference, and the perceived feasibility of response (Graham, 1983), all of which support a *culture of candor* within the organization.

Sanctioning Non-Transparent Behavior Unequivocally

In addition to the aforementioned factors, a transparent organizational culture should be supported by a set of reinforcing feedback mechanisms, typically a system of publicized rewards and punishments, to bolster communal understanding of the corporate ethics framework and provide symbolic support for adherence to transparency principles by its employees. Note that this goes beyond providing a supportive work environment to explicitly and visibly rewarding transparent behavior and penalizing non-transparent employee behavior. Within an organization, the role of sanctionability lies in reinforcing standards, upholding the value of conformity to shared norms, and generating a shared sense of justice and accountability.

Mild public sanctioning (known as transgression transparency) may also have other surprising benefits. Recent research adds color to a mostly black-and-white perspective by finding that instead of leading to stigmatization and shaming, making minor transgressions transparent may actually lead to social awareness of the transgression within the organization, leading colleagues to inquire about it and eventually leading the transgressor to construct a mutually acceptable narrative, which the authors call "personal narrative control" (Frey et al., 2022). As a result of wanting to maintain the narrative they have constructed, transgressors exercise greater self-control and avoid further transgressions, leading to their rehabilitation. This seems to suggest that being transparent about penalizing non-transparent work behaviors may produce transparency benefits. In summary, the key issues at the organizational level lie in considering what reward and penalty mechanisms to use, how to introduce and maintain them within the organization, and how to assess their effects.

Summary. From the work of organizational scholars over the last fifty years or longer, we know a lot about how to build a transparent organizational culture and various factors that may impede this objective. Yet even as digital technology pervades organizations and social norms about work and the workplace continues to evolve, our pace of understanding how these changes affect the cultural aspects of organizational transparency is somewhat lagging. A key challenge is that these interactions of the changing context with organizational transparency and its constituent processes often produce counter-intuitive and challenging results that need to be understood and incorporated into evolving management theory. The flavor of these challenges will be apparent in the next section where research on the recently popular area of pay transparency is examined.

Pay Transparency and the Gender Wage Gap

The large and quickly growing body of research on pay transparency provides a specific concrete context to explore the nuances underlying organizational transparency and to appreciate the subtle and surprising ways in which the impulse for transparency manifests in and affects individual and organizational outcomes. Simply stated, pay transparency is a particularly resonant form of organizational transparency because it is seen as an effective way to minimize the pay gap due to gender, increase employee engagement, build trust, and increase job satisfaction (Wong et al., 2022). After all, if an organization professes to endorse and facilitate the free flow of useful authentic information, shouldn't its employees know and benefit from knowing the wages their peers, supervisors, executives, and others earn? Strikingly, a corpus of studies spanning several decades has provided evidence for a large and persistent *gender wage gap* (e.g., Blau & Kahn, 2017; Card et al., 2016; Goldin, 2014; Warner & Lehmann, 2019), which offers a good starting point to explore pay transparency research.

The Gender Wage Gap

The literature on the gender wage gap is vast, and while an in-depth exploration is beyond our scope, three significant points about this body of work are relevant to the current discussion. First, from our perspective, the organization-level gender wage gap is a *consequence* of organizational transparency (or lack of it), and how it is operationalized, explained, and remedied provides valuable insights into organizational transparency. A common operationalization of the gender wage gap used by many researchers is aggregate-level *men-women earning ratios*, commonly reported and tracked at the country level (Goldin, 2014). For instance, it was famously noted that in the 1970s, women made 59 cents for every dollar earned by men in the United States; by the early 2000s, this value had increased to 77 cents, and in 2020, it stood at 84 cents (Barroso & Brown, 2021).

At the aggregate level, there is little doubt that the gender wage gap exists within organizations, remains significant to the present, or that it is shrinking gradually (There are also other demographically relevant wage gaps, such as the gaps between different racial groups, age groups, religious affiliation groups, and so on; however, these gaps have received significantly less scholarly attention thus far; Trotter et al., 2017). However, aggregate measures of wage gaps are only partially helpful. For individual workers, the personally relevant measures are statistics about wages by gender for their employer and even more so for wages earned by coworkers doing the same job as them. For this reason, much of the research and public policy discussion focuses on more granular, organization-specific pay transparency measures.

Second, given the robust confirmation of the gender wage gap, research shows that a significant portion of the gender wage gap can be ascribed to systemic differences in the labor of men and women.

As Goldin (2014) puts it, "The wage is also a summary statistic for an individual's education, training, prior labor force experience, and expected future participation. The gender gap in wages is a summary statistic for gender differences at work" (p. 1093). There is a long list of gender differences in labor that affect wages in the literature. They include, among others, occupation, industry, experience, workforce interruptions, the impact of motherhood, career progression, firm-specific pay premiums, the share of service work, and traits such as locus of control, risk preferences, and agreeableness (see Blau & Kahn, 2017; Olivetti & Petrongolo, 2016, for reviews).

Interestingly, one relevant behavioral gender difference identified as responsible for the gender wage gap is the variability in the inclination to negotiate or bargain about the wage during the recruitment process, with women displaying a lower propensity to negotiate than men (Card et al., 2016; Leibbrandt & List, 2015; Maitra et al., 2021). At first glance, these factors do not seem germane to our analysis of organizational transparency. However, as developed below, this is far from the case.

A significant proportion of the gender wage gap cannot be explained even after accounting for all known factors. This is what Goldin (2014) calls the "residual portion" of the gender wage gap, and researchers ascribe this portion to *gender discrimination* (Blau & Kahn, 2017; Maitra et al., 2021; Trotter et al., 2017), which itself can be a function of various factors such as implicit biases of employers, differential evaluation and promotion standards used by them, and the structure of pay (Blau & Kahn, 2017). Additionally, specific policies implemented by many organizations having to do with transparency, such as pay secrecy policies that prohibit employees from discussing wages or when and how information about wages is shared, may exacerbate the gender wage gap (Cullen & Perez-Truglia, 2022).

Third, the extant research seems to suggest that both systemic factors, such as the differential propensity to negotiate and the residual effect from gender discrimination, can be potentially affected by wage disclosure so as to bridge the gender wage gap (Obloj & Zenger, 2022; Ramachandran, 2011). For example, although women may be less inclined to negotiate than men, if information about wages for the job they are applying for is made available or if they know what peers in the same role are earning at the firm, they may feel empowered and be more willing to negotiate for a higher salary. Indeed, research shows that even with relatively simple cues, such as providing an explicit statement that wages are negotiable, gender differences in negotiation tend to disappear (Leibbrandt & List, 2015). This is one example where compared to secrecy, even a moderate amount of transparency benefits the worker.

Furthermore, the disclosure of wages may also attenuate discrimination by employers, whether its roots are explicit or implicit. Under implicit bias, the disclosure of wages may shift hiring and the determination of compensation to a more deliberate process of valuing a candidate's qualifications and experience such that the hiring manager may become more likely to consider the upshot of offering lower wages to women candidates and be instead nudged toward using a wage parity default criterion. For those discriminating explicitly, shining light on wages and wage differences by gender at a job level may serve as a concrete deterrent to discriminatory conduct and the potential penalties that may accrue from such behavior.

Pay Transparency

Given the significant adverse individual and societal repercussions of the pay gaps that arise from gender, race, age, and other worker characteristics, the regulatory environment, and the corporate culture have become more favorable toward supporting *pay transparency*, also known variously as wage or salary transparency. Pay transparency refers to specific actions taken by the organization to provide information about employee wages to job seekers and current employees; in practice, this openness is manifested in varying degrees of disclosure and provision of wage information. For example, an organization may make the wage measures available on a website or document to everyone publicly or only provide it to those who ask.

The degree of detail about wages varies significantly across organizations, with averages or median values at the aggregate or by groups being far more common than what individual employees or employee roles earn. Pay transparency also covers the degree of autonomy employees have to share information about their wages with their peers openly. Finally, in recent work, Wong and colleagues (2022) point out the helpful distinction between *process transparency*, i.e., the information given to employees about the procedures used to determine pay and monetary rewards such as bonuses, *outcome transparency*, i.e., information about actual wages, wage levels or ranges of individual employees or groups such as gender or work roles, and *communications transparency*, i.e., information about the company's policy regarding the ability of employees to share information about their wages with coworkers.

The Disparity of Pay Transparency Regulations

In the UK, organizations with more than 250 employees have had to publish gender-based wage statistics since July 2018. As of this writing, the EU is considering a proposal to implement pay transparency measures that give job seekers the right to know the pay levels of employees doing the same work and gender-based pay differences in the company and prohibit employers from asking job seekers about their pay history. In Germany, employees have the right to know the median salary earned by a group of comparable employees in organizations with 200 employees, whereas New York City requires virtually all employers to provide the expected salary range that they believe they would pay for each advertised job starting from spring 2022 (Bennedsen et al., 2019; Cutter, 2022).

Finally, in the US, Executive Order 13,665 prohibited employers with contracts valued at $10,000 or more with the US government from retaliating against employees for disclosure and discussion of compensation information (Trotter et al., 2017). As these examples illustrate, pay transparency regulations, even when they exist, vary considerably from one place to another, and new ones continue to be written and enacted at different governmental levels. Obviously, as organizations change their pay disclosure policies to comply with new regulations, their effects offer fertile ground for research in theory building for organizational transparency research.

Effects of Pay Transparency on the Gender Wage Gap

Even though the specific wage information disclosed may vary based on local regulations, the logic behind it is widely applicable. It is that disclosing wage information provides two significant benefits to workers. First, it makes the job application process, including the choice of whether or not to apply, more efficient for potential job seekers and evens the playing field during salary negotiations. Second, pay transparency allows current employees to compare their wages to salaries earned by their peers or salaries quoted in advertised job openings, making it harder for the organization to sustain various forms of wage gaps and systematically underpay certain employees or employee groups.

Supporting the optimistic view of organizational transparency that has dominated this chapter, there is some evidence from extant research suggesting that *pay transparency* reduces the gender wage gap. In a Danish study, for instance, Bennedsen and colleagues (2019) leveraged a 2006 legislation implementation in Denmark that required firms with more than 35 employees to report salary data by gender for employee groups and inform employees of the wage gap, to study the effects of mandatory pay transparency on the gender wage gap. They found that wages of male employees went down and those of female employees went up after the regulation went into effect, thus lowering the gender wage gap in the country by about 13%, with greater reductions reported in the wage gap for lower and middle-level wages. Women were also hired in greater numbers, about 5% more, presumably because fairer wages made the jobs more attractive. The wage gap reduction, however, did not affect the financial performance of organizations as the savings in wages resulting from wage balancing were counteracted by lower employee productivity. Similarly, in a study conducted in Canada, upon passing of laws that provided public access to individual faculty salaries beyond certain thresholds such as $50,000, the gender pay gap declined significantly from 6% initially to 1% by the end of the study period (Baker et al., 2021).

In contrast, studies conducted in Austria after a 2011 law requiring firms above a specific size to publish internal reports on the gender wage gap have found that "the policy had no discernible effects on male and female wages, thus leaving the gender wage gap unchanged" (Gulyas et al., 2021, p. 1; see also Böheim & Gust, 2021). An additional positive effect of disclosure is found in reputational effects and the results are nuanced. A recent study examined the changes in employees' evaluations of their employers on the review site Glassdoor and found that after gender pay rates were disclosed, those companies that reported parity derived a short-lived reputational boost through improvement in employee evaluations, but there was little adverse reaction for companies that reported substantial gender wage gaps (Sharkey et al., 2022). Clearly, this is an evolving area of research, but there is reason to be hopeful that the adoption of wage disclosure laws combined with the prevailing popularity of diversity, equity, and inclusion corporate programs will continue to lower the gender wage gap.

The Downsides of Pay Transparency

An alternate title for this section could well be "Ignorance is bliss" because research has found a surprising number of significant downsides for workers from pay transparency, including for those workers who may be expected to benefit from the additional information about wages. When wages are disclosed within an organization, the information can result in unfavorable social comparisons for employees when they see their supervisors' higher wages, generating jealousy, envy, and frustration. These emotional responses, in turn, affect behavior adversely. Several studies provide evidence of adverse effects.

Breza et al. (2018) conducted a month-long experiment by setting up factory workshops in India and varying whether workers received the same pay or different pay than their peers. Although researchers did not disclose wages directly in this study, the workers routinely talked about their pay with peers, resulting in culture-generated organizational transparency. The researchers found that sharing information about pay inequality in these circumstances led to lower productivity and attendance among workers and, unsurprisingly, reduced work group cohesion. The workers were unhappy *when they knew* they were being paid less than their peers for the same work.

In another field study, Card et al. (2012) chose a random subset of University of California employees and informed them of a new website that listed the individual wages of all University employees, then surveyed them a few days later. The authors found that those from this subset who were paid below the median in their department and occupation group reported lower pay satisfaction, job satisfaction, and greater intentions to search for a new job than other University employees who had not been told about the website. Interestingly, those who were paid more than the median did not show any differences. The authors argued that *extreme* pay transparency, defined as disclosure about the pay of individual workers, can lead to *inequality aversion*, whereby specific unfavorable comparisons reduce worker satisfaction, but favorable comparisons do not produce any benefit, in effect indicating that no one benefits from the disclosure of individual wages.

Cullen and Perez-Truglia (2018) conducted a field experiment with the employees of a large corporation. They found that a vast majority of employees perceived asking a coworker their salary to be unacceptable, indicated they would feel uncomfortable doing so, and reported an unwillingness to disclose their salary to coworkers. The authors called this widespread aversion of workers to talk about specific wages the "salary taboo." The salary taboo is an exemplar of the maxim that where organizational transparency (and indeed, other forms of business transparency) is concerned, the content of the information matters, as does the identity of the provider and the recipient, and the "more transparency is better" maxim rarely holds. Furthermore, recent research shows that outcome pay transparency leads to more counterproductive workplace behaviors, i.e., behaviors intended to cause harm to the organization (e.g., absenteeism) or coworkers (e.g., harassment), especially among workers who learn that they are being paid less than peers performing similar work and feel a sense of unfairness (SimonTov-Nachlieli & Bamberger, 2021).

Interestingly, research shows that the adverse psychological effects of transparency on those affected by the disclosure extend beyond wages to income more generally. Perez-Truglia (2020) studied Norwegian citizens between 1985 and 2013, a period that included a regulatory change that occurred in the country in 2001 when tax records became publicly available. Citizens could access the incomes of every Swedish citizen. Perez-Truglia found that the increased income transparency increased the happiness gap between rich and poor individuals by 29% and the gap in levels of life satisfaction by 21% and concluded that these changes were driven by self-perceptions of relative income of Norwegians, and its potential effects such as better versus worse treatment for richer and poorer individuals, respectively.

Furthermore, when organizations adopt pay transparency practices, the fallout can extend to managers with little control over setting wages. In a recent study, Wong and colleagues (2022) found that the immediate brunt of making pay transparent was borne by supervisors who now had to explain the reasons for the revealed pay differentials to their indignant reports, consuming their time and taxing their psychological resources. The authors also found that pay transparency led to wage compression as the wage differentials were reduced through adjustments by those setting pay and the greater adoption of personalized rewards through what the authors called "idiosyncratic deals," including non-financial benefits like additional training for career development during the pay negotiation process. It seems that as wages become more transparent, employee pay for the same role shrinks, but differences in opaque, non-monetary benefits expand. It is not clear that pay transparency reduces the total earnings gap. The authors concluded that "when it comes to pay transparency, such "sunlight," by compressing the observable forms of remuneration while extending more hidden forms, may result in pay transparency becoming a moving target" (p. 48).

Summary. Based on the extant research evidence, we can conclude that even though it might reduce disparities between employees and contribute to labor equity within an organization, the full disclosure of how much each worker earns to coworkers is undesirable and aversive to all parties involved, the recipients of this information and wage-earners alike. However, a moderate level of transparency, such as information about mean and median wages earned by workers performing the same task, further broken down by gender, age, and other relevant group descriptors, may have significant benefits to workers, particularly those likely to be affected adversely by discrimination.

All indications are that further providing context and interpretability to this information, such as levels of mean and median industry wages for the same role, could further add value to this moderate disclosure, although this remains to be studied. Equally important is linking workers' performance to their pay as objectively and cut and dried as possible. Indeed, it may even make sense to increase the transparency of performance rewards and the link between them when pay transparency is instituted within the organization.

References

Albu, O. B., & Flyverbom, M. (2019). Organizational transparency: Conceptualizations, conditions, and consequences. *Business & Society, 58*(2), 268–297.

Allen, T. D. (2006). Rewarding good citizens: The relationship between citizenship behavior, gender, and organizational rewards 1. *Journal of Applied Social Psychology, 36*(1), 120–143.

Alvesson, M., & Einola, K. (2019). Warning for excessive positivity: Authentic leadership and other traps in leadership studies. *Leadership Quarterly, 30*(4), 383–395.

Anteby, M., & Chan, C. K. (2018). A self-fulfilling cycle of coercive surveillance: Workers' invisibility practices and managerial justification. *Organization Science, 29*(2), 247–263.

Arkan, O., Nagpal, M., Scharding, T. K., & Warren, D. E. (2022). Don't just trust your gut: The importance of normative deliberation to ethical decision-making at work. *Journal of Business Ethics*, 1–21.

Barroso, A., & Brown, A. (2021, May 25). *Gender pay gap in the US held steady in 2020*. Pew Research Center. https://www.pewresearch.org/fact-tank/2021/05/25/gender-pay-gap-facts/

Beer, M. (2021, December). *To change your company's culture, don't start by trying to change the culture*. Harvard Business School Working Knowledge. https://hbswk.hbs.edu/item/to-change-your-companys-culture-dont-start-by-trying-to-change-the-culture

Bennedsen, M., Simintzi, E., Tsoutsoura, M., & Wolfenzon, D. (2019). *Do firms respond to gender pay gap transparency?* (Working paper 24345). National Bureau of Economic Research.

Bennis, W., Goleman, D., O'Toole, J., & Biederman, P. W. (2008). *Transparency: How leaders create a culture of Candor*. Jossey-Bass.

Bernstein, E. (2014). The transparency trap. *Harvard Business Review, 92*(10), 58–66.

Bernstein, E. S. (2012). The transparency paradox: A role for privacy in organizational learning and operational control. *Administrative Science Quarterly, 57*(2), 181–216.

Bernstein, E. S. (2017). Making transparency transparent: The evolution of observation in management theory. *Academy of Management Annals, 11*(1), 217–266.

Blau, F. D., & Kahn, L. M. (2017). The gender wage gap: Extent, trends, and explanations. *Journal of Economic Literature, 55*(3), 789–865.

Böheim, R., & Gust, S. (2021). *The Austrian pay transparency law and the gender wage gap* (CESifo Working Paper 8960).

Bovens, M. (1998). *The quest for responsibility: Accountability and citizenship in complex organizations*. Cambridge University Press.

Breza, E., Kaur, S., & Shamdasani, Y. (2018). The morale effects of pay inequality. *The Quarterly Journal of Economics, 133*(2), 611–663.

Brown, A. J., Vandekerckhove, W., & Dreyfus, S. (2014). *The relationship between transparency, whistleblowing, and public trust* (pp. 30–58). Edward Elgar.

Card, D., Cardoso, A. R., & Kline, P. (2016). Bargaining, sorting, and the gender wage gap: Quantifying the impact of firms on the relative pay of women. *The Quarterly Journal of Economics, 131*(2), 633–686.

Card, D., Mas, A., Moretti, E., & Saez, E. (2012). Inequality at work: The effect of peer salaries on job satisfaction. *American Economic Review, 102*(6), 2981–3003.

Coser, R. L. (1961). Insulation from observability and types of social conformity. *American Sociological Review, 26*(1), 28–39.

Cullen, Z., & Perez-Truglia, R. (2022). How much does your boss make? The effects of salary comparisons. *Journal of Political Economy, 130*(3), 766–822.

Cullen, Z. B., & Perez-Truglia, R. (2018). *The salary taboo: Privacy norms and the diffusion of information* (Working paper 25145). National Bureau of Economic Research.
Cutter, C. (2022, January 28). You'll soon get to see pay on NYC job postings. *Wall Street Journal*. https://www.wsj.com/articles/goldman-google-and-just-about-every-nyc-employer-will-soon-have-to-disclose-pay-secrets-11643365982
Denison, D. R., & Mishra, A. K. (1995). Toward a theory of organizational culture and effectiveness. *Organization Science, 6*(2), 204–223.
Detert, J. R., & Burris, E. R. (2007). Leadership behavior and employee voice: Is the door really open? *Academy of Management Journal, 50*(4), 869–884.
Detert, J. R., & Burris, E. R. (2016). Can your employees really speak freely. *Harvard Business Review, 94*(1), 80–87.
Flint, J. (2021, October 13). Netflix employee group calls for walkout amid tensions over Dave Chappelle show. *Wall Street Journal*. https://www.wsj.com/articles/netflix-employee-group-calls-for-walkout-amid-tensions-over-dave-chappelle-show-11634169211
Flyverbom, M. (2016). Transparency: Mediation and the management of visibilities. *International Journal of Communication, 10*, 110–122.
Frey, E., Bernstein, E., & Rekenthaler, N. (2022). Scarlet letters: Rehabilitation through transgression transparency and personal narrative control. *Administrative Science Quarterly, 67*(4), 968–1011.
Gardner, W. L., Avolio, B. J., Luthans, F., May, D. R., & Walumbwa, F. (2005). "Can you see the real me?" A self-based model of authentic leader and follower development. *Leadership Quarterly, 16*(3), 343–372.
Gilliom, J., & Monahan, T. (2013). *SuperVision: An introduction to the surveillance society*. University of Chicago Press.
Goldin, C. (2014). A grand gender convergence: Its last chapter. *American Economic Review, 104*(4), 1091–1119.
Graham, J. W. (1983). *Principled organizational dissent* (Unpublished dissertation). Northwestern University.
Gulyas, A., Seitz, S., & Sinha, S. (2021). *Does pay transparency affect the gender wage gap? Evidence from Austria* (Discussion Paper 21–076). Center for European Economic Research. https://papers.ssrn.com/sol3/papers.cfm?abstract_id=3949832
Kaptein, M. (2008). Developing and testing a measure for the ethical culture of organizations: The corporate ethical virtues model. *Journal of Organizational Behavior, 29*(7), 923–947.
Karlsson, P., Turner, M., & Gassmann, P. (2019). Succeeding the long-serving legend in the corner office. *Strategy & Business, 95*. https://www.strategy-business.com/article/Succeeding-the-long-serving-legend-in-the-corner-office

Koblin, J., & Sperling, N. (2021, October 20). Netflix employees walk out to protest Dave Chappelle's special. *New York Times.* https://www.nytimes.com/live/2021/10/20/business/news-business-stock-market#netflix-protest-dave-chappelle

Landier, A., Sraer, D., & Thesmar, D. (2009). Optimal dissent in organizations. *Review of Economic Studies, 76*(2), 761–794.

Leibbrandt, A., & List, J. A. (2015). Do women avoid salary negotiations? Evidence from a large-scale natural field experiment. *Management Science, 61*(9), 2016–2024.

Maitra, P., Neelim, A., & Tran, C. (2021). The role of risk and negotiation in explaining the gender wage gap. *Journal of Economic Behavior & Organization, 191,* 1–27. https://doi.org/10.1016/j.jebo.2021.08.021

Meijer, A. (2014). Transparency. *The Oxford handbook of public accountability* (pp. 507–524). Oxford University Press

Mollick, E. R., & Rothbard, N. (2014). *Mandatory fun: Consent, gamification and the impact of games at work* (Wharton School Research Paper Series).

Morrison, E. W. (2011). Employee voice behavior: Integration and directions for future research. *Academy of Management Annals, 5*(1), 373–412.

Morrison, E. W., & Milliken, F. J. (2000). Organizational silence: A barrier to change and development in a pluralistic world. *Academy of Management Review, 25*(4), 706–725.

Obloj, T., & Zenger, T. (2022). The influence of pay transparency on (gender) inequity, inequality and the performance basis of pay. *Nature Human Behaviour, 6*(5), 646–655.

O'Reilly, C. A., III., Chatman, J. A., & Doerr, B. (2021). When "me" trumps "we": Narcissistic leaders and the cultures they create. *Academy of Management Discoveries, 7*(3), 419–450.

Olivetti, C., & Petrongolo, B. (2016). The evolution of gender gaps in industrialized countries. *Annual Review of Economics, 8,* 405–434.

Perez-Truglia, R. (2020). The effects of income transparency on well-being: Evidence from a natural experiment. *American Economic Review, 110*(4), 1019–1054.

Ramachandran, G. (2011). Pay transparency. *Penn State Law Review, 116*(4), 1043–1080.

Schnackenberg, A. K., & Tomlinson, E. C. (2016). Organizational transparency: A new perspective on managing trust in organization-stakeholder relationships. *Journal of Management, 42*(7), 1784–1810.

Sharkey, A., Pontikes, E., & Hsu, G. (2022). The impact of mandated pay gap transparency on firms' reputations as employers. *Administrative Science Quarterly, 67*(4), 1136–1179.

SimanTov-Nachlieli, I., & Bamberger, P. (2021). Pay communication, justice, and affect: The asymmetric effects of process and outcome pay transparency on counterproductive workplace behavior. *Journal of Applied Psychology*, *106*(2), 230.

Smith, K. J., & Harris, L. M. (2014). Drafting an effective employee handbook. *Employment Relations Today*, *41*(1), 71–79.

Testa, J., Friedman, V., & Paton, E. (2020, July 26). Everlane's promise of 'radical transparency' unravels. *New York Times*. Available online at: https://www.nytimes.com/2020/07/26/fashion/everlane-employees-ethical-clothing.html

Thiel, C. E., Bonner, J., Bush, J. T., Welsh, D. T., & Garud, N. (2022). Stripped of agency: The paradoxical effect of employee monitoring on deviance. *Journal of Management*, in press.

Trotter, R. G., Zacur, S. R., & Stickney, L. T. (2017). The new age of pay transparency. *Business Horizons*, *60*(4), 529–539.

Turco, C. J. (2016). *The conversational firm: Rethinking bureaucracy in the age of social media*. Columbia University Press.

Van Scotter, J. R., & Roglio, K. D. D. (2020). CEO bright and dark personality: Effects on ethical misconduct. *Journal of Business Ethics*, *164*(3), 451–475.

Warner, A. S., & Lehmann, L. S. (2019). Gender wage disparities in medicine: time to close the gap. *Journal of General Internal Medicine*, *34*, 1334–1336.

Wayne, S. J., Shore, L. M., Bommer, W. H., & Tetrick, L. E. (2002). The role of fair treatment and rewards in perceptions of organizational support and leader-member exchange. *Journal of Applied Psychology*, *87*(3), 590.

Whelan, R., & Sayre, K. (2022, March 22). Disney workers walk out to protest company's response to Florida bill. *Wall Street Journal*. https://www.wsj.com/articles/disney-workers-walk-out-to-protest-companys-response-to-florida-bill-11647991140

Wong, M. N., Cheng, B. H., Lam, L. W. Y., & Bamberger, P. A. (2022). Pay transparency as a moving target: A multi-step model of pay compression, I-deals, and collectivist shared values. *Academy of Management Journal*. https://doi.org/10.5465/amj.2020.1831

CHAPTER 5

Transparent Business Leadership

Abstract This chapter reviews key concepts and findings from the vast authentic leadership and relational transparency literatures that privilege honesty, self-awareness, truthfulness in communication practices, humility, relational alignment, and concordant behaviors as traits and practices contributing to transparent leadership and leading to significant positive downstream consequences. Critiques of these literatures are also examined in this chapter, which argue that mainstream treatments of transparent leaders tend to be overly simplistic, one-dimensional, static, decontextualized, unrealistic and positively biased, detracting from academic rigor, and direct practical application.

Keywords Transparency · Authentic leadership · Relational transparency · Self-awareness · Humility

> I think the currency of leadership is transparency. You've got to be truthful. I don't think you should be vulnerable every day, but there are moments where you've got to share your soul and conscience with people and show them who you are, and not be afraid of it.—Howard Schultz

What are the attributes of an ideal leader? This question has occupied humans for millennia and business scholars in the present academic epoch for at least a century (e.g., Barnard, 1938; Cha et al., 2019; Prastacos et al., 2013). Despite the collective efforts of great minds over all this time, an unequivocal answer to this question remains to be found. What research suggests is that many leadership styles, even seemingly contradictory ones, can be effective; leadership efficacy depends a lot on the organizational setting, the environmental context, and to a lesser extent, the leader's qualities. Depending on how and when effectiveness is assessed, Elon Musk, Carlos Ghosn, or Ratan Tata could each rise to the top of a "Most Effective Business Leaders" list despite the dramatic differences in their leadership styles and dispositions.

Nevertheless, one characteristic of successful leaders, very much relevant to our investigation of business transparency, that rises prominently to the surface in many of these studies is *authenticity*. As George (2016) puts it, "being authentic is the most effective and sustainable way to lead" (p. 30), and Ibarra (2015) says that "authenticity has become the gold standard for leadership" (p. 54). An authentic business leader is imbued with many of the virtues that are also prized in other domains of human endeavor, such as honesty, sincerity, self-awareness, optimism, humility, patience, empathy, morality, resilience, collegiality, and compassion. What's more, in many significant respects, an authentic business leader is attuned to transparency, not just on their account but also in fostering attitudes and practices that advance transparency within the organization and in nurturing the development of transparent employees.

In an era where concerns about diversity, equity, and inclusion have taken center stage in many organizations, and the results of conventional methods to achieve DEI objectives such as mandatory diversity training, hiring tests, and performance ratings, are often found wanting (Dobbin & Kalev, 2022), authentic business leadership offers a compelling alternative means to revitalize stagnant or underperforming DEI initiatives (e.g., Anderson et al., 2017; Houser et al., 2014; Rahim-Dillard, 2021). For example, recent research shows that when a CEO demonstrates sociopolitical activism, defined as a public and costly expression of personal political values, job seekers, especially those holding congruent attitudes, are attracted to the organization (Appels, 2022). Transparent leadership is perhaps more valued today than at any other time.

A vast literature on authentic business leadership has sprung up in the scholarly and popular writing domains over the past fifty years or so, and different aspects of transparency feature prominently in it. In this chapter, we will review some key concepts and findings from the influential work in this area and consider the implications of transparency for management and leadership. We will conclude this chapter by examining critiques of authentic leadership research, considering what these challenges mean for transparent leadership.

In academic studies of authentic leadership, transparency is conceptualized as a positive managerial trait that can be inculcated to a certain extent by the business leader, but which also arises from the person's experiences and life circumstances to some degree and is a vital contributor to a host of positive individual, interpersonal, and organizational outcomes. Combined with a penetrating self-awareness, transparency in values, attitudes, and behaviors forms a significant aspect of the authentic leader's persona. There is a large and still growing body of research, especially spanning the last two decades, that has found that authentic business leaders put themselves and their egos in the background, seek to align their internal sense of self with external expressions, deliberately encourage diverse viewpoints, and support the mentorship of employees, along with the formation of communities and organizational structures that allow for the nurturance and expression of diverse perspectives (Cha et al., 2019; George, 2015). Employees at every level, and thus the organization as a whole, benefit substantially from the authentic leader's demeanor, orientation, and decisions. As one exemplar capturing the general tenor of this thesis, one experimental study reported that leader transparency, which the authors defined as the ready ability of group members to observe the leader's actions, led to significantly more cooperation among group members, higher group earnings, and reduced variation in contribution from group members (Houser et al., 2014). Authentic leadership is positively associated with employee well-being, their ability to have a voice, work engagement, empowerment, organizational citizenship behaviors, and employee performance. It is negatively associated with intentions to leave and burnout (Avolio & Walumba, 2014; Lemoine et al., 2019).

THE PRESENT SIGNIFICANCE OF AUTHENTIC LEADERSHIP

In addition to the challenges with DEI initiatives and the aforementioned beneficial effects on employees, another evolving set of phenomena has posed severe challenges to organizations across industries and fueled the value of authentic leadership. They include the frequent instances of workplace misconduct taking various forms, including scandalous, callous, immoral, and even illegal behaviors by executives and business leaders and the resultant loss of public trust in business leaders, the unceasing high levels of scrutiny afforded by digital technologies to a broader set of interested constituents such as investors, customers, journalists, and others, a widespread social culture of skepticism and negativity, and the steady decline in the effectiveness of hierarchical management structures (Avolio et al., 2004; Cillizza, 2015; George, 2016; Karlsson et al., 2019; Larcker & Tayan, 2016; Perna, 2020; Scott & Davis, 2015; Vogelgesang, 2008). Authentic leadership is offered up as a solution to ameliorate all these and other growing challenges for organizations.

What Is Authentic Leadership?

Management scholars and practitioners have used phrases such as "raw honesty" (Thacker, 2016), "an internal alignment between beliefs and actions" (Keleman et al., 2022), "following their True North" (George, 2016), "the unvarnished truth," "reflecting sincere choices" (Iszatt-White & Kemper, 2019), "moral self-concordance" (Lemoine et al., 2019), and "straight talk" (O'Toole & Bennis, 2009) to characterize authentic leadership. The large body of research on authenticity as a psychological construct identifies four broad components: (1) self-awareness, characterized by an understanding of and trust in one's values, motivations, thoughts, and feelings, (2) an objective or unbiased recognition and understanding of one's attributes, (3) acting consistently with one's values and attitudes, and (4) supporting honesty and openness in one's relationships (Gardner et al., 2011; Kernis & Goldman, 2006). With these background ideas, the perspectives of a number of prominent business leadership scholars on what it means to be an authentic leader are now briefly explored.

A useful scholarly definition of authentic leadership was provided by Luthans and Avolio (2003) as "a process that draws from both positive psychological capacities and a highly developed organizational context, which results in both greater self-awareness and self-regulated positive behaviors on the part of leaders and associates, fostering positive self-development" (p. 243). In another paper, Avolio and colleagues (2004) defined authentic leaders as those who "act in accordance with deep personal values and convictions, to build credibility and win the respect and trust of followers by encouraging diverse viewpoints and building networks of collaborative relationships with followers, and thereby lead in a manner that followers recognize as authentic" (p. 806). In a well-cited paper, Gardner and colleagues (2005) observed that for managers, authenticity "involves both owning one's personal experiences (values, thoughts, emotions and beliefs) and acting in accordance with one's true self (expressing what you really think and believe and behaving accordingly)" (p. 344), and business leaders achieve authenticity "through self-awareness, self-acceptance, and authentic actions and relationships" (p. 345).

Walumbwa and colleagues (2008) built on these definitions and provided the following expanded, widely used definition of authentic leadership "as a pattern of leader behavior that draws upon and promotes both positive psychological capacities and a positive ethical climate, to foster greater self-awareness, an internalized moral perspective, balanced processing of information, and relational transparency on the part of leaders working with followers, fostering positive self-development" (p. 94). Leroy and colleagues (2015) provided the following definition: Authentic leadership in the workplace occurs when leaders enact their true selves and is manifest in behaviors such as being honest with oneself (e.g., admitting personal mistakes), being sincere with others (e.g., telling others the hard truth), and behaving in a way that reflects one's personal values" (p. 1678). Finally, George (2016) posited that "Authentic leaders align people around shared purpose and values, and empower them to lead authentically to create value for all stakeholders" (p. 32).

As will be evident to the reader, several common themes emerge from these different authors' perspectives regarding the attributes entailed in authentic leadership. They include self-awareness, honesty, an emphasis on moral decisions and stances, the development of followers and building productive relationships with them, and consistency in values, attitudes, and behaviors consistency. These definitions also distinguish between the leader's *personal transparency*, i.e., the degree of clarity about one's own internal states, some of which is captured by self-awareness, and *interactional transparency*, i.e., expressing consistency and clarity in interactions with others. Together, these forms come under *relational transparency*.

Authentic Leadership in Practice

Next, let's consider the prescriptions from two influential practitioner perspectives regarding how to cultivate authentic leadership, comparing and assessing their suggestions. First, O'Toole and Bennis (2009) provided eight prescriptive guidelines to business leaders and managers to cultivate authentic leadership, many of which, not surprisingly, involve engaging in more transparent behaviors. They include: (1) consistently telling the truth, which eventually results in a reputation for honesty, (2) encouraging workers to be truthful to their colleagues and managers, (3) listening to and rewarding contrarian perspectives that go against the accepted perspectives, (4) practicing to have unpleasant conversations that involve delivering bad news, (5) diversifying sources of information used for decision making, for example, by talking to employees, customers, and competitors with different and contradictory views, (6) admitting one's mistakes candidly, (7) building organizational support for transparency through specific programs such as protecting whistle-blowers and hiring employees with a track record of candor, and (8) reducing constraints on information to the extent feasible by making it widely available within the organization. When adopted and practiced over time consistently, these attributes contribute to fostering a climate of organizational cultural transparency, covered in detail in Chapter 4 (Bennis et al., 2008; O'Toole & Bennis, 2009).

Second, George (2015, 2016) provided a shorter list of four personal projects to become an authentic leader: (1) cultivating self-awareness, explained as understanding one's life story, process and accepting one's crucibles, and then cultivating habits involving reflection and honest feedback; (2) understanding one's values through introspection, extending it to develop one's business philosophy, and then undertake to adhere to them in all business situations; (3) integrating one's life, defined as seeking a mindful balance between work and personal aspects of one's life; and (4) seeking fulfillment by separating the purpose of leadership from the trappings of leadership that may accrue such as financial rewards, fame, and power. Relational transparency is material in both these practitioner guidelines.

As pointed out earlier and evident in these lists, authentic leadership can significantly positively contribute to an organization's DEI initiatives. The activities of authentic leaders are centered around serving others, particularly their subordinates, by empowering them to make a difference (George, 2003). They recognize and appreciate individual differences paying particular attention to their subordinates' talents and proclivities, are open to diverse perspectives, and deliberately help them to hone these into differential strengths. They eschew coercive persuasion, instead emphasizing the shared values and attitudes to encourage activities in service of the organization's goals. Significantly, Hughes (2005) points out that authentic leadership is a root construct of leadership that can support different, seemingly incompatible leadership styles, such as the transformational, transactional, directive, or participative leadership styles. (But note that critics have raised this same point as evidence of conceptual confusion and redundancy of the authentic leadership construct in the scholarly literature.)

Interestingly, while the extensive academic literature provides a great deal of clarity about the precursors and benefits of authenticity in leadership, much less is known about the extent to which managers practice authentic leadership. There are reasons to believe that authentic leadership is far less common than claims from business leaders or the low-cost behavioral signaling that business leaders engage in routinely. For instance, Thacker (2016) points out that while concepts such as authentic leadership and relational transparency are widely acknowledged as having benefits, "the leadership practice of transparency, which creates honest, substantive conversations, is far from routine in most work environments" (p. 104). Relatedly, Eurich (2018) reports that while most people believe they are self-aware, a core facet of relational transparency, only 10–15% of respondents possess the required competencies to practice self-awareness. Finally, Alvesson and Einola (2019) offer a broad-based critique of authentic leadership research and argue that the "static, entity-oriented, fixed, and de-contextualized conceptualizations and empirical studies" (p. 387) paint a distorted picture of what effective leadership looks like in practice. Critiques of authentic leadership research are considered in greater detail later in this chapter.

Authentic leadership and transparency. Walumbwa and colleagues' (2008) ideas cited earlier, along with Gardner and colleagues' (2005) influential operationalization of authentic leadership as comprised of the self-awareness of one's values, identity, emotion, and motives, balanced processing, relational transparency, and authentic behavior establishes explicit bridges to transparency. Transparency, as concerned with understanding one's own identity as a leader and in fully conveying this identity and the associated values, attitudes, and actions to subordinates and others, known in the literature as *relational transparency*, is a core characteristic of authentic leadership (Walumbwa et al., 2008). It can be conceptualized as a trait and a cultivated set of work values and processes that any individual can adopt to bring about positive outcomes for themselves and their organization (Hughes, 2005; Thacker, 2016).

Baldoni (2008) points out two ramifications of relational transparency. First, its presence motivates employees, and its absence disrupts them by diminishing employee morale and ultimately reducing their productivity. Second, a key practical aspect of relational transparency is its ability to match the opportunities available within the organization to the aspirations and abilities of individual employees. To Avolio and colleagues (2004), these benefits only accrue when the business leader has a deep awareness of their own and their employees' values and moral perspectives, knowledge and strengths, and aspirations and motivators, along with the context within which their decisions and behaviors are enacted.

Furthermore, a significant body of research has theorized that authentic leaders possess and cultivate a range of attributes and orientations that are often derived from their personal history and key triggering events in their lives. In the words of Friedman (2008), "Effective leaders use their imaginations to connect the actual stories of their pasts with the hoped-for stories of their futures." Furthermore, these leaders support informed disagreement and challenges to the status quo from their peers and followers, consistently exhibit a high level of candor, act in accordance with their beliefs and values, encourage the flow of helpful information between different groups within their organizations and outside it to various other stakeholders, and deliberately set about to create a culture of candor and accountability that we considered at length in Chapter 4. The research on relational transparency is considered in greater detail next.

Relational Transparency

Given its foundational role in supporting and perhaps even constituting authentic leadership, *relational transparency* has received considerable attention in the organizational psychology and leadership literature (Gardner et al., 2005; Hughes, 2005; Walumbwa et al., 2008). In a nutshell, relational transparency is about being transparent in relations with others; in the business leadership context, it involves honesty and empathy about work issues in interactions with employees, customers, board members, and others.

There are a number of definitions in the literature which help to explore and understand this construct. Walumbwa and colleagues (2008) conceive of relational transparency as presenting one's authentic self (instead of a curated self) to others through judicious disclosures that involve openly sharing personal information and expressing one's true thoughts and feelings while at the same time minimizing displays of inappropriate emotions. Although their discussion focuses on business leaders, it is generally relevant to everyone. The authors measured relational transparency using items such as "I admit my mistakes to others," "I rarely present a "false" front to others," "I let others know who I truly am as a person," and "I openly share my feelings with others."

According to Kernis (2003), relational transparency "is relational in nature, inasmuch as it involves valuing and achieving openness and truthfulness in one's close relationships" (p. 15). Rego et al. (2021) define the concept as "showing one's true self to others, expressing true thoughts and emotions, and openly sharing information," while Hughes (2005) defines it as occurring "when one discloses along the person-relevant dimension of self-disclosure" (p. 35). Vogelgesang (2008) introduced and developed the related but distinctly named construct of *interactional transparency* as a form of candor developed and maintained through sustained interactions between leaders and followers and defines it as "interactions characterized by sharing relevant information, being open to giving and receiving feedback, being forthcoming regarding motives and the reasoning behind decisions, and displaying alignment between words and actions" (p. 43). The time factor comes into play more explicitly in this characterization, making the construct somewhat dynamic and dependent on a series of back-and-forths.

On the flip side, Gardner and colleagues (2021) caution that "the multi-faceted nature of the self and its social construction in the face of situational contingencies makes it tricky for leaders who strive for authenticity to gauge the appropriate level of transparency" (p. 4), and Alvesson and Einola (2019) point out that the leader's self that is to be transparently expressed in social interactions with subordinates is not one-dimensional, but is instead composed of multiple selves that are constructed adaptively in response to situational needs. Thus, rather than the overtly simplistic and positive perspective of relational transparency as uninhibited blanket disclosure, a more subtle conceptualization that acknowledges its dynamic, inconsistent, and situationally bound aspects is likely to be more fruitful. Stated figuratively, relational transparency operates like the light from a flickering star, sensitive to atmospheric densities, temperatures, and disturbances.

Thacker (2016) provides an extended example of Ford Motor's CEO Alan Mullaly, who famously said, "You can't manage a secret," and engaged in numerous practices representative of a relationally transparent leader, such as encouraging senior executives who reported to him to admit to the difficult challenges they were facing and then collaborate in good faith to solve the most complex problems. Research has shown that the leader's relational transparency not only contributes to authentic followership marked by the adoption of corresponding properties by followers as they model the leader, but it also has a significant impact on a range of downstream outcomes of followers such as trust, engagement, workplace well-being, positive emotions, creative performance, and sustainable job performance (Gardner et al., 2005; Hughes, 2005).

The authentic leadership literature suggests that self-awareness, truthful communication practices, and humility are core leadership qualities that constitute relational transparency. In addition, practical actions by the leader, such as rewarding the honesty and candor of subordinates even when they go against their self-interests, taking active steps to reduce the constraints on information sharing within their organization, and deliberately setting about to build an organizational culture of transparency, also matter. We will examine the components of relational transparency in detail, aside from aspects of organizational cultural transparency, which is covered in Chapter 4.

Self-Awareness

Perhaps the most intimate form of relational transparency is its personal form, by which the manager gains an understanding of oneself through self-reflection, with the explicit mechanisms of introspection, monitoring, and assessment. Psychologists classically define *self-awareness* as an attentional state, referring to those times when an individual focuses on events internal to their consciousness, personal history, or body (Duval & Wicklund, 1972). More recently, organizational psychologists have distinguished between *internal self-awareness*, which represents the individual's clarity about their values, passions, aspirations, fit with their environment, reactions (thoughts, feelings, behaviors, strengths, and weaknesses), and impact on others, and *external self-awareness*, which involves a penetrative understanding regarding how others view oneself along the same dimensions (Eurich, 2018).

While self- and other-directed understanding will no doubt be tremendously helpful in every life domain, its heft in managerial decision making and its role as an integral component of relational transparency is considered here. Management scholars have variously defined self-awareness in terms of having a deep understanding of one's emotions, competencies, behaviors, and skills, core beliefs and values, one's commitment to certain projects or organizational identities, and conversely one's aversion to other alternatives, along with an appraisal of oneself along one or more of these dimensions in comparison with specific others (e.g., peers within one's organization), or with generalized identities such as a company CEO, an emergency room nurse, and so on (see Caldwell & Hayes, 2016, for a review). Self-awareness includes both the formational processes and the actual state of the manager's granular understanding of who one is, what one believes, and where one stands with respect to issues, ideas, and other people; in psychological terms, it can be seen as a perception that one knows these things about oneself, i.e., it is the degree of belief that one is self-aware. Even more succinctly, self-awareness is simply self-transparency.

Hughes (2005) linked the disparate forms of self-awareness knowledge directly to relational transparency and its downstream consequences by construing it as self-disclosure and suggesting that self-disclosure consists of four specific aspects of self-awareness: goals and motives, identity, values, and emotions. The author further argued that self-knowledge in these four domains is an essential precursor for a manager to be able to engage in transparent workplace behaviors. Other researchers have pointed out that self-awareness is also necessary to regulate one's behaviors, align them with one's beliefs, values, and behavioral tendencies (Gardner et al., 2005), and demonstrate empathy toward others (Trentini et al., 2022).

In an influential article, Brown and Starkey (2000) pointed out that organizations, as defined by the collective psychological processes of their members, are prone to ego defenses such as denial, rationalization, idealization, fantasy, and symbolization, among others, that maintain the collective self-esteem of their members and support the continuity of their existing identities as a whole. Each of these ego defenses not only has potentially negative consequences on performance (for instance, denial can distort managers' decision making leading them to deploy their resources on the wrong strategies and ignore the more promising opportunities), but they hinder transparency and its benefits. Brown and Starkey (2000) suggested that engaging in critical self-reflection to understand and critique the bases of the organization's (and its members') identities is an effective way to break through the dysfunctional ego defenses and engage the virtues of organizational learning. Caldwell and Hayes (2016) went even a step further by positing that managers who engage in formal practices of self-awareness to assess the intersection of their abilities, their calling, positive marketplace responses, and the dictates of their conscience create greater value for their organization and are trusted to a greater degree when compared to managers who don't engage in these self-awareness activities. The bottom line is that the manager's self-awareness—its components and consequences—is integral to understanding relational transparency.

Truthful Communication Practices

As essential aspects of authenticity, honesty, and truthfulness are, not surprisingly, the core aspects of relational transparency. In seeking to build strong relations with subordinates and to foster trust, authentic leaders will help them to see both their positive and negative qualities while encouraging them to do the same (Gardner et al., 2021). The truthful communication practices extend to fact-finding and obtaining relevant information for decision making (e.g., marketing research about target customers to make decisions about the company's targeting and positioning strategy) and explaining the rationale behind decisions to employees in a meaningful way. As an example of the beneficial effects of such truthful disclosure from business leaders, Wilken and colleagues (2010) found that when salespeople with the authority to establish prices in negotiation with customers were provided information about costs by their managers, they were likely to negotiate more effectively, give fewer price concessions and earn higher final prices and profits for their employers.

Another aspect of truthful communication practices is what some practitioners have called *emotional transparency*, which has to do with sharing one's emotions in a concrete and complete way with followers. Thacker (2016) provided two examples of emotional transparency, one of Apple CEO Tim Cook's frank and inspiring assertions regarding his sexual orientation and Meta COO Sheryl Sandberg's candid and widely shared narrative of dealing with grief and fulfilling her responsibilities and obligations after her husband's unexpected demise from a heart attack.

In a broader sense beyond just the leader's directives and behaviors, this aspect is also given considerable weight in communications research as a part of the organization's "communication climate" and is considered to be a significant precursor to employee engagement. Transparent organizational communication is defined as "an organization's deliberate information dissemination coupled with employees' active participation in information acquisition and information distribution, in a manner that is truthful, substantial, and complete, to hold organizations accountable for their business practices and policies" (Jiang & Men, 2017, p. 4). With this perspective, it is the joint participation and active, volitional involvement of leaders and employees in communication practices that involve identifying, gathering, making sense of, and disseminating the information truthfully and without bias that drives positive outcomes (Cotterrell, 1999).

Humility

"More humility and less hubris" (Weick, 2001, p. 106) has been a popular leadership mantra for the past two decades. When a manager says, "I don't know," for example, it not only serves as a direct enactment of relational transparency, but it communicates a receptivity to subordinates that starts up a virtuous cycle of engagement, trust, and learning (Owens et al., 2011). Humility is a catalyst, contributing to relational transparency's downstream effects and amplifying its other components. At its core, humility refers to three interrelated characteristics of a business leader: (1) the capacity or willingness to evaluate oneself without exaggerating positive or negative attributes because of which they can produce a more accurate, non-defensive, and objective self-view for themselves, (2) the ability to view and assess the contributions and abilities of others, particularly peers and subordinates, in a positive way without feeling threatened by them, and (3) a receptivity to consider new ideas, points of view, feedback, and advice even when they run counter to one's established views, and again, especially from subordinates (Kelemen et al., 2022; Owens et al., 2011). In the context of relational transparency, humility can be seen as an evaluative extension of self-awareness (Ou et al., 2014), the principle of open understanding turned inward toward oneself. Where the self-awareness of one's beliefs and values reflects an understanding of what is important to oneself, humility reflects an evaluative assessment that explicitly acknowledges one's strengths and weaknesses based on that understanding.

There is a significant business literature on humility; however, focusing narrowly on the context of relational transparency, studies show that humility plays two key roles. First, it contributes to downstream consequences of relational transparency, and second, it amplifies the efficacy of its other components. Related to impacting downstream consequences, several studies find that the manager's humility positively affects their subordinates. As one example, Ou and coauthors (2014) found that CEO humility was positively associated with empowering leadership behaviors that make work more meaningful for employees, encourage their participation in making decisions, express confidence in their abilities, and provide autonomy, which in turn supported perceptions of empowerment among their organizations' top and middle managers. Others have found that the CEO's humility, as manifested by their willingness to seek feedback, contributes to other top management team members' humility (Ashford et al., 2018) and the performance of followers by increasing their relational energy and decreasing their emotional exhaustion (Wang et al., 2018). Furthermore, the influence of humility on performance is thought to occur through three distinct mechanisms: A greater and more accurate awareness about the time and effort that one would need to allocate to accomplish the task, greater attention given and benefits derived from observing others, in particular learning from strong performers, and greater receptivity to feedback, in turn, leading to faster and more efficient adjustments after a poor or mediocre performance (Owens et al., 2011).

Second, humility amplifies the effects of other components of relational transparency. As one example of its functioning, Rego et al. (2021) recently studied a sample of 114 leaders and 516 team members and found that humility moderated the effects of the manager's relational transparency on their respect for team members and their receptiveness to team members' relational transparency. Specifically, the authors distinguished between expressing a genuine self and being receptive to the expression of others' genuine selves and argued that because of the power asymmetry inherent in hierarchical work relationships, a relationally transparent manager would be more receptive to the relational transparency of subordinates only when they are themselves humble and respectful.

In the authors' words, "A relationally transparent leader, if he/she does not show humility, may be dogmatic, inflexible, uncompromising, and unable to acknowledge the imperfections and the positive qualities of either him/herself or of team members, thus refraining from entering into a relational dialog with team members and being unwilling to open up to their relational input." These studies conclude that it is not sufficient for a leader to be transparent as defined by other characteristics; humility is essential for relational transparency to produce its positive benefits.

However, one note of caution should be mentioned here. As the manager's career progresses and they take on new, more demanding, and more significant roles within their organization, they will naturally adapt and evolve, trying on new leadership styles and behaviors, and growing into new identities. This also requires that their humility be recalibrated to allow moving outside their comfort zone, taking on new tasks and learning skillful leadership techniques. Anchoring too rigidly to one's self-identity, and by implication, to prior anchors of what humility means personally may be counterproductive. Calling this an adaptive form of authenticity, Ibarra (2015) observes, "when we're looking to change our game, a too rigid self-concept becomes an anchor that keeps us from sailing forth" (p. 56). Essentially, as they progress and evolve in their careers, effective leaders need to remain humble but in different, more confident, and more motivationally relevant ways to practice relational transparency.

CRITIQUES OF AUTHENTIC LEADERSHIP AND RELATIONAL TRANSPARENCY

As we move toward the end of this chapter, one point of note is our hitherto-biased perspective. In particular, our coverage of authentic leadership and relational transparency research has been largely positive, focusing on the strengths and benefits of these concepts for the leaders themselves, their direct reports and employees, and their organization as a whole. However, we would be amiss if we ignored the negative aspects discussed in the literature. In particular, there are vociferous critiques concerning these concepts and the body of research on authentic leadership as a whole that need to be covered to come away with a balanced understanding.

Starting with popularity, perhaps because the ideas behind what it means to be authentic leaders and how they might impact their organizations are so intuitive and commonsensical, they resonate strongly with practitioners and laypeople. Accordingly, consultants and consulting firms (e.g., Feser et al., 2015), successful business leaders such as ex-CEOs (Bill George, the ex-CEO of Medtronic is one famous example; George, 2015), and numerous academic researchers cited throughout this chapter thus far have developed and advanced their respective views on authentic leadership.

The concern is that these perspectives often strike out on their own, trying to reinvent the wheel each time. They ignore or insufficiently credit extant work and do not adequately accommodate the existing ideas and findings, thus failing to develop a coherent, integrated, and ripening knowledge base. Even more perniciously, some competing views on authentic leadership flatly contradict each other, leading to confusion for those wanting to build on the literature or apply the findings to practice. As Gardner and colleagues (2011) observe, "the emergence of multiple practitioner and scholarly conceptions of AL has created ambiguity about what does and does not constitute AL, as well as the efficacy of strategies for its development" (p. 1120).

Compounding the problem, many of these writers rely on carefully chosen anecdotes and case studies of successful business leaders to advance their respective perspectives, falling prey to selection bias; rigorous empirical research that studies the nuanced consequences of authentic leadership within organizations in a balanced way using open science practices is scarce. Accordingly, our current understanding of transparent leadership practices is somewhat fuzzy and perhaps overly rosy-eyed; it is greatly influenced by the positive psychology and positive leadership studies paradigms within which many of its researchers are located, with a heavy accent on the "positive." Compared with other formulations of business transparency studied in this book, the question of how transparency of business leaders might backfire or cause harm to the leaders themselves or to employees or other constituents of the organization has been investigated to a much lesser degree.

Still, some researchers have raised serious and thought-provoking concerns about the current state of authentic leadership research. Alvesson and Einola (2019, 2021, 2022), in particular, have presented a vocal, multi-faceted, and significant critique of authentic leadership. Given space constraints, some of their key criticisms are described here, with readers encouraged to refer to the cited works for further detail. In a nutshell, Alvesson and Einola (2019) argue that the ideas underlying the authentic leadership research paradigm are overly simplistic, one-dimensional, static, decontextualized, and distorted by a positive bias and have yet to be sufficiently tested through rigorous academic scholarship. For these reasons, Alvesson and Einola conclude that the findings from this research are often misleading to apply in practice.

These authors posit that the theorizing behind authentic leadership is overly simplistic in the sense that it offers a Disneyfied vision of what it means to be a leader and unmoored in the sense that it isn't sufficiently grounded in the more fundamental question of what it means to be authentically human (Algera & Lips-Wiersma, 2012). In actual work settings, there is often an unresolvable tension and incompatibility between one's work role, which is primarily other-directed (e.g., oriented toward influencing subordinates and getting them to perform at a high level), and one's authentic self which is self-referential. Focusing too much on oneself is unproductive for other-oriented tasks, and vice versa. Numerous factors, such as the organization's social norms, political climate and extant alliances, conflicting loyalties, and inherent incompatibilities involved in the goals and interests of leaders and subordinates, make authenticity virtually impossible (Algera & Lips-Wiersma, 2012; Gardner et al., 2021).

On the flip side, experts have noted that many business leaders use authenticity as an excuse for bad behavior. As Gruenfeld and Zander (2011) point out, "What comes naturally can also get pretty nasty. When you are overly critical, non-communicative, crass, judgmental, or rigid, you are probably at your most real — but you are not at your best. In fact, it is often these most authentic parts of a leader that need the most management." In such circumstances, self-regulating thoughts and actions and lowering transparency may be the smart thing to do.

Alvesson and Einola (2019) also pointedly observe that authentic leadership research is bent on providing "easy, ideologically appealing solutions rather than on offering a qualified understanding of organizational life and manager-subordinate relations" (p. 383). Furthermore, from a theory development perspective, these authors argue that the constitutive elements of authentic leadership advanced by well-cited research do not form a coherent whole, conceptually or logically. They focus too much on the leader's personality and not sufficiently on social and situational factors that may be far more important in influencing mechanisms and organizational outcomes.

Criticisms have also been raised that authentic leadership research portrays a one-dimensional, overly rosy-eyed, positive, and unrealistic picture of effective leaders as saviors, ultimate problem-solvers, and exemplary moral individuals single-handedly responsible for inspiring workers throughout the organization, defeating competitors, and achieving financial success. These criticisms arise from the fact that, as mentioned earlier in this chapter, the prevailing conceptualizations of leader authenticity treat it as synonymous with other virtues like honesty, sincerity, morality, resilience, and compassion without attempting to disentangle the specific nuances of these concepts, or critically considering the realism behind them. Can the CEOs of multi-billion dollar corporations really be imbued with the traits of a Buddhist monk that has forsaken the world and lead their organization effectively?

Lehman and colleagues' (2019) recent attempt to tease out the different aspects of authenticity by distinguishing between the leader's *consistency* in internal values and external expressions, their *conformity* to the norms of the organization and other relevant social groups within which they operate, and the *connection* between the leader and the context in which leadership is practiced, and in considering the feasibility and roles of disclosure and observability in leadership and organizational decision making may be useful. Specifically, it may be possible to observe each facet of the leader's authenticity to different degrees acknowledging the underlying incompatibilities. For instance, no matter how candid and vocal a business leader may appear, it is still impossible to discern how consistent they are between their internal values and their words and actions; their internal values can be known only to them.

On the other hand, to the extent that organizational norms are spelled out, the degree to which the leader conforms to them is observable. Another aspect of one-dimensionality in this research arises from the fact that there is confusion regarding the theoretical content of the authentic leadership construct and its antecedents and outcomes. For example, Lehman and colleagues (2019) observed that the conceptual and empirical distinctions between authentic leadership and other forms, such as transformational, ethical, and servant leadership, are difficult to demarcate, even to the point that these constructs may be redundant.

Critics argue that the conclusions reached in this research are distorted because they give too much weight to the leader's personality and identity and not enough weight to the specific, nuanced, and context-bound decisions and actions that they must undertake using purposeful, patient and, in some cases devious or combative means to influence their subordinates to achieve challenging goals that may have little to do with transparency or its correlates. Instead of a stable, durable quality, authentic leadership may be "emergent from the narrative process in which others play a constitutive role in the self" (Sparrowe, 2005, p. 419).

Furthermore, Iszatt-White and Kempster (2019) point out that many theoretical treatments of authentic leadership fail to adequately consider or address the challenge associated with what they call "issues of intention vs. attribution," which is that a business leader can have intentions to be authentic and yet appear inauthentic to colleagues, and conversely, they may fake authenticity to appear authentic, while not being so. Putting it more bluntly, managers can both fail to convey transparency, and they can fake transparency, creating a chasm between the actual state of the manager's relational transparency and the assessments of relevant others, including colleagues, subordinates, and others, about how transparent they are. Even more abstractly, can anyone, including business leaders, ever be fully authentic in their day-to-day lives? Algera and Lips-Wiersma (2012) sagely assert that "inauthenticity is inevitable" (p. 122).

In many situations, business leaders may have valid reasons for faking transparency. In a detailed auto-ethnographic study of a senior hospital administrator, Kempster et al. (2019) found that during a period of intense challenge facing the organization, the manager felt it necessary to hide their experienced emotions and express desired emotions to colleagues to achieve leadership outcomes. The authors argued that this act of emotional labor shed light on two distinct dimensions of authenticity as experienced by managers in practice, *the strength of identification with the leadership role* (i.e., giving weight to their identity as managers and leaders relative to their other identities) and their *fidelity to the leadership role* (i.e., acting in accordance with specific goals to which they are committed in their leadership or managerial capacity). It is noteworthy that here again, like other forms of transparency covered throughout the book, we run into the importance and the substantial benefits (at least in the short-term) of creating an illusion of transparency to achieve desired goals, even when the transparency so generated deludes its creator as well as those influenced by them.

Some of the relations between the core constructs in the relational transparency nomological network are nuanced and deserve greater research attention. As one example, although Gardner, Avolio, and others studying authentic leadership have noted that the self-concept clarity resulting from introspection is positively associated with self-esteem, extraversion, and positive affect and negatively associated with depression and anxiety (e.g., Gardner et al., 2005), another line of research suggests the opposite relation, finding that people who introspect more tend to be less self-aware and report worse job satisfaction and well-being (Eurich, 2018). Grant et al. (2002) provide further insight, distinguishing between *self-reflection*, the inspection and evaluation of one's thoughts, feelings, and behavior, and *insight*, the clarity of understanding one's thoughts, feelings, and behavior. While insight benefits the individual through positive associations with cognitive flexibility and self-regulation and negative associations with depression, anxiety, and stress, self-reflection was correlated positively with anxiety and stress, suggesting that managers who self-reflect may be subject to dysfunctional rumination.

Eurich (2018) suggests that one reason for these adverse effects of self-reflection could be that when reflecting, leaders may be prone to invent answers that feel right even when many of the relevant thoughts, feelings, and motives remain unconscious and beyond their cognitive grasp. To deal with this problem, Eurich (2018) suggests that "to increase productive self-insight and decrease unproductive rumination, we should ask what, not why. "What" questions help us stay objective, future-focused, and empowered to act on our new insights." For instance, in evaluating a particular episode of negative feedback from subordinates, instead of framing the introspective question as "Why do my employees evaluate me so poorly," the leader could frame the question as "What are the concrete actions I need to take and changes I need to make to do a better job in the future?"

Summary. These critical perspectives on authentic leadership might seem harsh and unyielding; but they provide much-needed nuance to our understanding of the core psychological construct. Furthermore, these critical assertions and the proposed solutions echo the themes which have also emerged in other business settings identified in this book, and which are formalized in the integrative framework of Chapter 7. It is that the *transparency principle* in its absolute form is usually far too simple and non-rigorous a way to think about the desired level of business leadership transparency. What is needed instead is a scholarly approach that constructs, and then analyzes, a more complex, effortful, and realistic depiction and understanding of the managerial context and the organizational networks within which the business leader's lived professional experience unfolds, and in which they think their thoughts, move about, interact with others, and make business decisions.

References

Algera, P. M., & Lips-Wiersma, M. (2012). Radical authentic leadership: Co-creating the conditions under which all members of the organization can be authentic. *Leadership Quarterly, 23*(1), 118–131.

Alvesson, M., & Einola, K. (2019). Warning for excessive positivity: Authentic leadership and other traps in leadership studies. *Leadership Quarterly, 30*(4), 383–395.

Alvesson, M., & Einola, K. (2022). The gaslighting of authentic leadership 2.0. *Leadership, 18*(6), 814–831.

Anderson, H. J., Baur, J. E., Griffith, J. A., & Buckley, M. R. (2017). What works for you may not work for (Gen) Me: Limitations of present leadership theories for the new generation. *The Leadership Quarterly, 28*(1), 245–260.

Appels, M. (2022). CEO Sociopolitical activism as a signal of authentic leadership to prospective employees. *Journal of Management.* https://doi.org/10.1177/01492063221110207

Ashford, S. J., Wellman, N., Sully de Luque, M., De Stobbeleir, K. E., & Wollan, M. (2018). Two roads to effectiveness: CEO feedback seeking, vision articulation, and firm performance. *Journal of Organizational Behavior, 39*(1), 82–95.

Avolio, B. J., Gardner, W. L., Walumbwa, F. O., Luthans, F., & May, D. R. (2004). Unlocking the mask: A look at the process by which authentic leaders impact follower attitudes and behaviors. *Leadership Quarterly, 15*(6), 801–823.

Avolio, B. J., & Walumbwa, F. O. (2014). Authentic leadership theory, research and practice: Steps taken and steps that remain. In D. V. Day (Ed.), *The Oxford handbook of leadership and organizations* (pp. 331–356). Oxford University Press.

Baldoni, J. (2008, June 30). Start creating authentic leadership. *Harvard Business Review.* https://hbr.org/2008/06/start-creating-authentic-leade

Barnard, C. (1938). *The functions of the executive.* Harvard University Press.

Bennis, W., Goleman, D., O'Toole, J., & Biederman, P. W. (2008). *Transparency: How leaders create a culture of Candor.* Jossey-Bass.

Brown, A. D., & Starkey, K. (2000). Organizational identity and learning: A psychodynamic perspective. *Academy of Management Review, 25*(1), 102–120.

Caldwell, C., & Hayes, L. A. (2016). Self-efficacy and self-awareness: Moral insights to increased leader effectiveness. *Journal of Management Development, 35*(9), 1163–1173.

Cha, S. E., Hewlin, P. F., Roberts, L. M., Buckman, B. R., Leroy, H., Steckler, E. L., Ostermeier, K., & Cooper, D. (2019). Being your true self at work: Integrating the fragmented research on authenticity in organizations. *Academy of Management Annals, 13*(2), 633–671.

Cillizza, C. (2015, April 30). Millennials don't trust anyone. That's a big deal. *Washington Post.* https://www.washingtonpost.com/news/the-fix/wp/2015/04/30/millennials-dont-trust-anyone-what-else-is-new/

Cotterrell, R. (1999). Transparency, mass media, ideology and community. *Journal for Cultural Research, 3*(4), 414–426.

Dobbin, F., & Kalev, A. (2022). *Getting to diversity: What works and what doesn't*. Belknap Press.

Duval, S., & Wicklund, R. A. (1972). *A theory of objective self awareness*. Academic Press.

Einola, K., & Alvesson, M. (2021). Behind the numbers: Questioning questionnaires. *Journal of Management Inquiry, 30*(1), 102–114.

Eurich, T. (2018, January 4). What self-awareness really is (and how to cultivate it). *Harvard Business Review*. https://hbr.org/2018/01/what-self-awareness-really-is-and-how-to-cultivate-it

Feser, C., Mayol, F., & Srinivasan, R. (2015, January 1). Decoding leadership: What really matters. *McKinsey Quarterly*. https://www.mckinsey.com/featured-insights/leadership/decoding-leadership-what-really-matters

Friedman, S. D. (2008, November 6). Obama's authentic leadership—And yours. *Harvard Business Review*. https://hbr.org/2008/11/obamas-authentic-leadership-an

Gardner, W. L., Avolio, B. J., Luthans, F., May, D. R., & Walumbwa, F. (2005). "Can you see the real me?" A self-based model of authentic leader and follower development. *Leadership Quarterly, 16*(3), 343–372.

Gardner, W. L., Cogliser, C. C., Davis, K. M., & Dickens, M. P. (2011). Authentic leadership: A review of the literature and research agenda. *Leadership Quarterly, 22*(6), 1120–1145.

Gardner, W. L., Karam, E. P., Alvesson, M., & Einola, K. (2021). Authentic leadership theory: The case for and against. *Leadership Quarterly, 32*(6), 101495.

Grant, A. M., Franklin, J., & Langford, P. (2002). The self-reflection and insight scale: A new measure of private self-consciousness. *Social Behavior and Personality, 30*(8), 821–835.

George, B. (2003). *Authentic leadership: Rediscovering the secrets to creating lasting value* (Vol. 18). Wiley.

George, B. (2015). *Discover your true North: Becoming an authentic leader*. Jossey-Bass.

George, B. (2016). The rise of true north leaders. *Leader to Leader, 79*, 30–35.

Gruenfeld, D., & Zander, L. (2011, February). Authentic leadership can be bad leadership. *Harvard Business Review*. https://hbr.org/2011/02/authentic-leadership-can-be-ba

Houser, D., Levy, D. M., Padgitt, K., Peart, S. J., & Xiao, E. (2014). Raising the price of talk: An experimental analysis of transparent leadership. *Journal of Economic Behavior & Organization, 105*, 208–218.

Hughes, L. W. (2005). *Transparency, translucence or opacity? An experimental study of the impact of a leader's relational transparency and style of humor delivery on follower creative performance* (Unpublished doctoral dissertation). The University of Nebraska-Lincoln.

Ibarra, H. (2015). The authenticity paradox. *Harvard Business Review, 93*(1/2), 53–59.

Iszatt-White, M., & Kempster, S. (2019). Authentic leadership: Getting back to the roots of the 'root construct'? *International Journal of Management Reviews, 21*(3), 356–369.

Jiang, H., & Men, R. L. (2017). Creating an engaged workforce: The impact of authentic leadership, transparent organizational communication, and work-life enrichment. *Communication Research, 44*(2), 225–243.

Karlsson, P., Turner, M., & Gassmann, P. (2019). Succeeding the long-serving legend in the corner office. *Strategy & Business, 95*. https://www.strategy-business.com/article/Succeeding-the-long-serving-legend-in-the-corner-office

Kelemen, T. K., Matthews, S. H., Matthews, M. J., & Henry, S. E. (2022). Humble leadership: A review and synthesis of leader expressed humility. *Journal of Organizational Behavior*, in press.

Kempster, S., Iszatt-White, M., & Brown, M. (2019). Authenticity in leadership: Reframing relational transparency through the lens of emotional labour. *Leadership, 15*(3), 319–338.

Kernis, M. H. (2003). Toward a conceptualization of optimal self-esteem. *Psychological Inquiry, 14*(1), 1–26.

Kernis, M. H., & Goldman, B. M. (2006). A multicomponent conceptualization of authenticity: Theory and research. *Advances in Experimental Social Psychology, 38*, 283–357.

Larcker, D. F., & Tayan, B. (2016). *Scoundrels in the C-suite: How should the board respond when a CEO's bad behavior makes the news? Rock Center for Corporate Governance at Stanford University Closer Look Series: Topics, Issues and Controversies in Corporate Governance No. CGRP-57* (Stanford University Graduate School of Business Research Paper, 16–23).

Lehman, D. W., O'Connor, K., Kovács, B., & Newman, G. E. (2019). Authenticity. *Academy of Management Annals, 13*(1), 1–42.

Lemoine, G. J., Hartnell, C. A., & Leroy, H. (2019). Taking stock of moral approaches to leadership: An integrative review of ethical, authentic, and servant leadership. *Academy of Management Annals, 13*(1), 148–187.

Leroy, H., Anseel, F., Gardner, W. L., & Sels, L. (2015). Authentic leadership, authentic followership, basic need satisfaction, and work role performance: A cross-level study. *Journal of Management, 41*(6), 1677–1697.

Luthans, F., & Avolio, B. J. (2003). Authentic leadership development. In R. E. Quinn, J. E. Dutton, & K. S. Cameron (Eds.), *Positive organizational scholarship: Foundations of a new discipline* (pp. 241–258).

O'Toole, J., & Bennis, W. (2009). A culture of candor. *Harvard Business Review, 87*(6), 54–61.

Ou, A. Y., Tsui, A. S., Kinicki, A. J., Waldman, D. A., Xiao, Z., & Song, L. J. (2014). Humble chief executive officers' connections to top management team integration and middle managers' responses. *Administrative Science Quarterly, 59*(1), 34–72.

Owens, B. P., Rowatt, W. C., & Wilkins, A. L. (2011). Exploring the relevance and implications of humility in organizations. *Handbook of Positive Organizational Scholarship, 1,* 260–272.

Perna, G. (2020, January 20). *CEOs on leading through increased public scrutiny.* Health Evolution. https://www.healthevolution.com/insider/ceos-on-leading-through-increased-public-scrutiny/

Prastacos, G., Wang, F., & Soderquist, K. (2013). *Leadership through the classics: Learning management and leadership from ancient east and west philosophy.* Springer Science & Business Media.

Rahim-Dillard, S. (2021, April 19). How inclusive is your leadership? *Harvard Business Review.* https://hbr.org/2021/04/how-inclusive-is-your-leadership

Rego, A., & Giustiniano, L. (2021). Are relationally transparent leaders more receptive to the relational transparency of others? An authentic dialog perspective. *Journal of Business Ethics.* https://doi.org/10.1007/s10551-021-04792-6

Scott, W. R., & Davis, G. F. (2015). *Organizations and organizing: Rational.* Routledge.

Sparrowe, R. T. (2005). Authentic leadership and the narrative self. *Leadership Quarterly, 16*(3), 419–439.

Thacker, K. (2016). *The art of authenticity: Tools to become an authentic leader and your best self.* Wiley.

Trentini, C., Tambelli, R., Maiorani, S., & Lauriola, M. (2022). Gender differences in empathy during adolescence: Does emotional self-awareness matter? *Psychological Reports, 125*(2), 913–936.

Vogelgesang, G. R. (2008). *How leader interactional transparency can impact follower psychological safety and role engagement* (Doctoral dissertation). The University of Nebraska-Lincoln.

Walumbwa, F. O., Avolio, B. J., Gardner, W. L., Wernsing, T. S., & Peterson, S. J. (2008). Authentic leadership: Development and validation of a theory-based measure. *Journal of Management, 34*(1), 89–126.

Wang, L., Owens, B. P., Li, J. J., & Shi, L. (2018). Exploring the affective impact, boundary conditions, and antecedents of leader humility. *Journal of Applied Psychology, 103*(9), 1019.

Weick, K. E. (2001). Leadership as the legitimization of doubt. In W. Bennis, G. M. Spreitzer, & T. G. Cummings (Eds.), *The future of leadership: Today's top leadership thinkers speak to tomorrow's leaders* (pp. 91–102).

Wilken, R., Cornelißen, M., Backhaus, K., & Schmitz, C. (2010). Steering sales reps through cost information: An investigation into the black box of cognitive references and negotiation behavior. *International Journal of Research in Marketing, 27*(1), 69–82.

CHAPTER 6

Algorithmic Transparency and Consumer Disclosure

Abstract This chapter reviews the growing and evolving literature on algorithmic transparency and consumer disclosure. As algorithms are adopted widely in data-driven business decision making, often involving consumers, the questions of which data is collected and used, how it is analyzed, and the various unintended consequences it produces all gain in significance. In the endeavor to formulate a better understanding of business transparency, this chapter considers the research on the various means to formulate and increase algorithmic transparency and the challenges of doing so, along with the host of associated issues concerning consumers whose private data is at stake.

Keywords Transparency · Algorithms · Consumer disclosure · Artificial intelligence · Discrimination

> The near-ubiquitous use of algorithmically driven software, both visible and invisible to everyday people, demands a closer inspection of what values are prioritized in such automated decision-making systems.—Safiya Umoja Noble

Consider this ProPublica investigative story from October 2022. It reported on the popularity of a dynamic pricing software called Yield-Star, used by property managers throughout the United States, that is

© The Author(s), under exclusive license to Springer Nature Switzerland AG 2023
U. Dholakia, *Transparency in Business*,
https://doi.org/10.1007/978-3-031-12145-6_6

responsible for steep increases in apartment rents in cities from Seattle to Atlanta to Denver (Vogell, 2022). The service relies on an algorithm that considers apartment characteristics like square footage, the number of bedrooms, the floor level, etc., the forthcoming availability of apartments within the complex, and the locations and actual rents paid for apartments in that complex and at proximal competitors to calculate the rent to charge for each apartment. The rent recommendations are dynamically updated daily by the software.

Furthermore, the company recommends its clients avoid negotiating with potential renters and favor lower occupancy over lower rents. The algorithm runs using lease transaction data from over 13 million rental transactions, which contains actual rents paid (vs. advertised rents; Kovatch, 2022), but the details of how it calculates its output, i.e., precisely which variables are used, how they are combined, and how the rent estimates are calculated, remain entirely opaque to landlords using the software and their renters. The upshot is that tens of thousands of US renters have suffered significant hardship by paying significantly higher rents for the same apartments or undertaking an inconvenient and costly move with little understanding of why rents are increasing.

As this case illustrates, on the frontlines in the battle between disclosure and secrecy, the fiercest skirmishes are being fought in using algorithms for business purposes. Algorithms, defined as "encoded procedures for transforming input data into a desired output, based on specified calculations… [that] name both a problem and the steps by which it should be solved" (Gillespie, 2014, p. 167), have been adopted in a variety of business applications. Their popularity is driven by a confluence of factors, including a managerial preference for data-driven decision making and personalized offerings, the greater availability of behavioral data (like the YieldStar example), and services that provide cheap data storage and processing (Edelman & Abraham, 2022).

Algorithms driven by artificial intelligence are used routinely to moderate consumers' posts, comments, and reviews on content and social media sites, detect and prevent fraudulent financial transactions, audit contracts and financial statements, assess the creditworthiness of buyers, trade financial instruments, recognize voices and faces for automated conversations and identity verification, screen rental applications, set insurance rates by monitoring driving behavior, and set and change prices dynamically (Gillespie, 2020), leading Pasquale (2015) to coin the term "the scored society" for the ubiquitous use of algorithmic scoring in business practice.

As algorithm use proliferates in business, so do collateral concerns from those affected by their outputs. They include concerns about privacy, particularly the fact that many algorithmic applications rely on comprehensive but proprietary private and personal data about their targets, and the collection, storage, and use of the data is often based on insufficient explanation and often violates contextual norms of privacy (Martin, 2012). Equally, salient is the issue of transparency for both parties, those who adopt and use algorithms and those who are affected by them. For algorithm users, typically businesses or third parties that sell services to them, there are questions about how much information about the algorithm and the data used to provide its output can and should be disclosed. For those affected by algorithm outputs, such as customers or renters, the core questions are about understanding which of their personal information is collected, what other data sources are used, and how exactly the algorithm calculates scores for them that affect their choices. These are evolving topics, and there is growing scholarly literature studying them, which loosely falls under the title of "algorithmic transparency," which we will consider in this chapter. It should be noted that, as a whole, this academic literature has more questions than answers and is a few steps behind practice which continues to advance rapidly; however, it is still worth understanding current perspectives to round out our understanding of business transparency.

THE ALGORITHMIC TRANSPARENCY CHALLENGE

In one sense, applying algorithms with artificial intelligence to make business decisions has the veneer of openness and objectivity we have encountered throughout this book. After all, many aspects of algorithms are "objective;" they are well-defined computational procedures tasked with solving computational problems that are equally well-articulated, and the inputs, outputs, and goals all need to be written out mathematically. What could be more visible, communicable, and interpretable than a mathematical formula that produces clearly defined actions and replaces subjective human decision making that could be susceptible to biases? In the YieldStar case, for example, it can be argued that potential racial discrimination in quoting rent is bypassed completely because renter demographic characteristics are not included in the model.

Yet, a serious concern is that despite the good intentions of managers and statisticians, using algorithms may unintentionally lead to harmful consequences for those affected by these applications, such as the inadvertent promotion of bias and discrimination in various forms, the propagation of falsehoods such as domain-specific misinformation, conspiracy theories, and toxic speech, and the promotion of inequity by reducing access to information and services to certain groups (Commerford et al., 2022; Green & Viljoen, 2020; Lewandowsky & Kozyreva, 2022; Seele et al., 2021). As Gillespie (2014) puts it, there are "warm human and institutional choices that lie behind these cold mechanisms" (p. 169) that need to be considered and understood. Even in the case of the YieldStar algorithm that excludes demographic variables, the rapid increase in rents because of its dynamic pricing outputs has disproportionately affected lower-income Black and Hispanic renters (Mijares Torres & Marte, 2022).

Compounding this challenge, many artificial intelligence-based methods, such as deep learning, are "inscrutable" (Raj, 2020), inherently lacking explainability. The combined opacity in the mechanism and the surrounding human and social factors make it impossible for the working, rationale, or output to be *learned or understood by anyone*, including the coders and implementers of these algorithms. Furthermore, even within a single application domain, the concurrent use of different algorithms, AI methods, and algorithmic decision making (ADM) systems mean there is often significant variation in transparency within the same setting (Gorwa et al., 2020).

All of this is to say that in any given application, understanding the transparency of algorithms being used is itself ridden with dilemmas and open questions. Pasquale (2015) provides a concrete example of this challenge by asking, "Should a credit card company be entitled to raise a couple's interest rate if they are seeking marriage counseling? If so, should cardholders know this?" (p. 5). Such questions can easily be extended into a lengthy series in this context or extrapolated to other business applications of algorithms.

Defining Algorithmic Transparency

By now, it should be clear that beyond technical considerations such as scalability, efficiency, and accuracy, the future broad-based adoption and success of business applications of algorithms, its regulatory approval by governments, and by extension, its acceptance by consumers or employees who are affected by its outputs in consequential ways, hinges on achieving *algorithmic transparency*. Thus, as a starting point, we need to seek clarity about the concept itself and understand current conceptualizations of it.

At a basic level, algorithmic transparency refers to the user's and, to a lesser and more abstract extent, the target's ability to understand the inputs, outputs, and the process followed by the model to convert inputs into outputs (Arrieta et al., 2020) and an actionable way to hold users accountable. Diakopoulos (2020) persuasively argues that managers must adopt transparency and accountability as key considerations when adopting ADM systems at the outset and then use them (see also Ananny & Crawford, 2018).

Transparency in ADM Systems

ADM systems typically use an algorithm-based process to generate a judgment or decision such as a dollar value (in the case of price), score, ranking, or classification, which is then used as an input into the creation or cocreation of digitally automated services such as the ones described earlier. For example, ADM systems calculate and change prices in dynamic pricing applications. In some cases, the algorithm's output may be marketed as the core service itself, for example, a potential renter's "shadow credit score" that is sold to landlords for screening purposes (Smith & Vogell, 2022) or an estimate of the asking rent using the YieldStar software (Vogell, 2022). In other applications, the algorithm's output may be used as part of a more extensive service, such as recommendations about other things to buy or watch used by online retailers and streaming services (Vanderbilt, 2016).

Some researchers studying algorithmic transparency rely on a core availability-based definition, defining algorithmic transparency as "the availability of information about an actor allowing other actors to monitor the workings or performance of this actor" (Meijer, 2014). Another line of research focuses on the opposite end of the conceptual spectrum by considering *algorithmic opacity*, defined as the lack of knowledge of the involved parties (those writing and using the algorithm and those affected by it) stemming from the partial or total ignorance about the inputs used in the algorithm, and a definite sense of how or why a particular outcome was derived from the inputs. Yet, there are specific nuances of "availability" (also called "explainability" in some strains of this literature) in this view of transparency that need to be teased out. For example, some of this ignorance is remediable, while some is not; and which party (user or target) is the focus of the remediation also matters.

Warm Human and Institutional Factors

When compared to other types of business transparency covered in this book, one unique aspect of algorithmic transparency is that it is reasonable to conceive of it not just as the algorithm's property (as, say, it is for a business leader or a supply chain), but instead it is the property of the overall system and the sum of processes that are employed in its service. These include the means used by the modeler to develop the algorithm (including the modeler's mindset and ideological orientation), the specific mathematical steps embedded in the algorithm, the sources, and the management of the relevant data (for instance, how the data is cleaned, missing values dealt with, etc.), and the method of utilization of the algorithm's output in the cocreation of the service (Creel, 2020).

Thus, both technical factors and human factors play roles in contributing to the ADM system's transparency. In this sense, ADM systems are sociotechnical systems that "do not contain complexity but enact complexity by connecting to and intertwining with assemblages of humans and non-humans" (Ananny & Crawford, 2018, p. 974). Furthermore, social, cultural, and political factors also play a role in how human decisions fit into the algorithm's workings and output (Gorwa et al., 2020) and ultimately dictate the net effects of transparency, including user perceptions.

As a particular case of a warm institutional factor, Burrell (2016) points out that in business applications, a common reason for algorithmic opacity is *intentional corporate secrecy*. A company may intentionally wish to keep its algorithms hidden and private to derive a durable advantage over its competitors and differentiate its brand by delivering unique benefits to customers; in fact, it may even take legal steps to do so by claiming its algorithms as intellectual property and trade secrets (Foss-Solbrekk, 2021). For example, Google frequently changes its PageRank algorithm, but both the algorithm itself and its changes are proprietary. Businesses looking to raise their ranking have no visibility into the actual inputs; in fact, marketing scholars have argued that algorithmic opacity is a significant reason for relatively little research on SEO marketing in academic journals (Dholakia, 2022).

It is noteworthy that hidden behind the cover of justified corporate secrecy, the algorithms used by the company could result in discrimination, unfair advantage, and other adverse outcomes, with targets being none the wiser. This idea is explored in more detail later on in the chapter. It also provides new insight into other forms of business transparency considered in previous chapters by suggesting that it may be more meaningful to view transparency as a property of a business setting that includes institutional and human factors rather than the property of an individual or group within the organization. As one example, this perspective advances the possibility that a business leader's transparency as a personally held value could easily interact with an organization's cultural transparency to amplify or attenuate the effects we expect from the individual forms. In sum, the idea of "warm institutional factors" urges us to break down the extant silos between the different areas of business transparency to get at the root of its significance and effects.

Event Versus Process Algorithmic Transparency

Furthermore, researchers have also identified two distinct forms of transparency that are relevant for assessing an ADM: transparency in the outcomes of the ADM's output and transparency in the processes behind the algorithm's development and use. As Ananny and Crawford (2018) put it, "transparency is thus not a precise end state where everything is clear and apparent, but a system of observing and knowing that promises a form of control" (p. 975). Heald's (2006) broad distinction between event and process transparency in governance provides some valuable insights. When the discloser adopts *event transparency*, they shed light on the inputs, outputs, and outcomes, typically measured by proxy variables. Process transparency goes further with respect to understanding by providing information about the processes that convert the inputs to outputs and the linkage processes that lead from outputs to outcomes.

We can distinguish between these forms concretely by considering the algorithmic transparency of shadow credit scores used for tenant screening. In this case, the variables used to calculate the scores are the inputs. Their sources, the processes by which they are encoded, recorded, and used for analysis (Holland et al., 2018), the methods to ascertain their accuracy, how they are weighted in the algorithm, the nature of non-compensatory rules and potential biases that might arise from their application (e.g., is a criminal conviction grounds for rejecting the tenant regardless of their creditworthiness, or does a higher credit score compensate for a prior conviction? If a criminal conviction is treated as absolute grounds for rejection, will that harm certain groups disproportionately, and is that acceptable to the user?), the roles played by human agents vis-à-vis the technology in the final output and its use for decision making are all facets of the ADM system's conversion processes.

The final shadow credit scores assigned to potential renters are the outputs. Their behaviors as renters over the lease period and afterward constitute the outcomes. Finally, the psychological or sociological processes through which the shadow credit scores explain the renter's future behavior constitute the linkage process. Through this lens, consistent with the earlier discussion, perfect algorithmic transparency is hypothetical and idealized, whereby an external observer would have perfect insight into every one of these steps in the renter's experience. Practically, how much insight observers can get into this entire process characterizes the algorithmic transparency of shadow credit score deployment.

Ribeiro et al. (2016) distinguish between "trusting a model" and "trusting its prediction," which adds meaningfully to this discussion. Trusting a model relates to the belief that the model is correct and will yield good results when used. On the other hand, trusting its prediction has to do with whether the user trusts an individual prediction made by the model enough to act based on its output. These two types of trust affect different entities (the modeler and the decision maker, respectively) and require different actions to support them.

The Algorithmic Transparency Continuum

In generating a potential renter's shadow credit score, a company may use not only financial variables that are typically used to generate a credit score but also other publicly available data that may only be tangential, if at all related, such as criminal records, speeding tickets, and data on previous evictions. Which specific variables are chosen, their provenance (i.e., reliability and accuracy), and how they are used in the algorithm are just as important as the specific AI method used (e.g., a sparse linear model) and its limitations, how the resulting score is interpreted, what thresholds are established to deem the renter as acceptable, and so on. The roles played by human actors such as data analysts and modelers in utilizing the technology and their skills, and in particular, how much autonomy they have and how they use it, all affect the ADM system's transparency. This results in an *algorithmic transparency continuum*.

The level of transparency varies, inadvertently or by design. In some cases, transparency is the *bare minimum*, disclosing that an algorithm is being used to those affected by its output without additional information or contextualization. At the other end, in-depth information regarding each stage of the scoring process is provided, indicative of the *maximum possible* transparency. In analyzing algorithmic content moderation, Gorwa et al. (2020) argue that while some models are "inherently interpretable" (Rai, 2020) because of a confluence of technical complexity, commercial secrecy, and subjectivity introduced by a wide range of subjective factors, many ADM systems are so complex they cannot be deciphered even by experts. Thus, the *maximum possible* transparency is far from *perfect transparency*.

Much like transparency in other business settings covered in this book, algorithmic transparency is virtually never defined in binary (i.e., present or absent) and rarely in one-dimensional (i.e., high or low transparency) terms. Instead, it is seen as a continuous multi-dimensional concept that considers various factors, each of which is defined in degree for a given ADM system. We will consider Creel's (2020) perspective when we discuss process-based transparency in Chapter 7.

Gillespie (2014, 2020) also provides an insightful analysis to help understand multi-dimensional aspects of algorithmic transparency. According to him, first, the visibility into the underlying dataset on which the algorithm is run is crucial. The sources of data, the collection policies, and the data collection practices, such as explicit user consent and the methods of processing data, all affect algorithmic transparency.

Second, what Gillespie (2014) calls "cycles of anticipation" influence transparency in many business applications. The primary purpose of algorithms is to predict the behavior of a target, say customers, and act in specific ways at the correct time using this prediction, which relies on understanding the target as comprehensively as possible and collecting data about every possible characteristic. An infamous example is the use of detailed customer demographics and purchase behavior, such as unscented lotion and magnesium supplements, by the US-based retailer Target to generate a "pregnancy prediction" score that not only predicted whether a particular customer was pregnant but the likely due date for those who were pregnant. While the retailer's goal was to use these predictions to send targeted promotions to customers, its unintended byproduct was widespread outrage at the intrusion of privacy (Duhigg, 2012).

The non-specific data trawling impedes algorithmic transparency by making it hard to justify or explain the use of certain variables (e.g., unscented lotion purchase) to predict outcomes (e.g., the customer's pregnancy). At an abstract level, this approach falls in the same genre as the questionable research practice of "fishing for significance" that was widely used by social science researchers with its attendant ethical problems before the replication crisis awakening of the early 2010s (John et al., 2012).

Third, the degree to which the criteria used by the algorithm in determining the relevance of different input variables can be explained is important. As algorithms utilizing artificial intelligence learning techniques like unsupervised learning are employed repeatedly, they become more attuned to contextual information. They evolve from using relatively few and clearly explainable variables to a larger, more diffuse set of variables where the connection to the outcome is unclear. As Gillespie (2014) points out, "'relevant' is a fluid and loaded judgment, as open to interpretation as some of the evaluative terms that media scholars have already unpacked, such as "newsworthy" or "popular." As there is no independent metric for what are the most relevant search results for any given query, engineers must decide what results look "right" and tweak their algorithm to attain that result, or make changes based on evidence from their user" (p. 175). We can call this *intuitive, unexplainable subjectivity*, and it is detrimental to algorithmic transparency because it undermines understanding and trust.

The fourth issue is related to Gillespie's (2014) conception of "entanglement with practice," which consists of two separate ideas. One is that in line with the omnibus transparency definition we adopted in Chapter 1, the objectives for using the algorithm are rooted in corporate strategy and are often quite specific. Why did Target choose to predict which of its customers was pregnant and when they would give birth, and not some other event like when they would purchase a house or retire, which are commonly used by other retailers? It was because the marketing strategy of Target privileged new parents; the company's senior executives were interested in pursuing this particular customer segment because they saw it as lucrative (Duhigg, 2012). Another retailer might have chosen different segments, events, triggers, and algorithmic inputs and outputs. Simply put, when the reason for an important decision has antecedents terminating at executive preference, formulating a coherent explanation has a natural, and often inadequate, backstop that ends with a manager's or group's judgment.

The second idea is that the results of using algorithms are accretive; when one project is successful, it reinforces and pushes the company in the direction of building on its success and further fine-tuning the algorithms that work. This results in more sophisticated, data-intensive, and potentially complex algorithms over time and in the adoption of a more nuanced and hidden organizational decision calculus. An initial rupture eventually grows into a chasm between what the modeler envisioned and how the outputs are used in practice. As this discussion should make apparent, algorithmic transparency issues are full of rich theoretical considerations that have only recently begun to be unpacked and understood.

Enhancing Algorithmic Transparency

To deal with some of the potential challenges to algorithmic transparency identified thus far, Green and Viljoen (2020) propose the intriguing solution that it is important for ADM system users to painstakingly identify the boundaries within which their tools can work effectively and stay within them. Specifically, they suggest that as artificial intelligence applications expand their scope, they are bound to be applied to problems and settings where they are unsuitable or where their net effects (after accounting for unintended consequences) are negative. They ascribe the lack of transparency to the dominant mode of problem-solving within computer science, which they call "algorithmic formalism," which privileges objectivity, neutrality, internalism, and universalism. To increase transparency and mitigate the unintended negative consequences of ADM systems, Green and Viljoen (2020) propose replacing algorithmic formalism with "algorithmic realism," marked by "a reflexive political consciousness, a porousness that recognizes the complexity and fluidity of the social world, and contextualism" (p. 20). This point is pursued further in Chapter 7.

The Right to an Explanation

Intriguingly, many legal experts argue that when algorithms are used primarily or solely in making decisions that materially impact consumers, those affected adversely have a "right to an explanation" for the reasoning that led to the unfavorable outcome. The European General Data Protection Regulation (GDPR), a set of comprehensive regulations covering the collection, storage, and use of personal information of consumers adopted by the European Parliament in 2016, further intensified the debate about the importance of the right to an explanation, with experts seeing it as "one tool for scrutinizing, challenging, and restraining algorithmic decision making" (Edwards & Veale, 2017, p. 6). A heavily analyzed and debated section of the GDPR involves the individual's right to an explanation, which is scaffolded around the contents of Articles 15 and 22.

Article 15 of the GDPR provides consumers with the rights not only to obtain confirmation about whether the organization is using their personal data but also such things as "the purposes of the processing," "the categories of personal data concerned," and "the existence of automated decision-making, including profiling, … and, meaningful information about the logic involved, as well as the significance and the envisaged consequences of such processing for the data subject."

Furthermore, Article 22 of the GDPR states that the consumer "shall have the right not to be subject to a decision based solely on automated processing, including profiling, which produces legal effects concerning him or her or similarly significantly affects him or her." Companies using the consumer's data "shall implement suitable measures to safeguard the data subject's rights and freedoms and legitimate interests, at least the right to obtain human intervention on the part of the controller, to express his or her point of view and to contest the decision" (Goodman & Flaxman, 2017).

As the stipulations make clear, being able to explain how the ADM system works and how it is being used to make individual decisions is key information that the business must be able to provide affected consumers (Edwards & Veale, 2018). These ideas, particularly the level of power afforded to consumers, have not yet fully carried over to the United States, but the topic of the "right to an explanation" is full of intriguing and potentially promising possibilities to provide more balance and fairness to algorithmic transparency applications, particularly in digital marketing settings.

Comprehensibility, Understandability, and Explainability

In exploring the nuances behind mechanisms to enhance algorithmic transparency, many researchers use several terms in the literature that are often overlapping and used interchangeably. Arrieta and colleagues (2020) provide a useful typology of terms and an explanation of the nuances of the specific meanings that helps clarify algorithmic transparency in practice. The first term is *comprehensibility*, defined as the ability of a learning algorithm to represent its learned knowledge in a form that an expert human user can understand at a minimum and by lay people at a much higher level. Many researchers also use *comprehensibility* interchangeably with *interpretability*, which is seen as a measure of the model's complexity (Guidotti et al., 2018).

Second, *understandability or intelligibility* refers to the property of the model by which a layperson can understand its functioning, specifically how the model works, without any further need to explain its internal structure or technical details behind the algorithm or methods used to process the data. Third, *explainability* refers to an active characteristic of a model, denoting the affordances that allow it to take actions or implement a procedure with the primary purpose of clarifying or detailing its internal functioning. Building on this notion of explainability, Arrieta et al. (2020) defines explainable AI as "one that produces details or reasons to make its functioning clear or easy to understand" (p. 85). Each of these specific mechanisms contribute to unwrapping and clarifying the algorithm's operation to users and targets.

Post hoc explainability. Another way to increase the transparency of ADM systems is to use post hoc explainability methods for models that are not readily interpretable to begin with. A number of techniques are currently being used, with improvements constantly occurring in this active research space, each of which relies on using expository methods used by humans. These include text explanations that rely on a verbal description, using appropriate mathematical symbols to describe the functioning of the model, visual explanations that use visualization means like graphs, charts, and infographics to depict the model's functioning, local explanations that segment the relatively more complex solution space and provide verbal or visual explanations of simpler subspaces, explanations by example that extract and describe selected data samples to construct vivid examples, e.g., of a prototypical sample member, explanation by simplification which relies on constructing simplified, cruder, and more tractable models that provide the gist of the original model to the observer, and feature relevance explanation methods that describe the inner functioning of a model by computing relevance scores for key input variables, thus allowing observers to understand the relative importance of the different inputs. Note that within a particular application context, multiple post hoc explainability methods may be used concurrently to improve the understanding of the model to interested observers.

The benefits of explainable ADM systems. Explainable ADM systems have at least six significant benefits that support their use and make them more accountable to users and those affected by their outputs (Arrieta et al., 2020; Guidotti et al., 2018). First, explainable models engender user trust because they bolster users' beliefs that the model will run as intended for a given problem. Second, they help to establish causality by making it easier to find relationships between variables for further tests to investigate causal linkages. Third, explainable models make it easier to establish the boundaries within which a model may be used, leading to more effective implementations. For example, a credit-scoring model that heavily weighs several years of historical financial behaviors may be unsuitable for scoring a teenager or new immigrant with insufficient or sparse prior information. Another benefit is porting the explainable model to other similarly structured problems is easier.

Fourth, explainable models support extrapolation by providing more information to the decision maker about using the model output to make effective decisions. Simply put, these models are concurrently more informative and more restrictive. Fifth, by giving visibility into the structural elements that make the model robust and stable, explainable models lend greater confidence to decision makers to interpret and use the model's output. They ease the burden on non-technical or non-expert users in interacting with them. Finally, somewhat optimistically, Arrieta and colleagues (2020) argue that explainability can be considered as the capacity to reach and even guarantee fairness in ADM systems. Users can get involved in improving the models to the extent that they can make sense of the machinery inside.

Customer Transparency

The discussion so far in this chapter has focused on the use of algorithms by businesses and how they can manage algorithmic transparency to maintain their relationships with those affected by the algorithms' outputs. However, the consideration of algorithmic transparency also raises a host of issues that are squarely focused on the discloser's (i.e., the target's) side of the information exchange, most of which fall within the domain of consumer behavior because they involve customers.

A particularly significant form of relevant transparency with multifaceted and nuanced impacts is *customer disclosure*, defined here as *the personal information customers choose to reveal, are required to reveal, or inadvertently reveal about themselves to the business, the exchange partners on a platform, other customers, or (known and unknown) third parties throughout their buying and consumption journeys*. Customer disclosure is a double-edged sword. On the one hand, the more the marketer knows about the customer, the better they will be able to serve them, for example, by employing more nuanced and explainable algorithms. This so-called *principle of customer orientation*, which is to understand the customer and then design and deliver customized, compelling offerings to suit their preferences and tastes, lies at the heart of marketing strategy (Day, 1999) and has been robustly shown to affect customer well-being using a slew of measures (Arora et al., 2008). Indeed, with the advent of digital technology, many ethical marketers have embraced the concept of personalizing offerings for individual customers to increase the delivered value (Wind & Rangaswamy, 2001). However, there's a significant downside for customers as well; revealing personal information creates the potential for them to be exploited and discriminated against by the marketer, other customers, and third parties that access the customer's information.

Nowhere is the potential harm that disclosure can cause customers more clearly evident than in the seminal study of orchestra audition policies (Goldin & Rouse, 2000). When orchestras switched during the 1970s and 1980s from open auditions, where hiring juries could see the candidate, to blind auditions, where musicians were hidden behind screens during the audition, the percentage of female musicians hired by orchestras increased substantially, with as much as 55% of the increase attributed to the reduced transparency during the hiring process. Simply stated, anonymity reduced gender discrimination in hiring musicians. Disclosing customer information is analogous to "seeing" musicians in this study; the more the personal information is disclosed, the more visible the customer becomes, and thus more susceptible they will be to overt or inadvertent biases.

Other influential research has found that job candidates with Black-sounding names are significantly less likely to receive callbacks for interviews when compared to candidates with White names across occupations and industries (Bertrand & Mullainathan, 2004). These are robust findings that have been replicated repeatedly and in different settings. In these and many other such examples, disclosure of personal information is a precursor to discrimination and exploitation. Thus, there is a clear economic danger to customers from revealing personal information to counterbalance or even outweigh any potential benefits of personalization. The tension between the benefits of transparency and the potential harm it can cause customers lies at the heart of studying customer disclosure. Marketing scholars refer to this as the *privacy-personalization paradox* (Aguirre et al., 2016).

Customer disclosure can encompass a wide range of variables and personal information, from *observed behaviors* such as browsing, viewing, and engagement behaviors online, purchases, reviews, recommendations, complaints, and cancelations to *expressed variables* provided through survey responses such as investment goals and risk tolerance, expectations, evaluations of performance and psychological traits, to *inferred data* such as preferences, demographic and psychographic descriptors, and behavioral tendencies inferred about the customer. We can also distinguish between *active disclosure*, where the customer knows they are sharing information about themselves, and *passive disclosure*, where the sharing happens incidentally without the customer's awareness. Complicating this distinction between active and passive disclosure is that even when customers sign up with service providers and agree to their terms of service, which typically provide details about what personal information will be collected and how it will be used, many of them fail to read or comprehend the dense description (Kim, 2017).

Accordingly, the customer transparency concept is nuanced on multiple levels. In a particular setting, the structure of customer transparency can be regulated, negotiated, or designed; it can be a resource or a feature; it can be interpreted from the standpoint of the seller, the platform, other customers, or the customer's standpoint; it can be deliberate, inadvertent, or completely unknown; and it can be a concession, attribute, activity, or antecedent in the analysis of a particular problem or issue. For instance, fair lending regulations require that US financial institutions make lending decisions without consideration of the applicant's race, gender, sexual orientation, or religion (among other defining characteristics). In such settings, observed or inferred data about customers along any of these defining characteristics cannot be used to score or assess them by the business, even if it is available.

In contrast, on two-sided platforms such as eBay and Airbnb, consumers have a fair degree of autonomy regarding how much of their personal information to share; the decision involves a trade-off between the benefits of disclosure, such as crafting a curated identity to impress transaction partners and generate desired outcomes, and its costs such as enduring racial or other forms of discrimination. Platforms can also embed designed disclosure constraints into their structure, dictating how much information customers can disclose and when. For instance, many platforms require their customers to identify themselves only by their first names and allow pseudonyms to give them anonymity.

While the affordance of anonymity is useful, from the customer's perspective, much like other forms of knowledge, understanding how much personal information they are disclosing and how sellers are using this information is often lacking or inaccurate. In other words, the same issues and dilemmas we saw in algorithmic transparency crop up for customer disclosure. During exchanges, where customers may deliberately and thoughtfully disclose certain information, a considerable amount may be inadvertent. Given the complexity of the nature of customer transparency, its implications play out in numerous consequential ways in business exchanges, from a greater likelihood of discrimination resulting from sharing one's racial, sexual, or gender identity on platforms to the likelihood of getting funded by telling compelling stories or even just "appearing trustworthy" (Duarte et al., 2012) on crowdfunding and peer-to-peer sites, and the counterintuitive beneficial effects of participating in shared medical appointments where customer transparency extends to peer disclosure. Next, we consider each of these research areas in further detail.

Racial Discrimination on Two-Sided Platforms

On Airbnb, short-term renters and hosts can provide personal information such as their name, a photograph, and a brief introduction. Although such transparency can be beneficial by humanizing a renter and reassuring potential hosts who may be nervous about letting strangers stay in their homes, it also has downsides. As one concrete example, research shows that disclosing one's racial identity on the Airbnb platform, inferred by the host through the renter's name, can lead to racial discrimination (Cui et al., 2020; Edelman et al., 2017). In one influential field experiment conducted on Airbnb by booking requests to approximately 6,400 rental listings, Edelman et al. (2017) found that when compared to booking requests from potential renters with distinctively white names like Anne Walsh and Brad Murphy, those with distinctively Black names like Tanisha Jackson and Tyrone Robinson were 16% less likely to be accepted (42% positive response versus 50%) even though every act of discrimination potentially cost the hosts between $65 and $100 in foregone revenue.

Furthermore, racial discrimination was widespread in the study; as the authors put it, "Our results are remarkably persistent. Both African American and white hosts discriminate against African American guests; both male and female hosts discriminate; both male and female African American guests are discriminated against. Effects persist both for hosts that offer an entire property and for hosts who share the property with guests. Discrimination persists among experienced hosts, including those with multiple properties and those with many reviews. Discrimination persists and is of similar magnitude in high- and low-priced units, in diverse and homogeneous neighborhoods" (p. 3).

Other studies have found that Airbnb hosts are also discriminated against, as measured by the average prices realized by minority hosts relative to white hosts (Kakar et al., 2018); women hosts earned an average of 12% less revenue, and Black hosts earned an average of 22% less revenue in a large multinational study (Törnberg, 2022). In other words, discouraging as it sounds, these studies show when there is disclosure, it prompts discrimination by virtually everyone using the disclosed information for decision making.

Encouragingly, a recent study by Cui et al. (2020) found that when a positive review is posted on their Airbnb profile page, the discrimination is reduced for potential renters. In their study, acceptance rates for white and black renters with at least one positive review were equivalent. Even negative reviews or ratings without evaluative content helped reduce the race-based acceptance difference. The implications of these findings for customer transparency in platform design are clear: managers may be best served by designing the platform for *less participant or customer transparency* as a whole and *more controlled and purposive transparency*, in particular, to achieve well-defined goals while still allowing participants the discretion to choose who to do business with (Fisman & Luca, 2016). The transparency principle articulated at the outset of this book needs to be dialed down.

There are many ways to moderate customer disclosure and encourage efficient and collegial transactions between renter and host. They may include concealing renter names and photographs until after the host confirms the booking, reducing the size of host photographs, and giving greater prominence to their experience and factual information about the rental. Additionally, renters and hosts could be encouraged to use pseudonyms instead of their real names, renters could be allowed to provide personal information about themselves beyond what they look like to things such as their hobbies and travel interests to reduce negative stereotyping, and members could be nudged by reminding them that they are subject to implicit biases. Hosts could be incentivized (or even mandated if there are complaints against them) to use the "Instant Book" feature whereby rental requests from any qualified renter is accepted automatically, and hosts and renters could be encouraged to post reviews after the stay. Note that in each of these examples, transparency is implemented in a controlled and purposive way to reduce discrimination, and the idea that "more transparency is better" is jettisoned.

The Benefits of Shared Medical Appointments

In the medical field, the concept of *shared medical appointments*, in which "patients receive one-on-one physician consultations in the presence of others with similar conditions" (Ramdas & Darzi, 2017), provides another intriguing setting to study a different form of *customer transparency*. Shared medical appointments have been used for various purposes, including patient education, physical exams, and treating chronic conditions requiring multiple visits. They are seen as a way to deliver medical care efficiently using available physician resources. Instead of affording complete privacy from a transparency perspective, the method employs *designed co-interaction*, resulting in the inadvertent disclosure of one's medical information to peers.

Recent research suggests that greater patient transparency in shared medical appointments has unexpected benefits. Beyond the obvious efficiency benefits from the physician providing the core, common information once to the group instead of repeating it to each patient, patients also feel more engaged in this setting, spending more time with the physician than they would in a one-to-one setting, sharing camaraderie and solidarity with peers and learning from the physician's interactions with them. Buell et al. (2021) conducted a randomized control trial with one thousand patients undergoing glaucoma treatment over three years at an Indian eye hospital and found that when they met with the physician in a group setting, the patients demonstrated greater engagement using a variety of behavioral measures like questions asked and answered, comments made, attentiveness, and head wobbling when compared to those who participated in one-on-one appointments. Clearly, the patient's loss of privacy was more than counterbalanced by the learning and camaraderie in this setting. An obvious open question is whether these beneficial effects of greater customer transparency are culture-specific (e.g., Indians may be socially and culturally accustomed to less privacy than other cultures; Larson and Medora [1992]) and whether they carry over to, say, the United States, where patient privacy is the holy grail of medical practice.

Effects of Customer Transparency on Crowdfunding and Peer-to-Peer Lending

Financially-oriented platforms where peers undertake economic exchanges offer powerful insights into the nuanced roles and double-edged nature of customer transparency. The purpose and parameters of the economic exchange vary depending on the platform. On crowdfunding platforms, the economic exchange relationship is that of creators and patrons: creators seek funding for commercial, social, or creative projects, and patrons may receive something tangible in exchange, such as a product, or donate money to support the creator. P2P lending platforms, in contrast, are alternatives to traditional investment vehicles. On them, individual borrowers seek funding from individual investors or lenders. By disintermediating financial institutions, exchange partners can receive better terms, a lower interest rate for the borrower, and a higher risk-adjusted return for the investor.

On both crowdfunding and P2P lending platforms, there is a significant tension between maintaining arm's length and recipient anonymity and providing sufficient relevant information about the recipient for givers to feel comfortable about making financial contributions. Some disclosure by the receiver is essential, but too much may cause significant harm. Furthermore, the validity of the disclosure itself adds a layer of uncertainty and complexity to the giver's decision making.

Research has found that when previously unacquainted consumers engage in economic exchanges such as borrowing and lending money, they need a way to engender trust; self-disclosure, for instance, by providing a coherent and seemingly authentic narrative about themselves is one way to do so (Sonenshein et al., 2011). On Prosper.com, for example, a natural thing for most borrowers to do in their loan listing was to explain why they need the money, along with making claims about their identities. Herzenstein et al. (2011) studied the effects of such disclosure on borrowers' ability to receive funding and repay the borrowed money two years later.

They uncovered six different identity claims in borrowers' self-disclosures concerning their economic exchange relationship: trustworthy, successful, hardworking, economic hardship, moral, and religious. For instance, a trustworthy identity claim meant that the borrower's narrative centered around conveying that the lenders could trust the borrower to pay back the money on time. In contrast, the successful identity claim forwarded the narrative that the borrower is someone with a successful business, job, or career. The authors found that both the number and content of identity claims disclosed in the narratives of borrowers on Pro sper.com affected the lending decisions of borrowers. When borrowers disclosed more information about themselves by including more identity claims in their narrative, the loan funding, defined as the percentage of the requested amount given by lenders, went up. The content of the disclosure also mattered. Borrowers who disclosed narratives around their identities as being trustworthy or successful were associated with increased loan funding relative to those who composed and conveyed other identities like being moral or suffering economic hardship. Interestingly, later on, these borrowers were less likely to pay, suggesting that, unlike strategic herding, borrowers' narratives were inauthentic and constructed opportunistically, leading to adverse influence on lenders.

Summary. These three examples of consumer disclosure settings underscore the key point surfacing throughout this chapter, that transparency involving the acquisition of private consumer information, on the one hand, and its use in algorithms, on the other hand, is rarely amenable to simplification or idealization or generalization. Rarely is it the case in applications of algorithmic transparency and consumer disclosure that transparency can be defined clearly, provisions made to fully manage disclosure or its results, or entirely meaningful explanations and understanding can be generated. The key task, and accordingly, the highest-value scholarly contributions to the present and in the future, may lie mainly in identifying, explaining, and negotiating the boundaries of reasonable disclosure, and finding unique, deliberately formulated, and mutually considered solutions that are highly contextualized, resistant to extrapolation or generalization.

References

Aguirre, E., Roggeveen, A. L., Grewal, D., & Wetzels, M. (2016). The personalization-privacy paradox: Implications for new media. *Journal of Consumer Marketing, 33*(2), 98–110.

Ananny, M., & Crawford, K. (2018). Seeing without knowing: Limitations of the transparency ideal and its application to algorithmic accountability. *New Media & Society, 20*(3), 973–989.

Arora, N., Dreze, X., Ghose, A., Hess, J. D., Iyengar, R., Jing, B., Joshi, Y., Kumar, V., Lurie, N., Neslin, S., & Sajeesh, S. (2008). Putting one-to-one marketing to work: Personalization, customization, and choice. *Marketing Letters, 19*(3), 305–321.

Arrieta, A. B., Díaz-Rodríguez, N., Del Ser, J., Bennetot, A., Tabik, S., Barbado, A., García, S., Gil-López, S., Molina, D., Benjamins, R., & Chatila, R. (2020). Explainable artificial intelligence (XAI): Concepts, taxonomies, opportunities and challenges toward responsible AI. *Information Fusion, 58*, 82–115.

Bertrand, M., & Mullainathan, S. (2004). Are Emily and Greg more employable than Lakisha and Jamal? A field experiment on labor market discrimination. *American Economic Review, 94*(4), 991–1013.

Buell, R. W., Ramdas, K., & Sonmez, N. (2021). *Can shared service delivery increase customer engagement? A study of shared medical appointments* (Harvard Business School Technology & Operations Management Unit Working Paper, 21-001).

Burrell, J. (2016). How the machine 'thinks': Understanding opacity in machine learning algorithms. *Big Data & Society, 3*(1), 1–16.

Commerford, B. P., Dennis, S. A., Joe, J. R., & Ulla, J. W. (2022). Man versus machine: Complex estimates and auditor reliance on artificial intelligence. *Journal of Accounting Research, 60*(1), 171–201.
Creel, K. A. (2020). Transparency in complex computational systems. *Philosophy of Science, 87*(4), 568–589.
Cui, R., Li, J., & Zhang, D. J. (2020). Reducing discrimination with reviews in the sharing economy: Evidence from field experiments on Airbnb. *Management Science, 66*(3), 1071–1094.
Day, G. S. (1999). *The market driven organization: Understanding, attracting, and keeping valuable customers.* The Free Press.
Dholakia, U. M. (2022). *Advanced introduction to digital marketing.* Edward Elgar.
Diakopoulos, N. (2020). Transparency. In M. Dubber, F. Pasquale, & S. Das (Eds.), *The Oxford handbook of ethics of AI.* Oxford University Press.
Duarte, J., Siegel, S., & Young, L. (2012). Trust and credit: The role of appearance in peer-to-peer lending. *Review of Financial Studies, 25*(8), 2455–2484.
Duhigg, C. (2012, February 16). How companies learn your secrets. *New York Times.* https://www.nytimes.com/2012/02/19/magazine/shopping-habits.html
Edelman, D. C., & Abraham, M. (2022). Customer experience in the age of AI. *Harvard Business Review.* https://hbr.org/2022/03/customer-experience-in-the-age-of-ai
Edelman, B., Luca, M., & Svirsky, D. (2017). Racial discrimination in the sharing economy: Evidence from a field experiment. *American Economic Journal: Applied Economics, 9*(2), 1–22.
Edwards, L., & Veale, M. (2017). Slave to the algorithm? Why a 'right to an explanation' is probably not the remedy you are looking for. *Duke Law & Technology Review, 16,* 18–84.
Edwards, L., & Veale, M. (2018). Enslaving the algorithm: From a "Right to an explanation" to a "Right to better decisions"? *IEEE Security & Privacy, 16*(3), 46–54.
Fisman, R., & Luca, M. (2016). Fixing discrimination in online marketplaces. *Harvard Business Review, 94*(12), 88–95.
Foss-Solbrekk, K. (2021). Three routes to protecting AI systems and their algorithms under IP law: The good, the bad and the ugly. *Journal of Intellectual Property Law & Practice, 16*(3), 247–258.
Gillespie, T. (2014). The relevance of algorithms. *Media Technologies: Essays on Communication, Materiality, and Society, 167,* 167–194.
Gillespie, T. (2020). Content moderation, AI, and the question of scale. *Big Data & Society, 7*(2), 1–5.

Goldin, C., & Rouse, C. (2000). Orchestrating impartiality: The impact of "blind" auditions on female musicians. *American Economic Review, 90*(4), 715–741.

Gorwa, R., Binns, R., & Katzenbach, C. (2020). Algorithmic content moderation: Technical and political challenges in the automation of platform governance. *Big Data & Society, 7*(1), 1–15.

Goodman, B., & Flaxman, S. (2017). European Union regulations on algorithmic decision-making and a "right to explanation." *AI Magazine, 38*(3), 50–57.

Guidotti, R., Monreale, A., Ruggieri, S., Turini, F., Giannotti, F., & Pedreschi, D. (2018). A survey of methods for explaining black box models. *ACM Computing Surveys, 51*(5), 1–42.

Green, B., & Viljoen, S. (2020). Algorithmic realism: Expanding the boundaries of algorithmic thought. In *Proceedings of the 2020 Conference on Fairness, Accountability, and Transparency* (pp. 19–31).

Heald, D. (2006). Varieties of transparency. *Proceedings of the British Academy, 135*, 25–43.

Herzenstein, M., Sonenshein, S., & Dholakia, U. M. (2011). Tell me a good story and I may lend you money: The role of narratives in peer-to-peer lending decisions. *Journal of Marketing Research, 48*(SPL), S138–S149.

Holland, S., Hosny, A., Newman, S., Joseph, J., & Chmielinski, K. (2018). *The dataset nutrition label: A framework to drive higher data quality standards.* arXiv preprint arXiv:1805.03677

John, L. K., Loewenstein, G., & Prelec, D. (2012). Measuring the prevalence of questionable research practices with incentives for truth telling. *Psychological Science, 23*(5), 524–532.

Kakar, V., Voelz, J., Wu, J., & Franco, J. (2018). The visible host: Does race guide Airbnb rental rates in San Francisco? *Journal of Housing Economics, 40*, 25–40.

Kim, N. S. (2017). Relative consent and contract law. *Nevada Law Journal, 18*, 165–219.

Kovatch, S. (2022, October 28). *5 takeaways from our investigation into RealPage's rent-setting algorithm.* ProPublica. https://www.propublica.org/article/why-rent-is-so-high

Larson, J. H., & Medora, N. (1992). Privacy preferences: A cross-cultural comparison of Americans and Asian Indians. *International Journal of Sociology of the Family*, 55–66.

Lewandowsky, S., & Kozyreva, A. (2022, March). *Algorithms, lies, and social media.* OpenMind. https://www.openmindmag.org/articles/algorithms-lies-and-social-media

Martin, K. E. (2012). Diminished or just different? A factorial vignette study of privacy as a social contract. *Journal of Business Ethics, 111*(4), 519–539.

Meijer, A. (2014). Transparency. In *The Oxford handbook of public accountability* (pp. 507–524). Oxford University Press.

Mijares Torres, M. P., & Marte, J. (2022, August 10). The snowballing US rental crisis is sparing nowhere and no one. Bloomberg. https://www.bloomberg.com/news/features/2022-08-10/us-rental-housing-crisis-spirals-on-inflation-pressure-pandemic-migration?sref=d3S20v77

Pasquale, F. (2015). *The black box society: The secret algorithms that control money and information.* Harvard University Press.

Rai, A. (2020). Explainable AI: From black box to glass box. *Journal of the Academy of Marketing Science, 48,* 137–141.

Ramdas, K., & Darzi, A. (2017). Adopting innovations in care delivery—The case of shared medical appointments. *New England Journal of Medicine, 376*(12), 1105–1107.

Ribeiro, M. T., Singh, S., & Guestrin, C. (2016). Why should I trust you? Explaining the predictions of any classifier. *Proceedings of the 22nd ACM SIGKDD International Conference on Knowledge Discovery and Data Mining,* 1135–1144.

Seele, P., Dierksmeier, C., Hofstetter, R., & Schultz, M. D. (2021). Mapping the ethicality of algorithmic pricing: A review of dynamic and personalized pricing. *Journal of Business Ethics, 170,* 697–719.

Smith, E., & Vogell, H. (2022, March 29). How your shadow credit score could decide whether you get an apartment. ProPublica. Available online at: https://www.propublica.org/article/how-your-shadow-credit-score-could-decide-whether-you-get-an-apartment

Sonenshein, S., Herzenstein, M., & Dholakia, U. M. (2011). How accounts shape lending decisions through fostering perceived trustworthiness. *Organizational Behavior and Human Decision Processes, 115*(1), 69–84.

Törnberg, P. (2022). How sharing is the "sharing economy"? Evidence from 97 Airbnb markets. *Plos One, 17*(4). https://doi.org/10.1371/journal.pone.0266998.

Vanderbilt, T. (2016). *You may also like: Taste in an age of endless choice.* Alfred A. Knopf.

Vogell, H. (2022, October 15). Rent going up? One company's algorithm could be why. ProPublica. https://www.propublica.org/article/yieldstar-rent-increase-realpage-rent

Wind, J., & Rangaswamy, A. (2001). Customerization: The next revolution in mass customization. *Journal of Interactive Marketing, 15*(1), 13–32.

CHAPTER 7

An Integrative Perspective on Business Transparency

Abstract This chapter develops and presents an integrative framework of business transparency that actively seeks to build bridges across the business disciplines by identifying six common forms of transparency transcending disciplines, and parsing the information contained in the disclosure into its component characteristics that either facilitate or hinder understanding. On the basis of this theoretical development, a revised definition of business transparency is presented that expands its scope significantly by considering outcomes of mutual benefit, re-conceptualizing business transparency in a more balanced, interdisciplinary, versatile and integrative way than current definitions. Maximizing principles are dropped in favor of empathetic and satisficing mechanisms of disclosure.

Keywords Transparency · Disclosure · Information · Privacy · Comprehension · Understanding

> Today, power is gained by sharing knowledge, not hoarding it.—Dharmesh Shah.

Throughout this book, we have covered extensive ground by studying and drawing connections between the scholarly perspectives and the research findings on transparency in different business disciplines. One

© The Author(s), under exclusive license to Springer Nature Switzerland AG 2023
U. Dholakia, *Transparency in Business*,
https://doi.org/10.1007/978-3-031-12145-6_7

tension has recurred throughout these investigations: The conflict between the unalloyed positive narrative embedded in *the transparency principle*, which is the idea that more transparency is better because it makes business more accountable, efficient, and equitable, and glimpses of transparency's dark side, spotlighted in negative consequences such as exploitation by the discloser by using the disclosure strategically to persuade or mislead receivers, or conversely, exploitation of the disclosed information by the receiver and their resultant increased dyadic power, as the case may be. In business, transparency seems to exploit and cause harm to those involved almost as often as it benefits and enriches them.

On the whole, then, is transparency good or bad? How can we reconcile the fundamental inconsistency that seems to crop up when transparency is invoked? A significant goal of this final chapter is to try and answer these questions by providing a framework to think about these questions in *any* business setting. The answers may partly lie in a key insight we have encountered time and again throughout this book: *What is done with the disclosed information and by whom matters, and along with contextual details, dictates the meaning and outcomes of transparency*. It is the disposal of the disclosed information, a consideration of its effects on those involved, and the setting in which these processes occur that determine whether the net effects of transparency will be positive or negative and whether the discloser and the receiver will both benefit, only one of them will benefit, or whether one party will be rewarded at the other's expense. An important corollary to this point is that business transparency has several distinct forms that transcend business disciplines, and these forms affect the processes and net effects across business contexts.

Recall that in Chapter 1, after reviewing a selection of definitions of transparency from various business disciplines, we formulated an omnibus definition of transparency in Table 1.1 as "the degree to which valuable information is deliberately disclosed or made available through an uncovering process to relevant receivers to achieve a specific purpose." But now, given the recurrent contradiction of positive versus negative consequences, the incompleteness of this definition should be apparent to the reader. While it focuses on the information in the disclosure, the definition fails to consider what is done with the information and by whom in sufficient detail. Consequently, the omnibus definition conflates real transparency with the illusion of transparency and cannot distinguish between the two. To remedy this shortcoming, we will also set about the ambitious task of expanding the omnibus definition and re-conceptualizing business transparency in a more balanced, interdisciplinary, versatile, and integrative way in this chapter.

An Integrative Conceptual Framework of Business Transparency

The framework presented in Fig. 7.1 attempts to do this by making four claims. First, it distinguishes between two roles, the *discloser* and the *receiver*, conceiving each one as a volitional entity with certain affordances, constraints, abilities, and objectives; the information is provided by the discloser and is obtained and typically used by the receiver. Second, the framework identifies six meaningful forms of business transparency, each having certain configurations and structural features that generalize across disciplines and settings and govern the roles of the discloser and receiver and interactions between them. Third, the framework highlights the role of disclosure as information and elaborates on its properties that generate (or lessen) its value, individually or collectively. Fourth, the framework establishes the primary objective of transparency as *a striving towards generating understanding from the disclosure*, whether comprised of individual or joint effort, coordinated or discordant, mutually beneficial or a zero-sum game.

The entities playing the discloser and receiver roles depend on the transparency application and will vary across different applications. For example, in a customer relationship where the business wants access to personal information to deliver customized offerings, the discloser is typically the customer while the receiver is the business; in contrast, when prices or information about the supply chain are shared to close the sale or to engender trust, the discloser is the business while the receiver is the customer. The roles are specific to each disclosure; in multi-dimensional disclosures, the customer could be the discloser in some disclosures and concurrently play the receiver's role in other disclosures with the company. A further nuance is that many transparency applications entail *two-sided awareness*, marked by heightened awareness of each party by the other, which can affect their behaviors (Bernstein, 2017).

Furthermore, the discloser is most concerned with or affected by the issues of what is disclosed, why, and how, while the receiver is concerned with or affected most by the characteristics of the disclosed information

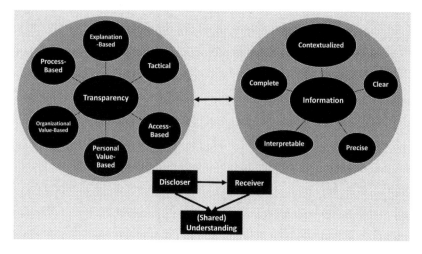

Fig. 7.1 An integrative framework of business transparency

that facilitate its sensemaking and use. To better understand business transparency, we need to understand the nature of the disclosed information, the mechanisms by which it is chosen, generated, and utilized, and the effects of these processes. As shown in Fig. 7.1, the integrative framework of business transparency parses the information contained in the disclosure into five component characteristics that facilitate or hinder *understanding*: clarity, precision, interpretation, completeness, and contextualization, which will be explored in greater detail.

The Six Forms of Business Transparency

The six forms of transparency shown in Fig. 7.1 need further explication. Given its diverse interpretations and the contexts encountered throughout this book, it is remarkable that six common forms emerged repeatedly. For instance, *process-based transparency* cropped up in research on operations, pricing strategy, and using algorithms. In each case, analyzing transparency entailed understanding the underlying process starting with the manager's objectives in deciding what information to disclose, where to find it, how to validate it, and how to share it with the receiver. In addition to process-based transparency, five other forms emerged throughout the book and are captured in the integrative framework: explanation-based, tactical, access-based, personal value-based, and organizational value-based. Thus, the integrative framework of business transparency locates these six broadly applicable and versatile forms of business transparency and the five characteristics of the disclosed information as core concepts in its analysis.

Together, in their interactions with the disclosure and the received information, the discloser and the receiver move toward deriving an understanding of value to them. Importantly, the self-serving, strategic, and limiting aspects embedded in the constructs shown in the framework can undermine shared or even unitary understanding, whereas their negotiated, altruistic, and virtuous underpinnings provide the impetus to support individual or mutual understanding. Thus, the proposed framework can accommodate a range of potential effects of business transparency and explain the reasons behind them. These ideas and the concepts in Fig. 7.1 are now developed in greater detail, after which a revised expanded definition of business transparency is presented at the chapter's and the book's conclusion. We begin with a consideration of the six forms of transparency included in the framework.

Explanation-Based Transparency

In many business applications, transparency hinges on providing a sufficient and meaningful explanation for the disclosure or the observation process. An employee might ask their employer, "Why are you monitoring me?" and "What aspects of my behavior are you tracking?" A customer might ask a brand, "What personal information about me do you know, and how are you storing and using this data?" or "How exactly did the algorithm you used calculate my credit score?" In these instances, and many others, the discloser is affected significantly by how the information they have disclosed is processed, transformed, and utilized by the receiver; furthermore, they may have access to the outcomes of the observation process (a reprimand or accolades, a targeted promotional offer, and the credit score, respectively) but may not be privy to the specific inputs of observation, the intermediate steps used to convert them into outputs, or even the logic behind the disclosure.

To elicit cooperation, continue the relationship, and maintain one's reputation, the receiver must provide an explanation to the discloser. The lack of an explanation or an explanation deemed inadequate or specious may not only adversely affect perceptions about the receiver but also negatively impact the desired outcomes and the viability of the application. For example, when complex predictive models using machine learning are used to diagnose medical conditions without an adequate explanation for how the model came up with the diagnosis, both physicians and patients are more likely to distrust the software's recommendations and reject them even when they have proven to be effective in the past (Miotto et al., 2018).

We might say that explanation-based transparency is *two-way transparency* in the sense that disclosed information flows to the receiver, and an explanation for the disclosure flows to the discloser, which has the potential to enhance the discloser's understanding of the reasons behind the disclosure and how it is being used by the receiver, consequently increasing dyadic trust. Additionally, the process of constructing the explanation itself may be useful to the receiver if it sheds light on the potential fragility or unforeseen effects embedded in the mechanism by which the disclosure is processed and utilized and suggests ways of improving it (e.g., by using less intrusive observation methods or more explainable predictive models) to provide mutual benefits.

In many business applications, explanation-based transparency also has an important *feasibility component* that has to do with the degree to which an explanation is feasible. The field of explainable AI, covered in Chapter 6, is a case in point. Even though the receiver may wish to provide an explanation that makes sense to the discloser and other entities, it is not feasible to do so. The method of converting the disclosed information into the output may be reliant on black box methods that are incomprehensible even to the receiver, and as such, explanation-based transparency may hit the ceiling. The key point is that explanations provide a conduit to enhancing understanding and are a powerful and broadly applicable way of enhancing the net benefits in transparency applications.

Tactical Transparency

In contrast, there is also economical and reputational value in tactically withholding information from external entities such as customers, competitors, or suppliers or disclosing information deliberately and measuredly. The primary reason for this is pragmatic: Sharing proprietary information can diminish the power, and the receiver's understanding comes at the expense of the discloser, or vice versa. In many B2B industries and in luxury real estate and art sales, for example, prices are withheld until the seller has ascertained a prospect's purchase intent and wherewithal. Managers often view withholding prices as an essential competitive advantage and a powerful way to maintain pricing power (Baker et al., 2010; Dholakia, 2017; Maxwell, 2015). Similarly, in providing complex services with a significant back-office or technology component, the processes by which the service is produced are often opaque to customers and keeping customers in the dark about "how the sausage gets made" supports relationship maintenance (Bruni, 2005).

Withholding information is a matter of both degree and perception. Companies use this idea to craft tactics based on sharing seemingly or authentically significant, even proprietary, information and making a big deal of it. Thus, a unique and practically important form of business transparency lies in its tactical role in crafting and executing programs or activities directed toward customers, suppliers, investors, or another targeted audience to achieve one or more specific business objectives. In this form, transparency is about using disclosure in a deliberate, controlled, and limited way to devise and execute effective tactical programs.

Consider the following experiment by US grocery delivery service Instacart during widespread stockouts of popular items in grocery stores during the COVID-19 pandemic (Knight & Mitrofanov, 2022). The company added a "Likely out of stock" label to the description of items on its ordering platform that it estimated had low probabilities of being in stock. Furthermore, instead of simply adding these items to their baskets, customers had to "Request" the item, and when they did so, they were given the option of selecting replacement items if that item was not available. The researchers found that compared with a control condition, sharing this additional information about inventory levels and potential stockouts with customers led to a decrease in the number of items purchased (and replaced) on that shopping occasion, but it also led to an increase in total revenue earned and order frequency over six months. In a nutshell, disclosing the possibility of stockouts and getting customers to consider other options actively benefited both customers and the company.

Telling customers that an item is on sale only for the next two days is a form of disclosure as is providing them with precise information about labor costs to make a particular garment. We focused on tactical transparency mostly in the domain of service operations in Chapter 2 and price offers in Chapter 3, but as the Instacart example shows, the idea of selective disclosure is also applicable to other business tactics. Some examples of non-price-based tactical transparency include using devices and programs to engender perceptions of authenticity for the brand or the organization (Puzakova, Kwak, & Bell, 2015), providing information about ingredients, manufacturing processes, and so on, involving frontline employees to convey sincerity and engender stakeholder engagement (Cinelli & LeBoeuf, 2020; Ikonen et al., 2020; Sirianni et al., 2013), and selective disclosure by salespeople to engender trust in B2B negotiations (Boyer & Jap, 2022). Thus, we can think of tactical transparency as the execution of a defined campaign with performance metrics chosen beforehand based on a target audience and the judicious selection of a point on a continuum between complete secrecy (no information is shared) and full disclosure (all information about the issue is openly shared).

Access-Based Transparency

As mentioned earlier, secrecy is warranted in many business settings for the organization's financial success and sustainability (Dufresne & Offstein, 2008). For instance, proprietary algorithms drive search engines like Google, recommendations on news sites like New York Times, and social media platforms like TikTok (Smith, 2022), many of which "are often ineliminably opaque, to the detriment of our ability to give scientific explanations and detect artifacts" (Creel, 2020, p. 568). Even without this "ineliminable opacity" in technology companies, there are pragmatic reasons for secrecy. Whether companies sell drugs, specialty chemicals, enterprise software, or even a delicious soft drink or food product, unique ingredients, manufacturing methods, assembly processes, or recipes may confer differentiation and competitive advantage for the company. In an organizational context, when secrecy is orchestrated carefully, it can enhance the power of relatively low-power employees and increase receptivity to their proposed strategic initiatives (Toegel et al., 2022). There is a reason for this "real secrecy," which is to establish a barrier between proprietary information and unauthorized access by potential legitimate or illicit entities, to maintain this advantage (Albu, 2022; Pasquale, 2015).

However, the degree of access can also be used as a strategic business tool. Nowhere is this aspect of transparency more prominent than in sellers' selective and controlled access to prices. By and large, restricting access to prices has several significant benefits to sellers, with corresponding adverse effects on buyers by making it more difficult to use information about prices effectively in buying decisions (Dholakia, 2022). First, in many B2B settings, prices are seen as a source of competitive advantage by the seller and withholding them is seen as a way to maintain the upper hand in customer negotiations (Pauly & Burns, 2008). Second, hiding prices also hides the seller's logical flaws, inconsistencies, and inefficient practices that prices could reveal. As described in the preface and Chapter 3, US hospitals are notorious for obfuscating price information, to the point that many violate federal law requiring them to reveal prices online (Kliff & Katz, 2021; Levenson, 2022).

Third, making prices hard to find can increase the customer's zest for the product. Many luxury products, such as fashion labels and upscale art galleries, require interested buyers to call or reach out to learn prices, and fine dining restaurants sometimes use menus without prices, all to increase intrigue, generate an aura of exclusivity and high status (Dholakia, 2022), and perhaps even to raise the customer's commitment to the item by making them overtly ask for the price (Staw, 1997). Relatedly, not revealing prices could provide an avenue for the seller to learn how much potential customers value the product and show their willingness to pay (Clarke, 2018).

In some settings, the outlined benefits of lower access can be additive, making a strong case for withholding prices for as long and as much as possible. Consistent with previous discussions, in many settings and through different mechanisms, regulating access has the potential to benefit the business and shift the balance of power in its favor, concurrently harming its counterparties and constituents such as customers, suppliers, and workers.

The opposite can also be true. In product management situations, providing selected customers with substantial access to the company's inner workings and even having them participate in the product development process can pay off. As one example, Lego actively sought out, engaged, and provided access to proprietary company information to adult Lego enthusiasts and leaders of their user community called the Lego User Group. Eventually, these collaborations with customers led to developing innovative and popular products like the Lego Mindstorms NXT and the Lego Modular Buildings series (Antorini et al., 2012).

In this case, the chosen customers had significant access to proprietary information.

As should be clear from this discussion, there is some overlap between tactical transparency and access-based transparency in the sense that both have to do with withholding or disclosing information in a calibrated, goal-directed way. The core difference is that tactical transparency hinges on achieving specific narrowly defined business objectives, whereas access-based transparency is about pursuing strategic objectives with abstract, broader goals. Further research is needed to build theory around further delineating and explaining these two forms of business transparency.

Process-Based Transparency

Even though some discussions of business transparency treat it as a binary concept (e.g., CEO X was fired because he refused to be transparent, or Brand X owes its success to its radical transparency), in most applications it is worth considering transparency as a matter of degree on a continuum. Furthermore, instead of a monolithic characterization, the process by which transparency is pursued and achieved and the mechanism by which the deliberate disclosure or uncovering of information occurs provide more insight into its modulation and effects. Two examples are used here to illustrate the value of the process-based form of transparency.

First, in considering algorithmic transparency in a fine-grained way, Creel (2020) argues for distinguishing between three sequential and independent forms of transparency that explicate the process by which algorithms are constructed and implemented in business applications, *functional transparency*, which is about understanding the high-level, logical rules that are encoded in the algorithm to transform a given set of inputs into outputs (implying that the algorithms are constructed and understood by humans as opposed to artificial intelligence), *structural transparency*, which involves understanding how the algorithm is realized in code (i.e., how the code executes the algorithm typically by understanding the modular steps through which the algorithm is run), and *run transparency*, which refers to the receiver understanding the actual running of the program on a specific occasion, including understanding the hardware and input data that were used to derive the results so as to isolate unexpected effects caused from a particular hardware setup or a dataset.

These three forms of transparency are complementary, but they refer to different levels of abstraction and are, therefore, "dissociable," according to Creel (2020), in the sense that one form of transparency can occur without requiring the others. It should be clear from this brief discussion that considering transparency at different stages and levels of abstraction in the process of using algorithms gives greater insight into the feasibility issue as well, that is, to what degree understanding can be realized by those involved.

Second, in studying supply chains, disaggregating and carefully studying each step of the process by which ingredients or raw materials are sourced, then processed into components, and ultimately utilized in the manufacturing process, followed by the distribution channels to get the products and associated value-added services to the buyers and final users is valuable. As discussed in Chapter 2, transparency means different things and raises challenges and issues depending on the stage of the process. In the upstream stages, traceability issues, such as ascertaining the origins of the raw materials, the methods used in their extraction or creation, the welfare of the labor force involved in their extraction, and so on, are important (Astill et al., 2019). In the middle, concerns about visibility, which is getting relevant disclosures about the upstream supply chain to the appropriate personnel within the organization and supply chain partners, are significant. Finally, downstream transparency is concerned with managing post-purchase disclosure issues and synchronizing delivered services with customer expectations and behaviors in their consumption journeys becomes paramount (Shankar & Canniford, 2016). Each stage of the business process surfaces specific challenges associated with seeking, managing, and validating disclosures and involves different organizational partners. Without using a process orientation to understand transparency within a supply chain, key challenges would be conflated and remain unattended.

Personal Value-Based Transparency

The idea that transparency is implicated as a personal terminal value of business leaders and workers and affects business conduct by providing ethical direction is powerful; it has shaped scholarly thinking in different business areas. In Chapter 5, we reviewed authentic leadership research where the personal value-based conceptualization of transparency is central and has been deeply explored. In a nutshell, the business leadership perspective views transparency to be a constellation of virtuous traits possessed by managers that have to do with honest, unflinching introspection, and equally candid and authentic external presentation as manifested in the leader's talk and actions that involve sharing one's vulnerabilities, explaining one's motivations, attitudes, and feelings, and taking decisive actions based on one's beliefs and convictions, all of which are grounded in possessing transparency as a terminal, personal value. Simply put, embracing transparency as a value means being honest and behaving honestly no matter the short-term (or even long-term) costs to oneself and one's organization.

Interestingly, while much of the leadership research has focused on senior managers with authority, like CEOs and company founders, the theory behind personal value-based transparency is quite general because of its significant overlap with the individual bases of ethical conduct (e.g., Reidenbach & Robin, 1990). The findings of this literature can just as easily be extrapolated to rank-and-file workers in their day-to-day work activities as they can be extended to life domains outside work. Although current applications are scarce, there is also considerable potential to apply the precepts and the findings behind personal value-based transparency to practical dilemmas within business disciplines so as to harness the promise of the integrative framework presented here.

For instance, marketing managers face the challenge of choosing what is right versus what is profitable in many decisions (George, 2015; Schlegelmilch & Öberseder, 2010). Should we apologize to customers for poor service and refund their money or refuse to acknowledge that we made mistakes? Should we self-censor and conform to our customers' populist attitudes (even when we disagree), or should we be honest and express our real beliefs even if it means arousing the ire of customers and losing their business? Should we be candid about the limitations of our brands and products, or should we create an entirely positive but false narrative through our branding strategies? Should we seek endorsements from influential celebrities that will boost our sales even though we find their ideological stances repugnant? In answering questions such as these, personal value-based transparency has rarely been invoked in marketing scholarship; but clearly, the same precepts that support authentic leadership will provide direction in untangling these dilemmas and merit elaboration and research attention (e.g., Nunes et al., 2021).

Organizational Value-Based Transparency

In its final form included in the present integrative framework, transparency is conceptualized as a group-level construct reflecting a "we've nothing to hide" culture of open information sharing that is marked by a set of formally and informally used practices within an organization that support access, observation, and lateral and hierarchical candor among employees so as to "transcend bureaucracy with openness" (Turco, 2016, p. 8). Chapter 4 has extensively covered the positive aspects of organizational value-based transparency.

However, four negative aspects are described here to provide an overall balanced perspective to the reader. First, in hierarchical work relationships such as those between subordinates and supervisors, the idealistic notion of open information sharing can easily metamorphose into an oppressive mode of surveillance, defined as "monitoring people in order to regulate or govern their behavior" (Gilliom & Monahan, 2013, p. 2), and its attendant loss of privacy and the potential for exploitation. A significant body of research has shown that surveillance tools and processes in organizational settings can modify the behavior of those who are observed in ways that cause individual and organizational harm (Anteby & Chan, 2018; Bernstein, 2017; Sewell & Barker, 2006). Furthermore, Albu and Flyverbom (2019) point out that when transparency projects are implemented within organizations, conflicts and tensions can arise naturally from the prevailing social dynamics and the conflicting ideologies and goals of those involved. Identifying and understanding the boundaries where supportive processes of observation, sharing, and mentoring change into oppressive forms of control and coercion within organizations is an important open research question.

Second, organizational transparency often implies access to everyone, including senior executives and leaders, a perceived flattening of organizational structures, and innovative governance methods like *holacracy* that shift decision making from executives to fluid, self-organized employee teams (Bernstein et al., 2016). While flat structures can benefit the job performance of rank-and-file employees (Ivancevich & Donnelly, 1975), they also reduce authority and make it difficult for key decision makers to communicate clearly, act decisively, and make tough decisions. As Turco (2016) explains, "the lack of "clear messaging from the top" was basically inherent in this organization given its commitment to voice rights. In a space so thick with open dialogue, where hundreds of voices might chime in on the wiki on any given issue, it was challenging to arrive at consensus" (p. 86). This downside of organizational transparency is particularly significant to understand, as more startups and technology companies enthusiastically adopt conversational firm practices, while case-based evidence from companies like Zappos and Medium suggests that such adoption hasn't been sustainable (Bernstein et al., 2016).

Third, the forces of digitization and digitalization that have accelerated intra-organizational sharing of information in speed and scope and fostered greater organizational transparency have also made the asymmetric downsides of organizational transparency starker and multifaceted. As workers have become more connected, more easily accessible, and more "behaviorally visible" (Leonardi & Treem, 2020), the line between work and leisure has blurred or disappeared completely for many. Working for an organization with a transparent culture has often entailed being constantly on call and expected to provide input into every issue even when it falls outside the domain of the worker's expertise (Kelly & Moen, 2020), which contributes to stress and reduces productivity (Newport, 2016).

Fourth, organizational transparency is positively related to a number of dark-side variables that hurt workers and the organization as a whole. In an extensive review of the extant research, Bernstein (2017) points out that, not surprisingly, increases in organizational transparency are associated with increases in impression management, posturing, pandering, and political correctness by workers observed across all levels of the organization. What's more, instead of encouraging contrarian candor and honest opinions, people in organizations that purport to be transparent tend to present opinions that reinforce the majority's views by "increasing compliance through a form of self-discipline" (Bernstein, 2017, p. 42). All of this is to underscore the main point of this chapter that organization value-based transparency is neither a panacea nor a poison; its net effects are highly contingent on a variety of situational factors that should be the main focus of attention.

THE CHARACTERISTICS OF DISCLOSED INFORMATION

In the integrative framework presented in Fig. 7.1, the nature of the disclosed information lies at the core of the analysis of business transparency. It facilitates or hinders the understanding of disclosers and receivers in the sense that five information characteristics—clarity, precision, completeness, interpretation, and contextualization, contribute to whether the net effects of transparency for the involved parties turn out to be positive or negative.

In this section, we will examine these informational properties in more detail by considering specific examples from the research on price transparency. These examples illustrate how sellers can regulate the information about prices beyond availability to change the customers' degree of understanding of prices and affect their use in decision making. The main point is that moving beyond simple availability, it is the nature of the information contained in the available prices and the process by which the information is made available that dictates how the effects of price transparency play out.

Clarity

Clarity refers to how simple and coherent the disclosed information is to its users. A list of all the ingredients in a packaged food item printed on a nutritional label with their weights and calories has a high degree of clarity; in contrast, the ratings of different aspects of service in a fast-food restaurant using a scale of five or seven stars have relatively low clarity. In this latter case, the user must work out the correspondence between the number of stars and the level of quality of relatively abstract service features in a personally meaningful and usable way.

As standalone information, individual prices tend to be high in clarity when they are quoted as amounts (e.g., $3.99 for a dozen eggs). However, marketers can use numerous methods to reduce the clarity of prices, for example, by providing additional information that is vague or extraneous and makes the consumer's decision task more difficult (e.g., the eggs are "natural and barn-raised") or making them work out the final price instead of giving it directly (e.g., the regular price of eggs is $4.99, today's price is discounted 20%). In settings like grocery stores or online retailers, where shoppers may encounter dozens or even hundreds of prices during a single shopping journey, such manipulations of presentation that affect price clarity can add up to significant differences in the level of effort shoppers have to make in understanding prices, and their eventual decisions and experience (Dholakia, 2019).

Precision

In business transparency, precision refers to the level of detail of the disclosed information. As a simple example, stating that a particular vendor is paying fair wages to its workers is less precise than saying that it pays its workers an average of $11 per hour and its lowest wages are $7.50 per hour. Similarly, a narrow salary range (or even a single value) in a job posting is more precise than a wide price range. In the pricing domain, marketers can use price precision to create specific perceptions and generate desired consumer responses.

To give one famous example, a house may be listed for sale at $395,000 (a less precise price) or $395,425 (a more precise price). In a study of listed homes for sale in New York and Florida, Thomas et al. (2010) found that using more precise prices in listings resulted in an increase of 0.6% in the final sale price. In other settings, a large body of research has found that employing specific price endings can be used as a high price precision strategy to communicate a certain image about an offering. For instance, prices that end in 9 are often associated with "good value" and "low price," whereas a price that ends in 4 or 6 is considered to be a non-standard price ending and generates perceptions that "this seller sells unique products" and "this seller has set prices thoughtfully" (Dholakia, 2019). Precise information may not only provide real transparency, but boost transparency perceptions.

Completeness

Completeness refers to how comprehensive the information is in its function to address or solve the business issue at hand. In many transparency applications, such as machine learning-based algorithms in business applications (e.g., Creel, 2020), complete information is infeasible because a significant portion of the relevant information is outside the purview of all involved parties and is thus unknowable. In other cases, such as all-inclusive pricing or revealing first-level suppliers' names to customers, complete information can be feasibly given to facilitate the receiver's understanding.

Furthermore, completeness can be considered as orthogonal to clarity and precision in the pricing context. It captures the degree to which the customer can access prices in the form they want and can use at the requisite point in their decision making process. In Chapter 3, we covered this aspect of price information in detail when we considered the different meanings of price transparency at each stage in the organization's pricing process and the customer's buying journey. It should also be noted that in many applications, completeness of the information may not necessarily correspond to understanding in a linear, monotonic sense, such as when too much information makes it hard to discern usefulness and leads to adverse effects of information overload (e.g., Pasquale, 2015).

Interpretation and Contextualization

Interpretation is the degree to which the provider interprets or translates the information to the user's vocabulary or perspective to facilitate their understanding. As an example, reporting that the employees of a Nicaraguan supplier are paid C$11,000 cordobas per month may provide little meaning to many readers unless it is also explained that the minimum wage in Nicaragua is currently C$5,900 cordobas per month so that now it is clear that the supplier's employee wage rate is significantly above the national minimum wage. This additional information about the national minimum wage helps the receiver to better interpret the supplier's wages.

When the discloser provides individual numbers or metrics (e.g., our average customer satisfaction score is 7.8, or our occupancy last quarter was 58.9%), they need to be interpreted (and contextualized, as developed below) to make sense. This issue is relevant in business areas like pricing, marketing, consumer behavior, and investor relations, where many information receivers may have poor domain knowledge and little or no information in memory to make sense of the disclosed information and have to rely on assistance from marketers or disclosers more generally, to understand the disclosure.

Finally, *contextualization* refers to explicating the information further by elaborating on broader contextual details beyond its narrower interpretation focused on the disclosure to enhance the user's understanding. For the Nicaraguan supplier, contextualizing the C$11,000 cordobas monthly wage may include such things as explaining the exchange rate of cordobas to other currencies that receivers may be more familiar with, applying purchasing power parity values in carrying out these conversions, detailing the historical average and median wages in Nicaragua, providing the prices of common household items and consumer durables as references, and so on. There are innumerable ways to contextualize the disclosed information. Furthermore, contextualization is important not just for numerical information like wages or prices but also for subjective information such as descriptions of an organization's culture or a business leader's relational transparency, the state of consumer welfare, environmental impact, and social justice considerations, among others, and especially in cases where prevailing and evolving norms are significant to assess the disclosure's appropriateness (e.g., Martin, 2012).

In the pricing domain, a further complicating factor that affects understanding is that customers often have poor price knowledge and rely on external cues at the point of purchase to evaluate prices (Vanhuele & Drèze, 2002). For example, a customer may find a bottle of apricot preserves in a farmer's market priced at $15. Here, even though the price is accessible, the shopper may not be able to discern whether $15 is a good or bad price simply because they don't know what homemade apricot preserves should cost. The price has to be interpreted and contextualized for customer understanding.

This can be done in many different ways, such as by indicating that "Apricot preserves of this quality typically cost $15-$25," implying that $15 is reasonable or by indicating that the $15 price is a limited-time sale price, marked down from $20, or by providing a break-down of the costs to manufacture the preserves (Dholakia, 2019). These are all examples of enhancing the consumer's interpretation of the $15 price. Furthermore, the purchase of the apricot preserves could also be contextualized by describing how this amount constitutes a reasonable portion of the consumer's grocery, food, or shopping budgets, positioning it as an "affordable luxury" purchase, underscoring the consumer's motivation to support local small businesses in their hometown, or as reflecting a particularly valued aspect of the consumer's identity.

Thus, in pricing, interpretation is tantamount to calibrating how easy or difficult it is for customers to use prices in their decision making, using the price to trade-off against other attributes, and even controlling which cues or reference values they use for comparison purposes. In contrast, contextualization goes beyond these strategies to situate the purchase (along with the price) on multi-faceted and significant motivations, emotions, and decision heuristics of the consumer. Of all the characteristics of the disclosed information discussed here, contextualization is perhaps the most subtle and abstract aspect of disclosure, with many different avenues for those sharing information and using information for specific business purposes to influence understanding.

An Expanded Definition of Business Transparency

We are now ready to expand the business transparency definition to include the disclosed information's effects explicitly. The revised, expanded definition of business transparency can therefore be stated as: "*Business transparency is the degree to which valuable information is deliberately disclosed or made available through a carefully designed uncovering process to the relevant receiver to generate understanding for the discloser and the receiver.*"

The key difference is that the specific purpose that was left undefined in the Chapter 1 version of the definition is now defined more clearly as "to generate understanding for the discloser and the receiver." With this added perspective, in a successful and mutually beneficial business transparency application, the two parties involved in the information exchange move away from a tacit acceptance of the transparency principle and make the additional effort to thoughtfully consider and perhaps even mutually agree on how the process and the matter of the disclosure will impact each of them individually and mutually, and seek ways to design the disclosure such that it yields mutually beneficial results and shared understanding. Thus, the model of asymmetric exploitation that underlies many transparency applications and may often lead to frayed relations, financial loss, and burnt bridges is replaced by a deliberate mutual construction of transparent action centered around the disclosure.

Deliberately Designed Disclosure

Adopting this revised perspective on business transparency would entail three further considerations in many of the settings we have examined throughout the book, where the dark side of transparency is prevalent. First, instead of treating disclosure as an arbitrary activity or an urgent requirement that emerges from the demands of a situation or the whims of one particular powerful individual or group (e.g., the company's founder, an executive team, or an interested manager), in successful applications of transparency, the disclosure is *deliberately designed* with due consideration given to all involved parties, with respect to the specific information to be disclosed, its antecedents (where it resides, how it will be gathered, and how it will be shared) and its consequences (how it will be used, what impacts the disclosure will have, how to react to these effects), and so on. The upshot of deliberate design is that, more often than not, the goal of effective transparency should not be to maximize disclosure but to find a level and format of disclosure that leads to the most good and the least harm to the involved parties.

Negotiated Disclosure

Second, the revised definition of transparency explicitly acknowledges that the terms of the disclosure, the uncovering process, and its consequences are better *negotiated* and agreed upon than *imposed*, even when there is a power disparity between the discloser and the receiver. Effective transparency applications should strive for information flows in both directions, where information from the disclosure flows in one direction, and an explanation flows in the other direction through structured processes so that both parties achieve relevant understanding.

Mutually Beneficial Understanding

Third, and perhaps the most idealistic in this list, this revised perspective on business transparency contends that disclosure need not be a zero-sum game where one party wins only when the other party loses. Instead, more often than not, and even in situations that seem primed to be adversarial, or have traditionally been so, bringing empathy into the mix and considering the issue at hand from the counterparty's perspective is a worthwhile endeavor, not just because it is the right thing to do, but because it is likely to pay off, with respect to more positive psychological, organizational, and financial outcomes. The discloser and the receiver could then be labeled as the *empathizer* and the *satisficer* in the transparency exchange. The net effect of this revised perspective on business transparency would be to adopt more sustainable and just business practices that do away with maximizing principles and choose moderate stances on disclosure in favor of extremes with "enough" as the key consideration.

References

Albu, O. B. (2022). Betwixt and between: Trends in transparency and secrecy research. *Management Communication Quarterly, 36*(2), 377–387.

Albu, O. B., & Flyverbom, M. (2019). Organizational transparency: Conceptualizations, conditions, and consequences. *Business & Society, 58*(2), 268–297.

Anteby, M., & Chan, C. K. (2018). A self-fulfilling cycle of coercive surveillance: Workers' invisibility practices and managerial justification. *Organization Science, 29*(2), 247–263.
Antorini, Y. M., Muñiz, A. M., Jr., & Askildsen, T. (2012). Collaborating with customer communities: Lessons from the LEGO Group. *Sloan Management Review, 53*(3), 73–79.
Astill, J., Dara, R. A., Campbell, M., Farber, J. M., Fraser, E. D., Sharif, S., & Yada, R. Y. (2019). Transparency in food supply chains: A review of enabling technology solutions. *Trends in Food Science & Technology, 91*, 240–247.
Baker, W. L., Marn, M. V., & Zawada, C. C. (2010). *The price advantage* (2nd ed.). Wiley.
Bernstein, E. S. (2017). Making transparency transparent: The evolution of observation in management theory. *Academy of Management Annals, 11*(1), 217–266.
Bernstein, E., Bunch, J., Canner, N., & Lee, M. (2016). Beyond the holacracy hype. *Harvard Business Review*. Reprint R16078.
Boyer, S. L., & Jap, S. D. (2022). The big spaces in sales negotiation research. *Journal of Personal Selling & Sales Management, 42*, 181–192.
Bruni, F. (2005, July 27). Yes, the kitchen's open. Too open. *New York Times*. https://www.nytimes.com/2005/07/27/dining/yes-the-kitchens-open-too-open.html
Cinelli, M. D., & LeBoeuf, R. A. (2020). Keeping it real: How perceived brand authenticity affects product perceptions. *Journal of Consumer Psychology, 30*(1), 40–59.
Clarke, K. (2018). How much is that luxury home? It's a secret. Wall Street Journal, March 29. https://www.wsj.com/articles/how-much-is-that-luxury-home-its-a-secret-1522333800
Creel, K. A. (2020). Transparency in complex computational systems. *Philosophy of Science, 87*(4), 568–589.
Dholakia, U. M. (2017). *How to price effectively: A guide for managers and entrepreneurs*. Kindle Publishing Group.
Dholakia, U. M. (2019). *Priced to influence, sell & satisfy: Lessons from behavioral economics for pricing success*. Kindle Publishing Group.
Dholakia, U. M. (2022). *Advanced introduction to digital marketing*. Edward Elgar.
Dufresne, R. L., & Offstein, E. H. (2008). On the virtues of secrecy in organizations. *Journal of Management Inquiry, 17*(2), 102–106.
George, B. (2015). *Discover your true north: Becoming an authentic leader*. Jossey-Bass.
Gilliom, J., & Monahan, T. (2013). *SuperVision: An introduction to the surveillance society*. University of Chicago Press.

Ikonen, I., Sotgiu, F., Aydinli, A., & Verlegh, P. W. (2020). Consumer effects of front-of-package nutrition labeling: An interdisciplinary meta-analysis. *Journal of the Academy of Marketing Science, 48*(3), 360–383.
Ivancevich, J. M., & Donnelly Jr, J. H. (1975). Relation of organizational structure to job satisfaction, anxiety-stress, and performance. *Administrative Science Quarterly, 20*(2), 272–280.
Kelly, E. L., & Moen, P. (2020). *Overload: How good jobs went bad and what we can do about it*. Princeton University Press.
Kliff, S., & Katz, J. (2021, August 22). Hospitals and insurers didn't want you to see these prices. Here's why. *New York Times*. https://www.nytimes.com/interactive/2021/08/22/upshot/hospital-prices.html
Knight, B., & Mitrofanov, D. (2022, September 5). Why you should warn customers when you're running low on stock. *Harvard Business Review*. https://hbr.org/2022/09/why-you-should-warn-customers-when-youre-running-low-on-stock
Leonardi, P. M., & Treem, J. W. (2020). Behavioral visibility: A new paradigm for organization studies in the age of digitization, digitalization, and datafication. *Organization Studies, 41*(12), 1601–1625.
Levenson, M. (2022, May 21). She was told surgery would cost about $1,300. Then the bill came: $229,000. *New York Times*. https://www.nytimes.com/2022/05/21/us/colorado-hospital-lisa-french.html
Martin, K. E. (2012). Diminished or just different? A factorial vignette study of privacy as a social contract. *Journal of Business Ethics, 111*(4), 519–539.
Maxwell, P. (2015). Transparent and opaque pricing: The interesting case of lithium. *Resources Policy, 45*, 92–97.
Miotto, R., Wang, F., Wang, S., Jiang, X., & Dudley, J. T. (2018). Deep learning for healthcare: Review, opportunities and challenges. *Briefings in Bioinformatics, 19*(6), 1236–1246.
Newport, C. (2016). *Deep work: Rules for focused success in a distracted world*. Grand Central Publishing.
Nunes, J. C., Ordanini, A., & Giambastiani, G. (2021). The concept of authenticity: What it means to consumers. *Journal of Marketing, 85*(4), 1–20.
Pasquale, F. (2015). *The black box society: The secret algorithms that control money and information*. Harvard University Press.
Pauly, M. V., & Burns, L. R. (2008). Price transparency for medical devices. *Health Affairs, 27*(6), 1544–1553.
Puzakova, M., Kwak, H., & Bell, M. (2015). Beyond seeing McDonald's fiesta menu: The role of accent in brand sincerity of ethnic products and brands. *Journal of Advertising, 44*(3), 219–231.
Reidenbach, R. E., & Robin, D. P. (1990). Toward the development of a multi-dimensional scale for improving evaluations of business ethics. *Journal of Business Ethics, 9*, 639–653.

Schlegelmilch, B. B., & Öberseder, M. (2010). Half a century of marketing ethics: Shifting perspectives and emerging trends. *Journal of Business Ethics, 93*(1), 1–19.

Sewell, G., & Barker, J. R. (2006). Coercion versus care: Using irony to make sense of organizational surveillance. *Academy of Management Review, 31*(4), 934–961.

Shankar, A., & Canniford, R. (2016, September 29). *If Patagonia's business model is a paragon of virtue, should more companies follow suit?* The Conversation. https://theconversation.com/if-patagonias-business-model-is-a-paragon-of-virtue-should-more-companies-follow-suit-66188

Sirianni, N. J., Bitner, M. J., Brown, S. W., & Mandel, N. (2013). Branded service encounters: Strategically aligning employee behavior with the brand positioning. *Journal of Marketing, 77*(6), 108–123.

Smith, B. (2022). A former Facebook executive pushes to open social media's black boxes, New York Times, January 2. https://www.nytimes.com/2022/01/02/business/media/crowdtangle-facebook-brandon-silverman.html

Staw, B. M. (1997). The escalation of commitment: An update and appraisal. Organizational Decision Making, 191–215.

Thomas, M., Simon, D. H., & Kadiyali, V. (2010). The price precision effect: Evidence from laboratory and market data. *Marketing Science, 29*(1), 175–190.

Toegel, I., Levy, O., & Jonsen, K. (2022). Secrecy in practice: How middle managers promote strategic initiatives behind the scenes. *Organization Studies, 43*(6), 885–906.

Turco, C. J. (2016). *The conversational firm: Rethinking bureaucracy in the age of social media.* Columbia University Press.

Vanhuele, M., & Drèze, X. (2002). Measuring the price knowledge shoppers bring to the store. *Journal of Marketing, 66*(4), 72–85.

References

Abraham, A. T., & Hamilton, R. W. (2018). When does partitioned pricing lead to more favorable consumer preferences? *Meta-Analytic Evidence. Journal of Marketing Research, 55*(5), 686–703.

Aguirre, E., Roggeveen, A. L., Grewal, D., & Wetzels, M. (2016). The personalization-privacy paradox: Implications for new media. *Journal of Consumer Marketing, 33*(2), 98–110.

Ahearne, M., Atefi, Y., Lam, S. K., & Pourmasoudi, M. (2022). The future of buyer–seller interactions: a conceptual framework and research agenda. *Journal of the Academy of Marketing Science, 50*, 22–45.

Albu, O. B. (2022). Betwixt and between: Trends in transparency and secrecy research. *Management Communication Quarterly, 36*(2), 377–387.

Albu, O. B., & Flyverbom, M. (2019). Organizational transparency: Conceptualizations, conditions, and consequences. *Business & Society, 58*(2), 268–297.

Algera, P. M., & Lips-Wiersma, M. (2012). Radical authentic leadership: Co-creating the conditions under which all members of the organization can be authentic. *Leadership Quarterly, 23*(1), 118–131.

Allen, T. D. (2006). Rewarding good citizens: The relationship between citizenship behavior, gender, and organizational rewards 1. *Journal of Applied Social Psychology, 36*(1), 120–143.

Alvesson, M., & Einola, K. (2019). Warning for excessive positivity: Authentic leadership and other traps in leadership studies. *Leadership Quarterly, 30*(4), 383–395.

Alvesson, M., & Einola, K. (2022). The gaslighting of authentic leadership 2.0. *Leadership, 18*(6), 814–831.

Amed, I., Balchandani, A., Beltrami, M., Berg, A., Hedrich, S., & Rölkens, F. (2019). What radical transparency could mean for the fashion industry. *McKinsey Insights*. https://www.mckinsey.com/industries/retail/our-insights/what-radical-transparency-could-mean-for-the-fashion-industry

Ananny, M., & Crawford, K. (2018). Seeing without knowing: Limitations of the transparency ideal and its application to algorithmic accountability. *New Media & Society, 20*(3), 973–989.

Anderson, H. J., Baur, J. E., Griffith, J. A., & Buckley, M. R. (2017). What works for you may not work for (Gen) Me: Limitations of present leadership theories for the new generation. *The Leadership Quarterly, 28*(1), 245–260.

Anteby, M., & Chan, C. K. (2018). A self-fulfilling cycle of coercive surveillance: Workers' invisibility practices and managerial justification. *Organization Science, 29*(2), 247–263.

Antorini, Y. M., Muñiz, A. M., Jr., & Askildsen, T. (2012). Collaborating with customer communities: Lessons from the LEGO group. *Sloan Management Review, 53*(3), 73–79.

Appels, M. (2022). CEO Sociopolitical activism as a signal of authentic leadership to prospective employees. *Journal of Management*. https://doi.org/10.1177/01492063221110207

Arkan, O., Nagpal, M., Scharding, T. K., & Warren, D. E. (2022). Don't just trust your gut: The importance of normative deliberation to ethical decision-making at work. *Journal of Business Ethics*, 1–21.

Arora, N., Dreze, X., Ghose, A., Hess, J. D., Iyengar, R., Jing, B., Joshi, Y., Kumar, V., Lurie, N., Neslin, S., & Sajeesh, S. (2008). Putting one-to-one marketing to work: Personalization, customization, and choice. *Marketing Letters, 19*(3), 305–321.

Arrieta, A. B., Díaz-Rodríguez, N., Del Ser, J., Bennetot, A., Tabik, S., Barbado, A., García, S., Gil-López, S., Molina, D., Benjamins, R., & Chatila, R. (2020). Explainable artificial intelligence (XAI): Concepts, taxonomies, opportunities and challenges toward responsible AI. *Information Fusion, 58*, 82–115.

Ashenfelter, O., & Graddy, K. (2003). Auctions and the price of art. *Journal of Economic Literature, 41*(3), 763–787.

Ashford, S. J., Wellman, N., Sully de Luque, M., De Stobbeleir, K. E., & Wollan, M. (2018). Two roads to effectiveness: CEO feedback seeking, vision articulation, and firm performance. *Journal of Organizational Behavior, 39*(1), 82–95.

Ashforth, B. E., & Humphrey, R. H. (1993). Emotional labor in service roles: The influence of identity. *Academy of Management Review, 18*(1), 88–115.

Ashwin, S., Kabeer, N., & Schüßler, E. (2020). Contested understandings in the global garment industry after Rana Plaza. *Development and Change, 51*(5), 1296–1305.

Astill, J., Dara, R. A., Campbell, M., Farber, J. M., Fraser, E. D., Sharif, S., & Yada, R. Y. (2019). Transparency in food supply chains: A review of enabling technology solutions. *Trends in Food Science & Technology, 91*, 240–247.

Atefi, Y., Ahearne, M., Hohenberg, S., Hall, Z., & Zettelmeyer, F. (2020). Open negotiation: The back-end benefits of salespeople's transparency in the front end. *Journal of Marketing Research, 57*(6), 1076–1094.

Aung, M. M., & Chang, Y. S. (2014). Traceability in a food supply chain: Safety and quality perspectives. *Food Control, 39*, 172–184.

Avolio, B. J., & Walumbwa, F. O. (2014). *Authentic leadership theory, research and practice: Steps taken and steps that remain* (pp. 331–356). The Oxford Handbook of Leadership and Organizations.

Avolio, B. J., Gardner, W. L., Walumbwa, F. O., Luthans, F., & May, D. R. (2004). Unlocking the mask: A look at the process by which authentic leaders impact follower attitudes and behaviors. *Leadership Quarterly, 15*(6), 801–823.

Baker, M., Halberstam, Y., Kroft, K., Mas, A., & Messacar, D. (2019). *Pay transparency and the gender gap* (Working paper 25834). National Bureau of Economic Research..

Baker, W. L., Marn, M. V., & Zawada, C. C. (2010). *The price advantage* (2nd ed.). Wiley.

Baldoni, J. (2008, June 30). *Start creating authentic leadership.* Harvard Business Review. https://hbr.org/2008/06/start-creating-authentic-leade

Ball, C. (2009). What is transparency? *Public Integrity, 11*(4), 293–308.

Bamberger, P., & Belogolovsky, E. (2017). The dark side of transparency: How and when pay administration practices affect employee helping. *Journal of Applied Psychology, 102*(4), 658–671.

Barber, B. M., Lee, Y. T., Liu, Y. J., & Odean, T. (2009). Just how much do individual investors lose by trading? *The Review of Financial Studies, 22*(2), 609–632.

Barnard, C. (1938). *The functions of the executive.* Harvard University Press.

Barroso, A., & Brown, A. (2021, May 25). *Gender pay gap in the US held steady in 2020.* Pew Research Center. https://www.pewresearch.org/fact-tank/2021/05/25/gender-pay-gap-facts/

Bateman, A., & Bonanni, L. (2019, August 20). *What supply chain transparency really means.* Harvard Business Review. https://hbr.org/2019/08/what-supply-chain-transparency-really-means

Bayus, B. L. (1992). The dynamic pricing of next generation consumer durables. *Marketing Science, 11*(3), 251–265.

Bazerman, M. H., Curhan, J. R., Moore, D. A., & Valley, K. L. (2000). Negotiation. *Annual Review of Psychology, 51*(1), 279–314.

Beer, M. (2021, December). *To change your company's culture, don't start by trying to change the culture.* Harvard Business School Working Knowledge. https://hbswk.hbs.edu/item/to-change-your-companys-culture-dont-start-by-trying-to-change-the-culture

Bennedsen, M., Simintzi, E., Tsoutsoura, M., & Wolfenzon, D. (2019). *Do firms respond to gender pay gap transparency?* (Working paper 24345). National Bureau of Economic Research.

Bennis, W., Goleman, D., O'Toole, J., & Biederman, P. W. (2008). *Transparency: How leaders create a culture of Candor.* Jossey-Bass.

Bernstein, E. (2014). The transparency trap. *Harvard Business Review, 92*(10), 58–66.

Bernstein, E. S. (2012). The transparency paradox: A role for privacy in organizational learning and operational control. *Administrative Science Quarterly, 57*(2), 181–216.

Bernstein, E. S. (2017). Making transparency transparent: The evolution of observation in management theory. *Academy of Management Annals, 11*(1), 217–266.

Bernstein, E., Bunch, J., Canner, N., & Lee, M. (2016). Beyond the holacracy hype. *Harvard Business Review.* Reprint R16078.

Bertini, M., & Wathieu, L. (2010). How to stop customers from fixating on price. *Harvard Business Review, 88*(5), 84–91.

Bertini, M., Buehler, S., & Halbheer, D. (2020). *Pricing and supply chain transparency to conscientious consumers* (CESifo Working Paper No. 8675).

Besanko, D., & Winston, W. L. (1990). Optimal price skimming by a monopolist facing rational consumers. *Management Science, 36*(5), 555–567.

Bertrand, M., & Mullainathan, S. (2004). Are Emily and Greg more employable than Lakisha and Jamal? A field experiment on labor market discrimination. *American Economic Review, 94*(4), 991–1013.

Bitner, M. J., Ostrom, A. L., & Morgan, F. N. (2008). Service blueprinting: A practical technique for service innovation. *California Management Review, 50*(3), 66–94.

Blau, F. D., & Kahn, L. M. (2017). The gender wage gap: Extent, trends, and explanations. *Journal of Economic Literature, 55*(3), 789–865.

Blau, F. D., & Kahn, L. M. (2007). The gender pay gap: Have women gone as far as they can? *Academy of Management Perspectives, 21*(1), 7–23.

Blodgett, H. (2017, January 7). *Ray Dalio offers a radical solution to the threat of 'fake news' and details life inside Bridgewater.* Business Insider. https://www.businessinsider.com/ray-dalio-interview-henry-blodget-1-2017

Böheim, R., & Gust, S. (2021). *The Austrian pay transparency law and the gender wage gap* (CESifo Working Paper 8960).

Bosona, T., & Gebresenbet, G. (2013). Food traceability as an integral part of logistics management in food and agricultural supply chain. *Food Control*, *33*(1), 32–48.

Bovens, M. (1998). *The quest for responsibility: Accountability and citizenship in complex organizations*. Cambridge University Press.

Boyer, S. L., & Jap, S. D. (2022). The big spaces in sales negotiation research. *Journal of Personal Selling & Sales Management*, *42*, 181–192.

Brandeis, L. D. (1913, December 20). What publicity can do. *Harper's Weekly* (pp. 10–13).

Breza, E., Kaur, S., & Shamdasani, Y. (2018). The morale effects of pay inequality. *The Quarterly Journal of Economics*, *133*(2), 611–663.

Brown, A. D., & Starkey, K. (2000). Organizational identity and learning: A psychodynamic perspective. *Academy of Management Review*, *25*(1), 102–120.

Brown, A. J., Vandekerckhove, W., & Dreyfus, S. (2014). *The relationship between transparency, whistleblowing, and public trust* (pp. 30–58). Edward Elgar.

Brown, L. W., Manegold, J. G., & Marquardt, D. J. (2020). The effects of CEO activism on employees person-organization ideological misfit: A conceptual model and research agenda. *Business and Society Review*, *125*(1), 119–141.

Brown, M., Nyberg, A. J., Weller, I., & Strizver, S. D. (2022). Pay information disclosure: Review and recommendations for research spanning the pay secrecy–pay transparency continuum. *Journal of Management*, *48*(6), 1661–1694.

Bruni, F. (2005, July 27). Yes, the kitchen's open. Too open. *New York Times*. https://www.nytimes.com/2005/07/27/dining/yes-the-kitchens-open-too-open.html

Buell, R. W. (2019). Operational transparency. *Harvard Business Review*, *97*(2), 102–113.

Buell, R. W., & Kalkanci, B. (2021). How transparency into internal and external responsibility initiatives influences consumer choice. *Management Science*, *67*(2), 932–950.

Buell, R. W., Kim, T., & Tsay, C. J. (2017). Creating reciprocal value through operational transparency. *Management Science*, *63*(6), 1673–1695.

Buell, R. W., & Norton, M. I. (2011). The labor illusion: How operational transparency increases perceived value. *Management Science*, *57*(9), 1564–1579.

Buell, R. W., Porter, E., & Norton, M. I. (2021). Surfacing the submerged state: Operational transparency increases trust in and engagement with government. *Manufacturing & Service Operations Management*, *23*(4), 781–802.

Buell, R. W., Ramdas, K., & Sonmez, N. (2021). Can shared service delivery increase customer engagement? A study of shared medical appointments

(Harvard Business School Technology & Operations Management Unit Working Paper, 21-001).
Burrell, J. (2016). How the machine 'thinks': Understanding opacity in machine learning algorithms. *Big Data & Society, 3*(1), 1–16.
Butler, S. (2022, October 21). Zara enters resale market with pre-owned service. *The Guardian.* https://www.theguardian.com/business/2022/oct/21/zara-enters-resale-market-pre-owned-service.
Byrne, D. P., Martin, L. A., & Nah, J. S. (2022). Price Discrimination by negotiation: A field experiment in retail electricity. *The Quarterly Journal of Economics, 137*(4), 2499–2537.
Caldwell, C., & Hayes, L. A. (2016). Self-efficacy and self-awareness: Moral insights to increased leader effectiveness. *Journal of Management Development, 35*(9), 1163–1173.
Campbell, M. C., & Winterich, K. P. (2018). A framework for the consumer psychology of morality in the marketplace. *Journal of Consumer Psychology, 28*(2), 167–179.
Card, D., Cardoso, A. R., & Kline, P. (2016). Bargaining, sorting, and the gender wage gap: Quantifying the impact of firms on the relative pay of women. *The Quarterly Journal of Economics, 131*(2), 633–686.
Card, D., Mas, A., Moretti, E., & Saez, E. (2012). Inequality at work: The effect of peer salaries on job satisfaction. *American Economic Review, 102*(6), 2981–3003.
Castilla, E. J. (2015). Accounting for the gap: A firm study manipulating organizational accountability and transparency in pay decisions. *Organization Science, 26*(2), 311–333.
Cernansky, R. (2021, October 18). Why destroying products is still an "Everest of a problem" for fashion. Vogue Business.
Cha, S. E., Hewlin, P. F., Roberts, L. M., Buckman, B. R., Leroy, H., Steckler, E. L., Ostermeier, K., & Cooper, D. (2019). Being your true self at work: Integrating the fragmented research on authenticity in organizations. *Academy of Management Annals, 13*(2), 633–671.
Chakravarti, D., Krish, R., Paul, P., & Srivastava, J. (2002). Partitioned presentation of multicomponent bundle prices: Evaluation, choice and underlying processing effects. *Journal of Consumer Psychology, 12*(3), 215–229.
Cheema, A., Leszczyc, P. T., Bagchi, R., Bagozzi, R. P., Cox, J. C., Dholakia, U. M., Greenleaf, E. A., Pazgal, A., Rothkopf, M. H., Shen, M., & Sunder, S. (2005). Economics, psychology, and social dynamics of consumer bidding in auctions. *Marketing Letters, 16*(3), 401–413.
Cillizza, C. (2015, April 30). Millennials don't trust anyone. That's a big deal. *Washington Post.* https://www.washingtonpost.com/news/the-fix/wp/2015/04/30/millennials-dont-trust-anyone-what-else-is-new/

Cinelli, M. D., & LeBoeuf, R. A. (2020). Keeping it real: How perceived brand authenticity affects product perceptions. *Journal of Consumer Psychology, 30*(1), 40–59.

Clarke, K. (2018, March 29). How much is that luxury home? It's a secret. *Wall Street Journal.* https://www.wsj.com/articles/how-much-is-that-luxury-home-its-a-secret-1522333800

Colella, A., Paetzold, R. L., Zardkoohi, A., & Wesson, M. J. (2007). Exposing pay secrecy. *Academy of Management Review, 32*(1), 55–71.

Commerford, B. P., Dennis, S. A., Joe, J. R., & Ulla, J. W. (2022). Man versus machine: Complex estimates and auditor reliance on artificial intelligence. *Journal of Accounting Research, 60*(1), 171–201.

Consumer Reports (2019, January 3). *WT fee survey research report.* https://advocacy.consumerreports.org/wp-content/uploads/2019/09/2018-WTFee-Survey-Report-_-Public-Report-1.pdf

Cormen, T. H., Leiserson, C. E., Rivest, R. L., & Stein, C. (2022). *Introduction to algorithms.* MIT Press.

Coser, R. L. (1961). Insulation from observability and types of social conformity. *American Sociological Review, 26*(1), 28–39.

Cotterrell, R. (1999). Transparency, mass media, ideology and community. *Journal for Cultural Research, 3*(4), 414–426.

Cox, J. C. (2008). First price independent private values auctions. *Handbook of Experimental Economics Results, 1*(1), 92–98.

Creel, K. A. (2020). Transparency in complex computational systems. *Philosophy of Science, 87*(4), 568–589.

Cui, R., Li, J., & Zhang, D. J. (2020). Reducing discrimination with reviews in the sharing economy: Evidence from field experiments on Airbnb. *Management Science, 66*(3), 1071–1094.

Cullen, Z. B., & Perez-Truglia, R. (2018). *The salary taboo: Privacy norms and the diffusion of information* (Working paper 25145). National Bureau of Economic Research.

Cullen, Z., & Perez-Truglia, R. (2022). How much does your boss make? The effects of salary comparisons. *Journal of Political Economy, 130*(3), 766–822.

Cutter, C. (2022, January 28). You'll soon get to see pay on NYC job postings. *Wall Street Journal.* https://www.wsj.com/articles/goldman-google-and-just-about-every-nyc-employer-will-soon-have-to-disclose-pay-secrets-11643365982

D'Acunto, F., Hoang, D., & Weber, M. (2022). Managing households' expectations with unconventional policies. *The Review of Financial Studies, 35*(4), 1597–1642.

Dalton, M. (2018, September 6). Why luxury brands burn their own goods. *Wall Street Journal.* https://www.wsj.com/articles/burning-luxury-goods-goes-out-of-style-at-burberry-1536238351

Danovich, T. (2015, May 6). How do pay-what-you-want restaurants work? Eater. https://www.eater.com/2015/5/6/8556309/pay-what-you-want-restaurant-SAME-cafe-panera-cares

Day G. S. (1999). *The market driven organization: Understanding, attracting, and keeping valuable customers.* The Free Press.

Denison, D. R., & Mishra, A. K. (1995). Toward a theory of organizational culture and effectiveness. *Organization Science, 6*(2), 204–223.

DePillis, L. (2013, July 14). Panera's pay-as-you-go pricing experiment failed. Here's how they could fix it. *Washington Post.* https://wapo.st/2MyG1dh

Detert, J. R., & Burris, E. R. (2007). Leadership behavior and employee voice: Is the door really open? *Academy of Management Journal, 50*(4), 869–884.

Detert, J. R., & Burris, E. R. (2016). Can your employees really speak freely. *Harvard Business Review, 94*(1), 80–87.

Dholakia, U. M. (2022). *Advanced introduction to digital marketing.* Edward Elgar.

Dholakia, U. M. (2021). If you're going to raise prices, tell customers why. Harvard Business Review, June. https://hbr.org/2021/06/if-youre-going-to-raise-prices-tell-customers-why

Dholakia, U. M. (2019). *Priced to influence, sell & satisfy: Lessons from behavioral economics for pricing success.* Kindle Publishing Group.

Dholakia, U. M. (2017). *How to price effectively: A guide for managers and entrepreneurs.* Kindle Publishing Group.

Dholakia, U. M. (2015, July 6). The risks of changing your prices too often. *Harvard Business Review.* https://hbr.org/2015/07/the-risks-of-changing-your-prices-too-often

Dholakia, U. M., & Morwitz, V. G. (2002). The scope and persistence of mere-measurement effects: Evidence from a field study of customer satisfaction measurement. *Journal of Consumer Research, 29*(2), 159–167.

Diakopoulos, N. (2020). Transparency. In the *Oxford handbook of ethics of AI* (Eds., M. Dubber, F. Pasquale, & S. Das). Oxford University Press.

Diakopoulos, N., & Koliska, M. (2017). Algorithmic transparency in the news media. *Digital Journalism, 5*(7), 809–828.

Dilmé, F., & Li, F. (2019). Revenue management without commitment: Dynamic pricing and periodic flash sales. *The Review of Economic Studies, 86*(5), 1999–2034.

Dobbin, F., & Kalev, A. (2022). *Getting to diversity: What works and what doesn't.* Belknap Press.

Donnelly, G. E., Lamberton, C., Reczek, R. W., & Norton, M. I. (2017). Social recycling transforms unwanted goods into happiness. *Journal of the Association for Consumer Research, 2*(1), 48–63.

Duarte, J., Siegel, S., & Young, L. (2012). Trust and credit: The role of appearance in peer-to-peer lending. *Review of Financial Studies*, 25(8), 2455–2484.

Dufresne, R. L., & Offstein, E. H. (2008). On the virtues of secrecy in organizations. *Journal of Management Inquiry*, 17(2), 102–106.

Duhigg, C. (2012, February 16). How companies learn your secrets. *New York Times*. https://www.nytimes.com/2012/02/19/magazine/shopping-habits.html

Duval, S., & Wicklund, R. A. (1972). *A theory of objective self awareness*. Academic Press.

Ashforth, E., & B., E. Kreiner, G., A. Clark, M., & Fugate, M. (2007). Normalizing dirty work: Managerial tactics for countering occupational taint. *Academy of Management Journal*, 50(1), 149–174.

Edelman, B., Luca, M., & Svirsky, D. (2017). Racial discrimination in the sharing economy: Evidence from a field experiment. *American Economic Journal: Applied Economics*, 9(2), 1–22.

Edelman, D. C., & Abraham, M. (2022). Customer experience in the age of AI. *Harvard Business Review*. https://hbr.org/2022/03/customer-experience-in-the-age-of-ai

Edwards, L., & Veale, M. (2017). Slave to the algorithm? Why a 'right to an explanation' is probably not the remedy you are looking for. *Duke Law & Technology Review*, 16, 18–84.

Edwards, L., & Veale, M. (2018). Enslaving the algorithm: From a "Right to an explanation" to a "Right to better decisions"? *IEEE Security & Privacy*, 16(3), 46–54.

Edwards, L., & Veale, M. (2017). Slave to the algorithm: Why a right to an explanation is probably not the remedy you are looking for. *Duke Law and Technology Review*, 16, 18–84.

Eggers, J. P. (2015, June 15). Focus on the customers you want, not the ones you have. *Harvard Business Review*. https://hbr.org/2015/06/focus-on-the-customers-you-want-not-the-ones-you-have

Einola, K., & Alvesson, M. (2021). Behind the numbers: Questioning questionnaires. *Journal of Management Inquiry*, 30(1), 102–114.

Eurich, T. (2018, January 4). What self-awareness really is (and how to cultivate it). *Harvard Business Review*. https://hbr.org/2018/01/what-self-awareness-really-is-and-how-to-cultivate-it

Falvey, D. (2021, February 24). How are consumers shopping? *Furniture, Lighting & Décor*. https://www.furniturelightingdecor.com/how-are-consumers-shopping

Feser, C., Mayol, F., & Srinivasan, R. (2015, January 1). Decoding leadership: What really matters. McKinsey Quarterly. https://www.mckinsey.com/featured-insights/leadership/decoding-leadership-what-really-matters

Fisman, R., & Luca, M. (2016). Fixing discrimination in online marketplaces. *Harvard Business Review, 94*(12), 88–95.
Flint, J. (2021, October 13). Netflix employee group calls for walkout amid tensions over Dave Chappelle show. *Wall Street Journal.* https://www.wsj.com/articles/netflix-employee-group-calls-for-walkout-amid-tensions-over-dave-chappelle-show-11634169211
Flyverbom, M. (2016). Transparency: Mediation and the management of visibilities. *International Journal of Communication, 10,* 110–122.
Foss-Solbrekk, K. (2021). Three routes to protecting AI systems and their algorithms under IP law: The good, the bad and the ugly. *Journal of Intellectual Property Law & Practice, 16*(3), 247–258.
Fowler, E., Kobe, C., Roberts, K. J., Collins, C. L., & McKenzie, L. B. (2016). Injuries associated with strollers and carriers among children in the United States, 1990 to 2010. *Academic Pediatrics, 16*(8), 726–733.
Fråne, A., Dahlbom, M., Sanctuary, M., Malmaeus, M., Fjellander, L., & de Jong, A. (2021). *Towards sustainable consumption in the Nordic Region.* Nordic Council of Ministers.
Frey, E., Bernstein, E., & Rekenthaler, N. (2022). Scarlet letters: Rehabilitation through transgression transparency and personal narrative control. *Administrative Science Quarterly, 67*(4), 968–1011.
Friedman, D. A. (2020). Regulating drip pricing. *Stanford Law & Policy Review, 31*(1), 51–102.
Friedman, N. (2021, November 11). Homes now typically sell in a week, forcing buyers to take risks. *Wall Street Journal.* https://www.wsj.com/articles/homes-typically-sell-in-a-week-forcing-buyers-to-take-risks-11636632000
Friedman, S. D. (2008, November 6). Obama's authentic leadership—And yours. *Harvard Business Review.* https://hbr.org/2008/11/obamas-authentic-leadership-an
Garaus, M., Wolfsteiner, E., & Wagner, U. (2016). Shoppers' acceptance and perceptions of electronic shelf labels. *Journal of Business Research, 69*(9), 3687–3692.
Gardner, W. L., Avolio, B. J., Luthans, F., May, D. R., & Walumbwa, F. (2005). "Can you see the real me?" A self-based model of authentic leader and follower development. *Leadership Quarterly, 16*(3), 343–372.
Gardner, W. L., Cogliser, C. C., Davis, K. M., & Dickens, M. P. (2011). Authentic leadership: A review of the literature and research agenda. *Leadership Quarterly, 22*(6), 1120–1145.
Gardner, W. L., Karam, E. P., Alvesson, M., & Einola, K. (2021). Authentic leadership theory: The case for and against. *Leadership Quarterly, 32*(6), 101495.

Gartenberg, C. (2021, December 16). *Apple is reportedly going to make more of its chips*. The Verge. https://www.theverge.com/2021/12/16/22839850/apple-office-develop-chips-in-house-broadcom-skyworks

Gatter, S., & Hüttl-Maack, V. (2020). Any item, only $10! When and why same-price promotions can reduce regret and the pain of paying. *Advances in Consumer Research, 48*, 357–358.

Gelber, S. (2005). Horseless horses: Car dealing and the survival of retail bargaining. In P. N. Stearns (Ed.), *American behavioral history* (pp. 118–140). New York University Press.

George, B. (2016). The rise of true north leaders. *Leader to Leader, 79*, 30–35.

George, B. (2015). *Discover your true North: Becoming an authentic leader*. Jossey-Bass.

George, B. (2003). *Authentic leadership: Rediscovering the secrets to creating lasting value* (Vol. 18). John Wiley & Sons.

Gerlick, J. (2019). Transparency in apparel: Everlane as a barometer for global positive impact. *The International Journal of Ethical Leadership, 6*(1), 87–95.

Gerstner, L. (2014, August 29). *How to haggle for practically anything*. Kiplinger. https://www.kiplinger.com/article/spending/t050-c000-s002-how-to-haggle-for-practically-anything.html

Gijsbrechts, E. (1993). Prices and pricing research in consumer marketing: Some recent developments. *International Journal of Research in Marketing, 10*(2), 115–151.

Gillespie, T. (2014). The relevance of algorithms. *Media Technologies: Essays on Communication, Materiality, and Society, 167*, 167–194.

Gillespie, T. (2020). Content moderation, AI, and the question of scale. *Big Data & Society, 7*(2), 1–5.

Gilliom, J., & Monahan, T. (2013). *SuperVision: An introduction to the surveillance society*. University of Chicago Press.

Giovannucci, D., & Ponte, S. (2005). Standards as a new form of social contract? Sustainability initiatives in the coffee industry. *Food Policy, 30*(3), 284–301.

Godfrey, D. M., Price, L. L., & Lusch, R. F. (2022). Repair, consumption, and sustainability: Fixing fragile objects and maintaining consumer practices. *Journal of Consumer Research, 49*(2), 229–251.

Goldin, C. (2014). A grand gender convergence: Its last chapter. *American Economic Review, 104*(4), 1091–1119.

Gold, H. (2020, March 30). *Bernie sanders calls out everlane*. The Cut. https://www.thecut.com/2020/03/bernie-sanders-calls-out-everlane.html

Goldin, C., & Rouse, C. (2000). Orchestrating impartiality: The impact of "blind" auditions on female musicians. *American Economic Review, 90*(4), 715–741.

Goleman, D. (2007, May). Winning in an age of radical transparency. *Harvard Business Review*. https://hbr.org/2009/05/radical-transparency

Goleman, D. (2009). Winning in an age of radical transparency. *Harvard Business Review*. https://hbr.org/2009/05/radical-transparency

Gong, T., Yi, Y., & Choi, J. N. (2014). Helping employees deal with dysfunctional customers: The underlying employee perceived justice mechanism. *Journal of Service Research, 17*(1), 102–116.

Goodman, B., & Flaxman, S. (2017). European Union regulations on algorithmic decision-making and a "right to explanation." *AI Magazine, 38*(3), 50–57.

Goolsbee, A., & Syverson, C. (2008). How do incumbents respond to the threat of entry? Evidence from the major airlines. *Quarterly Journal of Economics, 123*(4), 1611–1633.

Gorwa, R., Binns, R., & Katzenbach, C. (2020). Algorithmic content moderation: Technical and political challenges in the automation of platform governance. *Big Data & Society, 7*(1), 1–15.

Graham, J. W. (1983). *Principled organizational dissent* (Unpublished dissertation). Northwestern University.

Grant, A. M., Franklin, J., & Langford, P. (2002). The self-reflection and insight scale: A new measure of private self-consciousness. *Social Behavior and Personality, 30*(8), 821–835.

Green, B., & Viljoen, S. (2020). Algorithmic realism: Expanding the boundaries of algorithmic thought. In *Proceedings of the 2020 Conference on Fairness, Accountability, and Transparency* (pp. 19–31).

Greenleaf, E. A., & Lehmann, D. R. (1995). Reasons for substantial delay in consumer decision making. *Journal of Consumer Research, 22*(2), 186–199.

Greenleaf, E. A., Johnson, E. J., Morwitz, V. G., & Shalev, E. (2016). The price does not include additional taxes, fees, and surcharges: A review of research on partitioned pricing. *Journal of Consumer Psychology, 26*(1), 105–124.

Grubb, M. D. (2015). Failing to choose the best price: Theory, evidence, and policy. *Review of Industrial Organization, 47*(3), 303–340.

Gruenfeld, D., & Zander, L. (2011, February). Authentic leadership can be bad leadership. *Harvard Business Review*. https://hbr.org/2011/02/authentic-leadership-can-be-ba

Guda, H., Dawande, M., & Janakiraman, G. (2021). *The economics of process transparency*. Available at SSRN. https://doi.org/10.2139/ssrn.3715037

Guidotti, R., Monreale, A., Ruggieri, S., Turini, F., Giannotti, F., & Pedreschi, D. (2018). A survey of methods for explaining black box models. *ACM Computing Surveys, 51*(5), 1–42.

Gulyas, A., Seitz, S., & Sinha, S. (2021). *Does pay transparency affect the gender wage gap? Evidence from Austria* (Discussion Paper 21–076). Center for European Economic Research. https://papers.ssrn.com/sol3/papers.cfm?abstract_id=3949832

Hafermalz, E., & Huysman, M. (2022). Please explain: Key questions for explainable AI research from an Organizational perspective. *Morals & Machines, 1*(2), 10–23.

Hall, P., & Gill, N. (2019). *An introduction to machine learning interpretability*. O'Reilly Media.

Hampson, D. P., Grimes, A., Banister, E., & McGoldrick, P. J. (2018). A typology of consumers based on money attitudes after a major recession. *Journal of Business Research, 91*, 159–168.

Hanna, R. C., Lemon, K. N., & Smith, G. E. (2019). Is transparency a good thing? How online price transparency and variability can benefit firms and influence consumer decision making. *Business Horizons, 62*(2), 227–236.

Hansen, H. K., & Weiskopf, R. (2021). From universalizing transparency to the interplay of transparency matrices: Critical insights from the emerging social credit system in China. *Organization Studies, 42*(1), 109–128.

Hastig, G. M., & Sodhi, M. S. (2020). Blockchain for supply chain traceability: Business requirements and critical success factors. *Production and Operations Management, 29*(4), 935–954.

Heald, D. (2006). Varieties of transparency. *Proceedings of the British Academy, 135*, 25–43.f

Heemsbergen, L. (2016). From radical transparency to radical disclosure: Reconfiguring (in) voluntary transparency through the management of visibilities. *International Journal of Communication, 10*, 138–151.

Heil, O. P., & Helsen, K. (2001). Toward an understanding of price wars: Their nature and how they erupt. *International Journal of Research in Marketing, 18*(1), 83–98.

Herzenstein, M., Sonenshein, S., & Dholakia, U. M. (2011). Tell me a good story and I may lend you money: The role of narratives in peer-to-peer lending decisions. *Journal of Marketing Research, 48*(SPL), S138–S149.

Hochschild, A. R. (1983). *The managed heart: Commercialization of human feeling*. University of California Press.

Holland, S., Hosny, A., Newman, S., Joseph, J., & Chmielinski, K. (2018). *The dataset nutrition label: A framework to drive higher data quality standards*. arXiv preprint arXiv:1805.03677.

Hood, C. (2006). Transparency in historical perspective. *Proceedings of the British Academy, 135*, 3–23.

Houser, D., Levy, D. M., Padgitt, K., Peart, S. J., & Xiao, E. (2014). Raising the price of talk: An experimental analysis of transparent leadership. *Journal of Economic Behavior & Organization, 105*, 208–218.

Hughes, L. W. (2005). *Transparency, translucence or opacity? An experimental study of the impact of a leader's relational transparency and style of humor delivery on follower creative performance* (Unpublished doctoral dissertation). The University of Nebraska-Lincoln.

Ibarra, H. (2015). The authenticity paradox. *Harvard Business Review, 93*(1/2), 53–59.

Ikonen, I., Sotgiu, F., Aydinli, A., & Verlegh, P. W. (2020). Consumer effects of front-of-package nutrition labeling: An interdisciplinary meta-analysis. *Journal of the Academy of Marketing Science, 48*(3), 360–383.

Iszatt-White, M., & Kempster, S. (2019). Authentic leadership: Getting back to the roots of the 'root construct'? *International Journal of Management Reviews, 21*(3), 356–369.

Ivancevich, J. M., & Donnelly Jr, J. H. (1975). Relation of organizational structure to job satisfaction, anxiety-stress, and performance. *Administrative Science Quarterly, 20*(2), 272–280.

Jiang, B., Sudhir, K., & Zou, T. (2021). Effects of cost-information transparency on intertemporal price discrimination. *Production and Operations Management, 30*(2), 390–401.

Jiang, H., & Men, R. L. (2017). Creating an engaged workforce: The impact of authentic leadership, transparent organizational communication, and work-life enrichment. *Communication Research, 44*(2), 225–243.

John, L. K., Loewenstein, G., & Prelec, D. (2012). Measuring the prevalence of questionable research practices with incentives for truth telling. *Psychological Science, 23*(5), 524–532.

Jönsson, S. (1988). *Accounting regulation and elite structures*. Wiley.

Jovane, F., Alting, L., Armillotta, A., Eversheim, W., Feldmann, K., Seliger, G., & Roth, N. (1993). A key issue in product life cycle: Disassembly. *CIRP Annals, 42*(2), 651–658.

Kakar, V., Voelz, J., Wu, J., & Franco, J. (2018). The visible host: Does race guide Airbnb rental rates in San Francisco? *Journal of Housing Economics, 40*, 25–40.

Kale, S. (2021, , October 6). Out of style: Will Gen Z ever give up its dangerous love of fast fashion? *The Guardian*. https://www.theguardian.com/fashion/2021/oct/06/out-of-style-will-gen-z-ever-give-up-its-dangerous-love-of-fast-fashion

Kalkanci, B., & Plambeck, E. L. (2020). Reveal the supplier list? A trade-off in capacity vs. responsibility. *Manufacturing & Service Operations Management, 22*(6), 1251–1267.

Kapferer, J. N. (2012). *The luxury strategy: Break the rules of marketing to build luxury brands*. Kogan Page Publishers.

Kaptein, M. (2008). Developing and testing a measure for the ethical culture of organizations: The corporate ethical virtues model. *Journal of Organizational Behavior, 29*(7), 923–947.

Karlsson, P., Turner, M., & Gassmann, P. (2019). Succeeding the long-serving legend in the corner office. *Strategy & Business, 95*. https://www.strategy-business.com/article/Succeeding-the-long-serving-legend-in-the-corner-office

Keefe, J. (2019, June 18). *Haggle on the high street: Tips & tricks for hidden discounts*. Money Saving Expert. https://www.moneysavingexpert.com/shopping/how-to-haggle-successfully/

Keiser, T. C. (1988, November). Negotiating with a customer you can't afford to lose. *Harvard Business Review*. https://hbr.org/1988/11/negotiating-with-a-customer-you-cant-afford-to-lose

Kelemen, T. K., Matthews, S. H., Matthews, M. J., & Henry, S. E. (2022). Humble leadership: A review and synthesis of leader expressed humility. *Journal of Organizational Behavior*, in press.

Kellogg, K. C., Valentine, M. A., & Christin, A. (2020). Algorithms at work: The new contested terrain of control. *Academy of Management Annals*, 14(1), 366–410.

Kelly, E. L., & Moen, P. (2020). *Overload: How good jobs went bad and what we can do about it*. Princeton University Press.

Kempster, S., Iszatt-White, M., & Brown, M. (2019). Authenticity in leadership: Reframing relational transparency through the lens of emotional labour. *Leadership*, 15(3), 319–338.

Kernis, M. H. (2003). Toward a conceptualization of optimal self-esteem. *Psychological Inquiry*, 14(1), 1–26.

Kernis, M. H., & Goldman, B. M. (2006). A multicomponent conceptualization of authenticity: Theory and research. *Advances in Experimental Social Psychology*, 38, 283–357.

Khazan, O. (2022, March 30). Why people are acting so weird. *The Atlantic*. https://www.theatlantic.com/politics/archive/2022/03/antisocial-behavior-crime-violence-increase-pandemic/627076/

Kim, J. Y., Natter, M., & Spann, M. (2009). Pay what you want: A new participative pricing mechanism. *Journal of Marketing*, 73(1), 44–58.

Kim, N. L., Kim, G., & Rothenberg, L. (2020). Is honesty the best policy? Examining the role of price and production transparency in fashion marketing. *Sustainability*, 12(17), 6800.

Kim, N. S. (2017). Relative consent and contract law. *Nevada Law Journal*, 18, 165–219.

Kim, T., Barasz, K., & John, L. K. (2019). Why am I seeing this ad? The effect of ad transparency on ad effectiveness. *Journal of Consumer Research*, 45(5), 906–932.

Kim, Y. H., & Davis, G. F. (2016). Challenges for global supply chain sustainability: Evidence from conflict minerals reports. *Academy of Management Journal*, 59(6), 1896–1916.

Kliff, S., & Katz, J. (2021, August 22). Hospitals and insurers didn't want you to see these prices. Here's why. *New York Times*. https://www.nytimes.com/interactive/2021/08/22/upshot/hospital-prices.html

Knight, B., & Mitrofanov, D. (2022, September 5). Why you should warn customers when you're running low on stock. *Harvard Business Review.* https://hbr.org/2022/09/why-you-should-warn-customers-when-youre-running-low-on-stock

Koblin, J., & Sperling, N. (2021, October 20). Netflix employees walk out to protest Dave Chappelle's special. *New York Times.* https://www.nytimes.com/live/2021/10/20/business/news-business-stock-market#netflix-protest-dave-chappelle

Kondo, M. (2015). *The life-changing magic of tidying: The Japanese art.* Random House.

Kovatch, S. (2022, October 28). *5 takeaways from our investigation into RealPage's rent-setting algorithm.* ProPublica. https://www.propublica.org/article/why-rent-is-so-high

Kraft, T., Valdés, L., & Zheng, Y. (2018). Supply chain visibility and social responsibility: Investigating consumers' behaviors and motives. *Manufacturing & Service Operations Management, 20*(4), 617–636.

Lal, R. (1986). Delegating pricing responsibility to the salesforce. *Marketing Science, 5*(2), 159–168.

Lamberton, C., & Stephen, A. T. (2016). A thematic exploration of digital, social media, and mobile marketing: Research evolution from 2000 to 2015 and an agenda for future inquiry. *Journal of Marketing, 80*(6), 146–172.

Landier, A., Sraer, D., & Thesmar, D. (2009). Optimal dissent in organizations. *Review of Economic Studies, 76*(2), 761–794.

Larcker, D. F., & Tayan, B. (2016). *Scoundrels in the C-suite: How should the board respond when a CEO's bad behavior makes the news?* Rock Center for Corporate Governance at Stanford University Closer Look Series: Topics, Issues and Controversies in Corporate Governance No. CGRP-57 (Stanford University Graduate School of Business Research Paper, 16–23).

Larson, J. H., & Medora, N. (1992). Privacy preferences: A cross-cultural comparison of Americans and Asian Indians. *International Journal of Sociology of the Family,* 55–66.

Larsson, T. (1998). How open can a government be? The Swedish experience. In V. Deckmyn & I. Thompson (Eds.), *Openness and transparency in the European Union* (pp. 39–52). European Institute of Public Administration.

Lehman, D. W., O'Connor, K., Kovács, B., & Newman, G. E. (2019). Authenticity. *Academy of Management Annals, 13*(1), 1–42.

Leibbrandt, A., & List, J. A. (2015). Do women avoid salary negotiations? Evidence from a large-scale natural field experiment. *Management Science, 61*(9), 2016–2024.

Lemoine, G. J., Hartnell, C. A., & Leroy, H. (2019). Taking stock of moral approaches to leadership: An integrative review of ethical, authentic, and servant leadership. *Academy of Management Annals, 13*(1), 148–187.

Leonardi, P. M., & Treem, J. W. (2020). Behavioral visibility: A new paradigm for organization studies in the age of digitization, digitalization, and datafication. *Organization Studies, 41*(12), 1601–1625.

Leroy, H., Anseel, F., Gardner, W. L., & Sels, L. (2015). Authentic leadership, authentic followership, basic need satisfaction, and work role performance: A cross-level study. *Journal of Management, 41*(6), 1677–1697.

Levenson, M. (2022, May 21). She was told surgery would cost about $1,300. Then the bill came: $229,000. *New York Times*. https://www.nytimes.com/2022/05/21/us/colorado-hospital-lisa-french.html

Lewandowsky, S., & Kozyreva, A. (2022, March). *Algorithms, lies, and social media*. OpenMind. https://www.openmindmag.org/articles/algorithms-lies-and-social-media.

Lieber, R. (2022, September 24). The discount data that some colleges won't publish. *New York Times*. https://www.nytimes.com/2022/09/24/your-money/college-common-data-set-merit-aid.html

Luthans, F., & Avolio, B. J. (2003). Authentic leadership development. In R. E. Quinn, J. E. Dutton, & K. S. Cameron (Eds.), *Positive organizational scholarship: Foundations of a new discipline* (pp. 241–258).

Madhavan, A., Porter, D., & Weaver, D. (2005). Should securities markets be transparent? *Journal of Financial Markets, 8*(3), 265–287.

Maitra, P., Neelim, A., & Tran, C. (2021). The role of risk and negotiation in explaining the gender wage gap. *Journal of Economic Behavior & Organization, 191*, 1–27. https://doi.org/10.1016/j.jebo.2021.08.021

Markenson, S., & Orgel, D. (2022). *Transparency in an evolving omnichannel world*. NielsenIQ—FMI Report.

Marshall, D., McCarthy, L., McGrath, P., & Harrigan, F. (2016). What's your strategy for supply chain disclosure? *Sloan Management Review, 57*(2), 37–45.

Martin, K. E. (2012). Diminished or just different? A factorial vignette study of privacy as a social contract. *Journal of Business Ethics, 111*(4), 519–539.

Mas, A. (2017). Does transparency lead to pay compression? *Journal of Political Economy, 125*(5), 1683–1721.

Mathur, A., Acar, G., Friedman, M. J., Lucherini, E., Mayer, J., Chetty, M., & Narayanan, A. (2019). Dark patterns at scale: Findings from a crawl of 11K shopping websites. *Proceedings of the ACM on Human-Computer Interaction, 3*, 1–32.

Maxwell, P. (2015). Transparent and opaque pricing: The interesting case of lithium. *Resources Policy, 45*, 92–97.

Mazumdar, T., Raj, S. P., & Sinha, I. (2005). Reference price research: Review and propositions. *Journal of Marketing, 69*(4), 84–102.

McCoy, E. (2020, April 2). *Struggling Napa wineries offer deep discounts and virtual tastings.* Bloomberg. https://www.bloomberg.com/news/articles/2020-04-02/struggling-napa-wineries-offer-deep-discounts-and-virtual-tastings?sref=d3S20v77

McGinnis, C. (2019, January 24). *Hotel resort fees anger readers.* SFGate. https://www.sfgate.com/travel/article/Hotel-resort-fees-anger-readers-13559852.php

Meijer, A. (2014). Transparency. *The Oxford handbook of public accountability* (pp. 507–524). Oxford University Press

Mejia, J., Urrea, G., & Pedraza-Martinez, A. J. (2019). Operational transparency on crowdfunding platforms: Effect on donations for emergency response. *Production and Operations Management, 28*(7), 1773–1791.

Merriam-Webster. (2022). *The Merriam-Webster dictionary* (New edition).

Miao, L., & Mattila, A. S. (2007). How and how much to reveal? The effects of price transparency on consumers' price perceptions. *Journal of Hospitality & Tourism Research, 31*(4), 530–545.

Michaels, D. (2012, July 9). The secret price of an airliner. *Wall Street Journal.* https://www.wsj.com/articles/SB10001424052702303649504577494862829051078

Mijares Torres, M. P., & Marte, J. (2022, August 10). *The snowballing US rental crisis is sparing nowhere and no one.* Bloomberg. https://www.bloomberg.com/news/features/2022-08-10/us-rental-housing-crisis-spirals-on-inflation-pressure-pandemic-migration?sref=d3S20v77

Mills, K. E., Han, Z., Robbins, J., & Weary, D. M. (2018). Institutional transparency improves public perception of lab animal technicians and support for animal research. *PloS One, 13*(2), e0193262.

Miotto, R., Wang, F., Wang, S., Jiang, X., & Dudley, J. T. (2018). Deep learning for healthcare: Review, opportunities and challenges. *Briefings in Bioinformatics, 19*(6), 1236–1246.

Mohan, B., Buell, R. W., & John, L. K. (2020). Lifting the veil: The benefits of cost transparency. *Marketing Science, 39*(6), 1105–1121.

Mohan, B., Schlager, T., Deshpandé, R., & Norton, M. I. (2018). Consumers avoid buying from firms with higher CEO-to-worker pay ratios. *Journal of Consumer Psychology, 28*(2), 344–352.

Mohr, J., & Thissen, C. (2022). Measuring and disclosing corporate valuations of impacts and dependencies on nature. *California Management Review, 65*(1), 91–118.

Mollick, E. R., & Rothbard, N. (2014). *Mandatory fun: Consent, gamification and the impact of games at work* (Wharton School Research Paper Series).

Monroe, K. B. (1973). Buyers' subjective perceptions of price. *Journal of Marketing Research, 10*(1), 70–80.

Morrison, E. W. (2011). Employee voice behavior: Integration and directions for future research. *Academy of Management Annals, 5*(1), 373–412.

Morrison, E. W., & Milliken, F. J. (2000). Organizational silence: A barrier to change and development in a pluralistic world. *Academy of Management Review, 25*(4), 706–725.

NACUBO (2021, November 11). *National Association of College and University Business Officers 2021 tuition discounting study.* Available online at: https://www.nacubo.org/Research/2021/NACUBO-Tuition-Discounting-Study

Napier, E., & Sanguineti, F. (2018). Fashion merchandisers' slash and burn dilemma: A consequence of over production and excessive waste? *Rutgers Business Review, 3*(2), 159–174.

Nassauer, S. (2022, August 17). Target's profit sinks as retailer unloads unwanted inventory. *Wall Street Journal.* https://www.wsj.com/articles/target-tgt-q2-earnings-report-2022-11660708780

National Economic Council. (2016). *The competition initiative and hidden fees.* Report prepared for the White House. https://obamawhitehouse.archives.gov/sites/whitehouse.gov/files/documents/hiddenfeesreport_12282016.pdf

New, S. (2010, October). The transparent supply chain. *Harvard Business Review.* https://hbr.org/2010/10/the-transparent-supply-chain

New, S., & Brown, D. (2011). The four challenges of supply chain transparency. *European Business Review,* 4–6. https://www.europeanbusinessreview.com/challenges-supply-chain-transparency/

Newport, C. (2016). *Deep work: Rules for focused success in a distracted world.* Grand Central Publishing.

Nunes, J. C., Ordanini, A., & Giambastiani, G. (2021). The concept of authenticity: What it means to consumers. *Journal of Marketing, 85*(4), 1–20.

Obloj, T., & Zenger, T. (2022). The influence of pay transparency on (gender) inequity, inequality and the performance basis of pay. *Nature Human Behaviour, 6*(5), 646–655.

O'Brien, T. (2021, February). *The move to kitchen transparency.* Foodservice Equipment and Supplies. https://fesmag.com/topics/trends/18984-the-move-to-kitchen-transparency

O'Reilly, C. A., III., Chatman, J. A., & Doerr, B. (2021). When "me" trumps "we": Narcissistic leaders and the cultures they create. *Academy of Management Discoveries, 7*(3), 419–450.

O'Toole, J., & Bennis, W. (2009). A culture of candor. *Harvard Business Review, 87*(6), 54–61.

Olivetti, C., & Petrongolo, B. (2016). The evolution of gender gaps in industrialized countries. *Annual Review of Economics, 8,* 405–434.

Osorio-Vega, P. (2019). The ethics of entrepreneurial shared value. *Journal of Business Ethics, 157*(4), 981–995.

Ou, A. Y., Tsui, A. S., Kinicki, A. J., Waldman, D. A., Xiao, Z., & Song, L. J. (2014). Humble chief executive officers' connections to top management team integration and middle managers' responses. *Administrative Science Quarterly, 59*(1), 34–72.

Owens, B. P., Rowatt, W. C., & Wilkins, A. L. (2011). Exploring the relevance and implications of humility in organizations. *Handbook of Positive Organizational Scholarship, 1,* 260–272.

Parmigiani, A., Klassen, R. D., & Russo, M. V. (2011). Efficiency meets accountability: Performance implications of supply chain configuration, control, and capabilities. *Journal of Operations Management, 29*(3), 212–223.

Pasquale, F. (2015). *The black box society: The secret algorithms that control money and information.* Harvard University Press.

Patagonia (2022). Our environmental responsibility programs. https://www.patagonia.com/our-responsibility-programs.html. Accessed on 25 November 2022.

Paton, E. (2018, September 6). Burberry to stop burning clothing and other goods it can't sell. *New York Times.* https://www.nytimes.com/2018/09/06/business/burberry-burning-unsold-stock.html

Pauly, M. V., & Burns, L. R. (2008). Price transparency for medical devices. *Health Affairs, 27*(6), 1544–1553.

Perez-Truglia, R. (2020). The effects of income transparency on well-being: Evidence from a natural experiment. *American Economic Review, 110*(4), 1019–1054.

Perkins, C. (2022, July 27). *Wonder about the impact of your daily cup of coffee on the planet? Here's the bitter truth.* TED Ideas. https://ideas.ted.com/truth-about-coffee-impact-on-environment-planet/

Perna, G. (2020, January 20). *CEOs on leading through increased public scrutiny.* Health Evolution. https://www.healthevolution.com/insider/ceos-on-leading-through-increased-public-scrutiny/

Petty, R. E., & Cacioppo, J. T. (1984). The effects of involvement on responses to argument quantity and quality: Central and peripheral routes to persuasion. *Journal of Personality and Social Psychology, 46*(1), 69–81.

Plinke, W. (1985). Cost-based pricing: Behavioral aspects of price decisions for capital goods. *Journal of Business Research, 13*(5), 447–460.

Poort, J., & Zuiderveen Borgesius, F. (2021). *Personalised pricing: The demise of the fixed price? Data-driven personalisation in markets, politics and law* (pp. 174–189). Cambridge University Press.

Prastacos, G., Wang, F., & Soderquist, K. (2013). *Leadership through the classics: Learning management and leadership from ancient east and west philosophy.* Springer Science & Business Media.

Puzakova, M., Kwak, H., & Bell, M. (2015). Beyond seeing McDonald's fiesta menu: The role of accent in brand sincerity of ethnic products and brands. *Journal of Advertising, 44*(3), 219–231.

Rahim-Dillard, S. (2021, April 19). How inclusive is your leadership? *Harvard Business Review*. https://hbr.org/2021/04/how-inclusive-is-your-leadership

Rai, A. (2020). Explainable AI: From black box to glass box. *Journal of the Academy of Marketing Science, 48*, 137–141.

Ramachandran, G. (2011). Pay transparency. *Penn State Law Review, 116*(4), 1043–1080.

Ramdas, K., & Darzi, A. (2017). Adopting innovations in care delivery—The case of shared medical appointments. *New England Journal of Medicine, 376*(12), 1105–1107.

Reidenbach, R. E., & Robin, D. P. (1990). Toward the development of a multi-dimensional scale for improving evaluations of business ethics. *Journal of Business Ethics, 9*, 639–653.

Rego, A., & Giustiniano, L. (2021). Are relationally transparent leaders more receptive to the relational transparency of others? An authentic dialog perspective. *Journal of Business Ethics*. https://doi.org/10.1007/s10551-021-04792-6.

Ribeiro, M. T., Singh, S., & Guestrin, C. (2016). Why should I trust you? Explaining the predictions of any classifier. *Proceedings of the 22nd ACM SIGKDD International Conference on Knowledge Discovery and Data Mining* (pp. 1135–1144).

Richards, H. (2021). Rethinking value: 'Radical transparency' in fashion. *Continuum, 35*(6), 914–929.

Rosenbaum, L. (2015). Scoring no goal—Further adventures in transparency. *New England Journal of Medicine, 373*(15), 1385–1388.

Rosenbloom, S. (2009, July 31). High-end retailers offering more discounts. *New York Times*. Available online at: https://www.nytimes.com/2009/08/01/business/01secret.html

Rotemberg, J. J. (2005). Customer anger at price increases, changes in the frequency of price adjustment and monetary policy. *Journal of Monetary Economics, 52*(4), 829–852.

Saigol, L., & Root, A. (2022, May 19). Boeing gets good news: It flipped ab Airbus customer. *Barron's*. https://www.barrons.com/articles/boeing-737-max-jets-iag-51652951588

Sampson, C. J., Arnold, R., Bryan, S., Clarke, P., Ekins, S., Hatswell, A., Hawkins, N., Langham, S., Marshall, D., Sadatsafavi, M., & Sullivan, W. (2019). Transparency in decision modelling: What, why, who and how? *PharmacoEconomics, 37*(11), 1355–1369.

Santana, S., Dallas, S. K., & Morwitz, V. G. (2020). Consumer reactions to drip pricing. *Marketing Science, 39*(1), 188–210.

Schaerer, M., Schweinsberg, M., Thornley, N., & Swaab, R. I. (2020). Win-win in distributive negotiations: The economic and relational benefits of strategic offer framing. *Journal of Experimental Social Psychology, 87*, 103943.

Schlegelmilch, B. B., & Öberseder, M. (2010). Half a century of marketing ethics: Shifting perspectives and emerging trends. *Journal of Business Ethics, 93*(1), 1–19.

Schmidt, J., & Bijmolt, T. H. (2020). Accurately measuring willingness to pay for consumer goods: A meta-analysis of the hypothetical bias. *Journal of the Academy of Marketing Science, 48*(3), 499–518.

Schnackenberg, A. K., & Tomlinson, E. C. (2016). Organizational transparency: A new perspective on managing trust in organization-stakeholder relationships. *Journal of Management, 42*(7), 1784–1810.

Schüll, N. D. (2012). *Addition by design: Machine Gambling in Las Vegas*. Princeton University Press.

Schwantes, J. (2019). *What the fee?! How cable companies use hidden fees to raise prices and disguise the true cost of service*. Consumer Reports.

Scott, W. R., & Davis, G. F. (2015). *Organizations and organizing: Rational*. Routledge.

Seele, P., Dierksmeier, C., Hofstetter, R., & Schultz, M. D. (2021). Mapping the ethicality of algorithmic pricing: A review of dynamic and personalized pricing. *Journal of Business Ethics, 170*(4), 697–719.

Seim, K., Vitorino, M. A., & Muir, D. M. (2017). Do consumers value price transparency? *Quantitative Marketing and Economics, 15*, 305–339.

Sewell, G., & Barker, J. R. (2006). Coercion versus care: Using irony to make sense of organizational surveillance. *Academy of Management Review, 31*(4), 934–961.

Shankar, A., & Canniford, R. (2016, September 29). *If Patagonia's business model is a paragon of virtue, should more companies follow suit?* The Conversation. https://theconversation.com/if-patagonias-business-model-is-a-paragon-of-virtue-should-more-companies-follow-suit-66188

Sharkey, A., Pontikes, E., & Hsu, G. (2022). The impact of mandated pay gap transparency on firms' reputations as employers. *Administrative Science Quarterly, 67*(4), 1136–1179.

Shelegia, S., & Sherman, J. (2022). Bargaining at retail stores: Evidence from Vienna. *Management Science, 68*(1), 27–36.

Shen, L. (2017, September 18). The truth about whether airlines jack up prices if you keep searching the same flight. *Time*. https://time.com/4899508/flight-search-history-price/

SimanTov-Nachlieli, I., & Bamberger, P. (2021). Pay communication, justice, and affect: The asymmetric effects of process and outcome pay transparency on counterproductive workplace behavior. *Journal of Applied Psychology, 106*(2), 230.

Simmel, G. (1950). *The sociology of Georg Simmel*. The Free Press.
Simpson, R., & Simpson, A. (2018). "Embodying" dirty work: A review of the literature. *Sociology Compass, 12*(6), e12581.
Sinha, I. (2000). Cost transparency: The net's real threat to prices and brands. *Harvard Business Review, 78*(2), Reprint R00210.
Sirianni, N. J., Bitner, M. J., Brown, S. W., & Mandel, N. (2013). Branded service encounters: Strategically aligning employee behavior with the brand positioning. *Journal of Marketing, 77*(6), 108–123.
Sjolin, S. (2015, July 26). *In this London pub, drink prices rise and fall like stocks*. MarketWatch. https://www.marketwatch.com/story/when-this-market-crashes-traders-get-trashed-2015-07-17.
Smith, B. (2022, January 2). A former Facebook executive pushes to open social media's black boxes. *New York Times*. https://www.nytimes.com/2022/01/02/business/media/crowdtangle-facebook-brandon-silverman.html
Smith, E., & Vogell, H. (2022, March 29). *How your shadow credit score could decide whether you get an apartment*. ProPublica. Available online at: https://www.propublica.org/article/how-your-shadow-credit-score-could-decide-whether-you-get-an-apartment
Smith, K. J., & Harris, L. M. (2014). Drafting an effective employee handbook. *Employment Relations Today, 41*(1), 71–79.
Sodhi, M. S., & Tang, C. S. (2019). Research opportunities in supply chain transparency. *Production and Operations Management, 28*(12), 2946–2959.
Sodhi, M., & Sodhi, N. (2008). *Six sigma pricing: Improving pricing operations to increase profits*. FT Press.
Soh, C., Lynne Markus, M., & Goh, K. H. (2006). Electronic marketplaces and price transparency: Strategy, information technology, and success. *MIS Quarterly, 30*(3), 705–723.
Solove, D. J., & Citron, D. K. (2017). Risk and anxiety: A theory of data-breach harms. *Texas Law Review, 96*, 737–786.
Sonenshein, S., Herzenstein, M., & Dholakia, U. M. (2011). How accounts shape lending decisions through fostering perceived trustworthiness. *Organizational Behavior and Human Decision Processes, 115*(1), 69–84.
Spann, M., Zeithammer, R., Bertini, M., Haruvy, E., Jap, S. D., Koenigsberg, O., Mak, V., Popkowski Leszczyc, P., Skiera, B., & Thomas, M. (2018). Beyond posted prices: The past, present, and future of participative pricing mechanisms. *Customer Needs and Solutions, 5*(1), 121–136.
Sparrowe, R. T. (2005). Authentic leadership and the narrative self. *Leadership Quarterly, 16*(3), 419–439.
Spiegler, R. (2016). Choice complexity and market competition. *Annual Review of Economics, 8*, 1–25.
Staw, B. M. (1997). The escalation of commitment: An update and appraisal. *Organizational decision making*(pp. 191–215).

Swanson, A. (2016). Americans are less trusting than ever before. That could also make us poor. *Washington Post*, Wonkblog. https://wapo.st/2wGVWeV
Swift, C., Guide, V. D. R., Jr., & Muthulingam, S. (2019). Does supply chain visibility affect operating performance? Evidence from conflict minerals disclosures. *Journal of Operations Management, 65*(5), 406–429.
Symonds, M. (2007). The traceability advantage. *Quality, 46*(10), 36–41.
Testa, J., Friedman, V., & Paton, E. (2020, July 26). Everlane's promise of 'radical transparency' unravels. *New York Times*. Available online at: https://www.nytimes.com/2020/07/26/fashion/everlane-employees-ethical-clothing.html
Thacker, K. (2016). *The art of authenticity: Tools to become an authentic leader and your best self*. Wiley.
Thiel, C. E., Bonner, J., Bush, J. T., Welsh, D. T., & Garud, N. (2022). Stripped of agency: The paradoxical effect of employee monitoring on deviance. *Journal of Management*, in press.
Thomas, M., Simon, D. H., & Kadiyali, V. (2010). The price precision effect: Evidence from laboratory and market data. *Marketing Science, 29*(1), 175–190.
Thompson, S. (2021, May 30). *Your customers want to know the progress you've made in diversity, inclusion and belonging*. Forbes, CMO Network. https://www.forbes.com/sites/soniathompson/2021/05/30/your-customers-want-to-know-the-progress-youve-made-in-diversity-inclusion-and-belonging/?sh=7db84c113abc
Toegel, I., Levy, O., & Jonsen, K. (2022). Secrecy in practice: How middle managers promote strategic initiatives behind the scenes. *Organization Studies, 43*(6), 885–906.
Törnberg, P. (2022). How sharing is the "sharing economy"? Evidence from 97 Airbnb markets. *Plos One, 17*(4), https://doi.org/10.1371/journal.pone.0266998.
Totzek, D., & Jurgensen, G. (2021). Many a little makes a mickle: Why do consumers negatively react to sequential price disclosure? *Psychology & Marketing, 38*(1), 113–128.
Trentini, C., Tambelli, R., Maiorani, S., & Lauriola, M. (2022). Gender differences in empathy during adolescence: Does emotional self-awareness matter? *Psychological Reports, 125*(2), 913–936.
Trotter, R. G., Zacur, S. R., & Stickney, L. T. (2017). The new age of pay transparency. *Business Horizons, 60*(4), 529–539.
Truong, N. A., & Masopust, G. (2021). Cost transparency: A sales tool or a solid brand component? *Innovative Brand Management II Special Issue*, 39–61.
Turco, C. J. (2016). *The conversational firm: Rethinking bureaucracy in the age of social media*. Columbia University Press.

Van Scotter, J. R., & Roglio, K. D. D. (2020). CEO bright and dark personality: Effects on ethical misconduct. *Journal of Business Ethics, 164*(3), 451–475.
Vanderbilt, T. (2016). *You may also like: Taste in an age of endless choice*. Alfred A. Knopf.
Vanhuele, M., & Drèze, X. (2002). Measuring the price knowledge shoppers bring to the store. *Journal of Marketing, 66*(4), 72–85.
Vogelgesang, G. R. (2008). *How leader interactional transparency can impact follower psychological safety and role engagement* (Doctoral dissertation). The University of Nebraska-Lincoln.
Vogell, H. (2022, October). Rent going up? One company's algorithm could be why. ProPublica 15. https://www.propublica.org/article/yieldstar-rent-increase-realpage-rent
Walumbwa, F. O., Avolio, B. J., Gardner, W. L., Wernsing, T. S., & Peterson, S. J. (2008). Authentic leadership: Development and validation of a theory-based measure. *Journal of Management, 34*(1), 89–126.
Wang, L., Owens, B. P., Li, J. J., & Shi, L. (2018). Exploring the affective impact, boundary conditions, and antecedents of leader humility. *Journal of Applied Psychology, 103*(9), 1019.
Warner, A. S., & Lehmann, L. S. (2019). Gender wage disparities in medicine: time to close the gap. *Journal of General Internal Medicine, 34*, 1334–1336.
Wayne, S. J., Shore, L. M., Bommer, W. H., & Tetrick, L. E. (2002). The role of fair treatment and rewards in perceptions of organizational support and leader-member exchange. *Journal of Applied Psychology, 87*(3), 590.
Weick, K. E. (2001). Leadership as the legitimization of doubt. In W. Bennis, G. M. Spreitzer, & T. G. Cummings (Eds.), *The future of leadership: Today's top leadership thinkers speak to tomorrow's leaders* (pp. 91–102).
Wellener, P., Hardin, K., Gold, S., Leaper, S., & Parrott, A. (2022, September). *Meeting the challenge of supply chain disruption*. Deloitte Insights.
Whelan, R., & Sayre, K. (2022, March 22). Disney workers walk out to protest company's response to Florida bill. *Wall Street Journal*. https://www.wsj.com/articles/disney-workers-walk-out-to-protest-companys-response-to-florida-bill-11647991140
White, S. (2020). *When shrouded prices signal transparency: Consequences of price disaggregation* (Doctoral dissertation). The University of Chicago.
Wilken, R., Cornelißen, M., Backhaus, K., & Schmitz, C. (2010). Steering sales reps through cost information: An investigation into the black box of cognitive references and negotiation behavior. *International Journal of Research in Marketing, 27*(1), 69–82.
Wind, J., & Rangaswamy, A. (2001). Customerization: The next revolution in mass customization. *Journal of Interactive Marketing, 15*(1), 13–32.

Wong, M. N., Cheng, B. H., Lam, L. W. Y., & Bamberger, P. A. (2022). Pay transparency as a moving target: A multi-step model of pay compression, I-deals, and collectivist shared values. *Academy of Management Journal*. https://doi.org/10.5465/amj.2020.1831

Wunderlich, S., & Gatto, K. A. (2015). Consumer perception of genetically modified organisms and sources of information. *Advances in Nutrition*, 6(6), 842–851.

Wursthorn, M., & Choi, E. (2020, August 20). Does Robinhood make it too easy to trade? From free stocks to confetti. *Wall Street Journal*. https://www.wsj.com/articles/confetti-free-stocks-does-robinhoods-design-make-trading-too-easy-11597915801

Zhang, X., Manchanda, P., & Chu, J. (2021). "Meet me halfway": The costs and benefits of bargaining. *Marketing Science*, 40(6), 1081–1105.

Index

A
Accountability, 118
Accountable, 2, 4, 19
African American, 152
Airbnb, 151, 152
Algorithm(s), 2, 4, 6, 8, 9, 13, 15, 16, 18, 136–147, 149, 156
Algorithmic decision making (ADM), 138–143, 145–148
Ambiguity, 126
Anonymity, 149, 151, 155
Artificial intelligence, 136–138, 144, 145
Authenticity, 2, 15, 112, 114, 115, 117, 119, 122, 125, 127–129
Authentic leadership, 113–118, 120, 125–130
Availability, 136, 139
Availability of information, 28, 29
Awareness, two-sided, 163

B
B2B, 54, 55, 57, 59, 62, 64, 68, 70
Bangladesh, 33

Beneficial, 93
Black, 138, 150, 152
Borrower, 154, 155
Brand, 2, 4, 12–15, 17
Burberry, 36, 37
Buying journey, 51, 53, 54, 63, 64, 74

C
Campaign, 168
Candor, 4, 5, 88, 116, 118–120
CEO, 170, 172
Competition, 136, 140
Complexity, 13, 15, 17
Comprehensibility, 147
Comprehensible, 6
Conformity, 84, 86, 97
Consent, 90
Consistency, 84, 87, 94
Consumer-brand relationship, 26
Conversational firm, 84, 96
Core value(s), 95, 121
Credit score(s), 139, 141, 142
Critique, 113, 117, 122, 125, 126

Crowdfunding, 40, 151, 154, 155
Culture, 83, 84, 91, 92, 94, 96, 97, 101, 104
Customers, 24–26, 28–44

D
Dark patterns, 43, 44
Decision making, 4, 12, 18
Decontextualized, 126
Deep learning, 138
Definition, 162, 163, 165, 179, 180
Dialog, 85, 87
Differentiation, 140
Digitalization, 174
Digitization, 174
Dirty work, 41, 42
Discloser/Disclosure, 2, 4, 5, 7–9, 11–14, 17–19, 162–168, 170, 171, 174, 177–180
Disclosure, active, 150
Disclosure, deliberately designed, 179
Disclosure, negotiated, 180
Disclosure, passive, 150
Discrimination, 137, 138, 141, 149–153
Dissent, 94, 97
Dominican Republic, 35
Downstream, 24, 29–32, 36, 37
Drip pricing, 56, 65

E
Earning ratio, 99
eBay, 151
Efficiency, 2, 15, 17
Emotion, 104
Empathizer, 180
Empathy, 112, 118, 121
Employee performance, 113
Entrepreneurship, 10
Equity, 13
Everlane, vii, viii, 52, 75, 76, 94

Expectations, 93–96
Explainability, 138, 139, 147, 148
Explanation, 137, 145–148, 156
Exploitation, 162, 173, 179

F
Fashion, 27, 28, 30, 35–37
Feasibility, 12, 171
Food, 26, 28–30, 32, 35, 39, 40
Founder, 37

G
Gender wage gap, 86, 99, 100, 103
General Data Protection Regulation (GDPR), 146
Google, 168

H
Harm, 88, 105
Holacracy, 173
Honesty, 112, 114–116, 118, 120, 122, 128
Humility, 112, 120, 123–125

I
Identification, 84
Identity, 117, 121, 128, 129
Impression management, 84, 85
Inconsistency, 162
Inequality aversion, 104
Information, accessibility, 54, 61
Information, clarity, 164, 175
Information, completeness, 164, 175–177
Information, contextualization, 164, 175, 177, 178
Information flow, 88–90
Information, interpretation, 164, 175
Information, precision, 164, 175, 176
Instacart, 167, 168

Integrative framework, 164, 165, 172–174
Interpretability, 106
Interpretation, 164, 177, 178
Introspection, 116, 120, 129
Inventory level(s), 167

L

Labor illusion effect, 41, 43
Leadership, 1, 5, 8–11, 15, 16, 18
Leadership success, 126
Lego, 169
Lender, 154, 155

M

Measurement, 84, 85, 99, 101, 102
Medical appointment, 151, 153, 154
Model output, 148
Monitoring, 9, 18, 87, 90, 91
Moral, 115, 118, 128
Motivation, 2, 5, 7, 12, 16, 18

N

New York Times, 168
Nike, 36, 37
Normative integration, 86

O

Observability, 84, 86, 90
One-dimensional, 119, 126–128
Opacity, 7, 15, 138, 140
Opaque, 55, 105, 136, 167, 168
Open, 4, 17, 19
Open dialogue, 173
Operations, 1, 8, 9, 11, 15, 17
Optimism, 112
Orchestration, 89
Organizational culture, 2, 9, 10, 83–85, 89, 91, 92, 94–98

Organizational transparency, 84–89, 91, 93, 95, 96, 98–100, 102–105
Outcome(s), 4, 5, 13, 15, 18, 19

P

Partitioned pricing, 56, 65
Patagonia, 30, 37
Pay, 6, 8, 9, 13
Peer-to-peer lending, 154
Performance, financial, viii, 36, 67, 103
Personality, 127, 128
Practice(s), 84, 87–90, 93–96, 101, 105
Prediction, 142, 143
Price availability, 50, 56, 61, 63–66
Price change frequency, 61, 63, 66
Price communication & negotiation, 53
Price comprehensibility, 56
Price knowledge, 55, 66, 178
Price negotiation, 59
Price offer complexity, 61, 63, 65, 66
Price promotions, 66, 72, 75, 76
Price realization, 53, 57–59
Prices, 2, 10, 12–16
Price setting, 53, 54
Price structure(s), 50, 72
Pricing, 4, 6, 8, 10, 12, 14, 15, 17
Pricing, change frequency, 17
Pricing, dynamic, 135, 138, 139
Pricing inputs, 52, 71, 73, 75
Pricing process, 51–54
Privacy, 4, 7, 16, 85, 88, 90
Privacy-personalization paradox, 150
Product development, 169
Proprietary information, 166, 168, 170

R

Receiver, 162–166, 170, 175–177, 179, 180
Regulation(s), 89, 102, 103, 146, 151
Renter, 136–139, 142, 152, 153
Reputation, 26, 33, 36
Restaurant(s), 39, 40, 43
Rules, 12

S

Safety, 25, 26, 30–33, 40
Sale, 163, 167, 172, 176, 178
Sanction, 98
Satisficer, 180
Score(s), 137, 139, 141–143, 148, 151
Secrecy, 2, 4, 9, 16
Secrecy, corporate, 141
Self-acceptance, 115
Self-awareness, 112–117, 120–123
Self-disclosure, 119, 121
Self-reflection, 120, 122, 130
Self-regulation, 130
Services, backstage, 24, 38
Services, frontline, 24
Shared values, 117
Silence, 84
Sincerity, 112, 128
Static, 117, 126
Subjugation, 88
Supplier, 23–26, 30–34, 42
Supplier capabilities, 27
Supplier risks, 32
Supply chain, 2, 9, 13, 15
Sustainable, 2, 3

T

Target (brand), 143, 144
TikTok, 168
Traceability, 24, 29, 30, 32
Tracking, 84, 89, 99
Transparency, 25
Transparency, access-based, 168, 170
Transparency, accessibility-based, 61–63, 66
Transparency, algorithmic, 137, 139–145, 147, 149, 151, 156
Transparency, consequences, 162
Transparency, cost, 52, 60, 71, 73, 74
Transparency, customer, 38, 39, 149–151, 153, 154
Transparency, disclosure-based, 62, 63, 73–76
Transparency, emotional, 122
Transparency, event, 141
Transparency, explanation-based, 165, 166
Transparency, illusion, 50, 162
Transparency, interactional, 115, 119
Transparency, internal, 30
Transparency, negative aspects, 4
Transparency, operational, 24, 25, 38–44
Transparency, organizational value-based, 165, 173
Transparency paradox, 90
Transparency, pay, 86, 89, 98, 99, 101–106
Transparency, personal value-based, 165, 171, 172
Transparency pledge, 74, 75
Transparency, positive aspects, 3, 6
Transparency, price, 50–53, 55–63, 65, 66, 69, 71, 73–76
Transparency principle, 3, 4, 130, 162, 179
Transparency, process, 38–40, 141
Transparency, process-based, 164, 170
Transparency, radical, 52, 71, 72, 75, 76
Transparency, relational, 115–125, 129

Transparency, supply chain, 25–30, 34–36, 38
Transparency, tactical, 166, 168, 170
Transparency, two-way, 166
Transparent behaviors, 116
Transparent leadership, 112, 113, 126
Trust, 3, 5, 15, 28, 34, 40, 42, 114, 120, 122, 123

U
Understandability, 147
Understanding, 2, 3, 5–7, 13, 17, 18, 164–166, 170, 171, 173–180

Upstream, 29, 30, 36

V
Value, 2, 3, 5, 7–9, 12, 14, 15, 17, 18
Visibility, 10, 24, 28–33, 87, 91, 96
Voice, 90, 91, 96

W
Wage gap, 18
White, 150, 152
Work engagement, 113
Work environment, 95, 97

Printed in the United States
by Baker & Taylor Publisher Services